The Racia   licing

The Racialisation of British Policing

Simon Holdaway

First published in Great Britain 1996 by
MACMILLAN PRESS LTD
Houndmills, Basingstoke, Hampshire RG21 6XS
and London
Companies and representatives
throughout the world

A catalogue record for this book is available
from the British Library.

ISBN 0–333–56394–8 hardcover
ISBN 0–333–56395–6 paperback

First published in the United States of America 1996 by
ST. MARTIN'S PRESS, INC.,
Scholarly and Reference Division,
175 Fifth Avenue,
New York, N.Y. 10010

ISBN 0–312–12939–4

Library of Congress Cataloging-in-Publication Data
Holdaway, Simon.
The racialisation of British policing / Simon Holdaway.
p.   cm.
Includes bibliographical references and index.
ISBN 0–312–12939–4 (cloth)
1. Police—Great Britain.   2. Discrimination in law enforcement-
–Great Britain.   3. Great Britain—Race relations.   I. Title.
HV8195.A2H65   1996
363.2'0941—dc20   95–42139
                                                                            CIP

10   9   8   7   6   5   4   3   2   1
05   04   03   02   01   00   99   98   97   96

Printed in Malaysia

Contents

List of tables

Preface

Robert Reiner suggested I might write this book in 1989, as one of a series he was editing, but before a contract could be issued his publisher had been the subject of a merger and the series was cancelled. The half written text stayed in a drawer until Frances Arnold from Macmillan visited my university department, scouting for manuscripts. I mentioned the fragment and the order was given to complete it! Catherine Gray at Macmillan finally saw the project to print. I am grateful to all of them for their important encouragement and advice. As the project progressed Marian Fitzgerald and Michael Banton read parts of the manuscript, making many helpful suggestions. Paul Rock's work has over the years provided me with more ideas than I can cope with. I want to recognise his contribution to my thinking. None of these people hold any responsibility for the finished text but I have benefited from their assistance. It may sound trite but Hilary, Ruth, Ben, David and Peter – my family – have to be mentioned, with love.

I have been researching and writing about the police for a considerable number of years, longer than I care to remember. Throughout this time my interest has been sustained in relationships between the police and minority ethnic groups. This takes me further back, to my years as a police officer. Throughout my police service I worked in areas of large minority ethnic settlement and have seen at first hand the ways in which ideas about 'race' mould police work. I have also had opportunities in recent years to research racialised relations within the police and listen to many black and Asian officers talk about their experience of police employment. This book brings together many ideas I have gathered as my research has progressed and I hope to have written a fairly comprehensive introduction to the sociological study of relations between the police and minority ethnic groups that will help students gain insight into their complexities. It is also my hope that the occasional new idea is found in the pages that follow.

My university work brings me into contact with professionals working in criminal justice institutions, undergraduates and probation and social work trainees. Many students come to the study of race issues within what we inappropriately call the 'criminal justice system' equipped with one, undefined concept – 'racism'. They are all too often unwilling to look carefully at the research evidence or reflect on their ideas. Clarification of concepts is resisted. In this book I hope to prompt readers to ask some questions about the adequacy of thinking in 'isms' and to reflect more carefully on the available evidence about aspects of racialised relations. I also hope to suggest tactfully that criminologists should consider more fully the vital contribution sociological theory can make to their subject.

One reason for this all too easy stance taken by students and some academics is the desire to see more harmonious relations between minority and majority populations in contemporary Britain. This is obviously good and to be encouraged but I hope it does not sound too middle-aged (and stereotypical) to say that it is based on a woefully simplistic understanding of the way in which social phenomena are constructed and sustained within organisational and cultural settings. This book tries to be relevant to policy reform, working from a framework of analysis that retains 'race' precisely within the organisational and cultural structures of policing. Once these contexts are taken into account it becomes rather more difficult to propose effective policy reform.

One hot summer's day in the 1970s I took two of my children to Alton Towers. We joined a long queue for the Log Flume, a ride in boats along rough water. As we got near the entrance to the ride, to one side and above, boats full of expectant occupants began their voyage along a waterfilled channel. Two Asian families waited in front of us. As a boat passed by water was splashed over them and the occupants, four youths, none over 13 years of age, shouted 'Pakis'. The families just continued waiting. This incident has remained in my memory. Waiting is frustrating, all the more so when accompanied by personal abuse. Was this a routine happening that could be accommodated within the daily round? How could the abusive kids be so vile? Why is it like this? How can we change the world?

Other incidents come to mind: to the elderly Asian man reporting to me in 1970 a 'kicking' he had received at the hands of skinheads near to Brick Lane; the gaze of many black people living in Notting Hill as I patrolled their streets; the racial jokes and remarks told by

officers; to the dilemmas of officers wanting to challenge and change
the police; the wonderful sense of pride and solidarity expressed by
officers launching their Black Police Association. Motivation to keep
researching and writing are affected by personal experiences like
these. Dare I remember these people and write the book for them as
much as for anyone else? We need change.

SIMON HOLDAWAY

Chapter One

Thinking about 'race'

Common-sense about 'race'

'Blacks today are repaying whites for their bad treatment in colonial
days. They aren't just against police but against all white people. The
police are an obvious target because they represent white supremacy.
Really, until blacks have taken over and evened up the score, the
problem won't be solved. I don't blame them really, when they get stuck
in places like Brixton. I know that PCs call them spooks, niggers and
sooties, but deep down the majority of PCs aren't really against them,
although there are some who really hate them and will go out of their
way to get them. I call them niggers myself now, but I don't really mean
it. I think a relief takes on a personality of its own. Although you still
have your own personality you lose a lot of it to the relief group
personality (Smith, D. *et al.*, 1986, p. 393).'

For many years the police have been the subject of fierce allegations
about their racially prejudiced and discriminatory treatment of black
and Asian people and here is a young officer from the London
Metropolitan Police, talking about 'blacks'.[1] What do you make of
her views? Do you think she is racially prejudiced? Remember, she
is careful to say, 'I call them niggers myself now, but I don't really
mean it.' Perhaps her racial prejudice can be related to distinct
personality characteristics, generally shared by police colleagues or
mostly found among a few officers who might be called 'racists': the
few who, as she puts it, 'really hate them and will go out of their way
to get them?' Or perhaps you think she is influenced strongly by the
attitudes of the group of officers, the relief, with whom she works –
'although you still have your own personality you lose a lot of it to

1

the relief group personality.' Are her explanations of police attitudes and behaviour – singly or together – adequate? What do you think?

Your initial conclusion about these explanations might be to give minimal credibility to any of her views. Perhaps you don't attach much weight to any explanations of racialised prejudice or discrimination that afford a primary place to officers' personal characteristics or the organisation of the police rank-and-file. Emphasising the apparent intransigence and embeddedness of racial discrimination in our society you conclude she is a member of a racist society with its inevitably racist police. In this scheme individuals and the wider terrain of 'society' form a seamless robe. But remember that she also has a theory of racial conflict in Britain. Are, as she puts it, 'blacks repaying whites for their bad treatment in colonial days?'; are they 'against all white people?' Is one consequence of the history of colonialism, that 'they get stuck in places like Brixton?' And do the police in Brixton and in other inner city areas therefore form 'an obvious target because they represent white supremacy?'

These are questions that beg a conceptualisation of what we mean by 'race' and 'race relations', as well as evidence to assess their adequacy, in this instance focusing on many different kinds of relationships between the police and black people. They are not a long way from the kinds of questions and conclusions about relationships between the police and minority ethnic groups proposed by sociologists, and this raises a serious question about the status of sociology as an academic discipline. If a police officer is able to analyse sociologically in an impromptu conversation, it is then fair to criticise sociology as a discipline claiming academic credibility when in fact its practitioners do little more than articulate common sense dressed-up in pretentious jargon – a view I happen to have more than a little sympathy with. On the other hand, I also want to argue that sociologists' interests are precisely in peoples' perceptions and explanations of the social world; in what people regard as common sense, even though, particularly in considerations of 'race', we might find their views wide of the mark and offensive. Hence my choice of a contentious quotation from a young police officer to begin a book about a contentious subject, 'race' and policing.

The police officer's views about 'race' are what might properly be called a lay sociological perspective. They include implicit explanations of the relationship between black and white people living in contemporary Britain, with reference to the history of colonialism; the effects of living in an inner city area on these relationships; the consciousness of black and Asian people; the relationship between attitudes of racial prejudice and the actions of police officers; and so on. All these 'lay views' are commentary on what sociologists call social structure and social action. They resonate different sociological perspectives on contemporary race relations and in themselves interest sociologists. None of this puts the discipline of sociology at risk; indeed, I want to argue that the close relationship between peoples' commonsensical understandings of subjects like 'race' and sociological analysis is a strength rather than a weakness.[2]

Many studies of race relations and policing will be discussed in this book but few will immediately illustrate my preferred analytical framework. I therefore want briefly to say more about the type of sociology that interests me. Where possible, the implications of the type of sociology I defend will be drawn out, hopefully with a light touch. Where this is not done it will be helpful for a reader to know where some of my preferences (and prejudices) lie.

Other people's common-sense views might be offensive and our initial response is to rule them out of order, at times motivated more by emotion than reason. This is particularly a problem when we are discussing and analysing 'race'. Anyone who has completed empirical research about 'race' knows that misunderstandings about the language used to describe black people – or is it black and Asian, or ethnic minority or minority ethnic people – can generate tensions between researchers and the sponsors of a project. The backcloth to this and other difficulties does of course have historical bearings. There are more than sufficient examples of the most vile oppression brought upon human beings because they belong to a supposed 'race' than we might dare to ponder. The Holocaust, slavery in the New World and, more recently, the Russian bombing of the people of Grozny and many other situations caution easy analyses and solutions. Research nevertheless continues in this sensitive context.

A view expressed in saloon bar conversation, for example, that black youths are innately criminal is offensive, unsupported by a shred of evidence. Perhaps you think it should be dismissed immediately on moral grounds and given no further consideration (Wolfgang and Cohen, 1970)? The point is an important one but remember that common sense is a powerful resource of knowledge that often guides action; it is what we consider any reasonable person might accept as truth if they stood in our shoes and viewed the world from our perspective (Schutz, 1967). Common sense is what we take for granted about the social world and its powerful character has an impact on the way people think and act.

Sociologists faced with common-sense views about race relations within the criminal justice system may well find the morality that underpins them repugnant. It is nevertheless my view that a central feature of sociology is precisely concerned with describing and analysing the content and structure of peoples' common-sense views of the world and, where possible, the relationships between common-sensical ideas and action. This does not mean that sociology is a kind of sophisticated tape recording of public and private views. It does not mean that sociologists adopt the values of the people studied. Neither does it mean that we are stuck without a language other than the everyday to explore our findings. But for all this, common-sense accounts of the world are an important starting point for sociological analysis – a starting point, not the last word.

If sociology is concerned in the first instance with others' common sense as its basic data, a question about the status of sociological knowledge is raised. Is sociology not just another version of common-sense reasoning, no more valid or accurate than the ideas of anyone you care to stop in the street? This is a tricky one, but perhaps the status of sociological knowledge depends on the logic of reasoning that supports its arguments and the transparency and consistency guiding methods of data collection and analysis used to support arguments. In this sense the conclusions of sociological analyses differ from common sense. Its principles of reasoning are known and shared, at least amongst a significant, reflective community of thinkers. Its methods of data collection and analysis are also transparent. Arguments are testable and capable of revocation on agreed grounds.[3]

Importantly, sociology should be concerned with the meaningful nature of human relationships, which returns us to the systematic documentation of the ways in which people understand the world. This also means that sociology must be continually reflexive, rethinking the ways in which its analytical conclusions about aspects of the social world are related to those of the people who are the subject of attention. I am not content with a sociology that fails to take into account the ways in which people attribute meaning to the social world, supplanting their ideas with a grand theory that analyses the changing dynamics of an entity called 'society', then extrapolating the nature of peoples' present and, often, future consciousness. It is not possible to interpret individuals' consciousness or the meanings people attribute to the social world from an aggregation of structural characteristics like occupation, an analysis of relations to the means of production, gender, age, 'race', social class, or whatever. This point stands to judge both empirical and wholly theoretical research.[4] Studies like these reduce relationships and consciousness to one or more common denominators, a Flatland of relationships rather than a contoured diversity (Rock, 1979). Diversity as much as similarity should be of interest to the sociologist.

This does not mean that people interpret and attribute meaning to the social world in wholly idiosyncratic ways. Social structures of phenomena like age, gender, 'race' and class form frameworks for and limitations to human consciousness and action but these structures are constituted by human action. Societies are constructed and continually reconstituted through human action and ultimately have no 'life' apart from that action (Berger and Luckmann, 1967; Giddens, 1979). For various reasons the world appears object-like, determinate rather than processual. But the ongoing task for the sociologist remains the documentation of how we construct and sustain this world through myriad processes.

In particular ways the occupational status, income level, gender, and so on of people of Afro-Caribbean and Asian (and British) background limit their action and the range of meanings they attribute to relationships, other people and phenomena. The description and analysis of these structural limits, sometimes expressed in statistical terms, is an aspect of sociology and many such studies will be discussed in this book. The history of immigration and recruitment of people into particular occupations, for example, is crucial to understanding the material circumstances of black and Asian people in contemporary Britain (Miles, 1982). Their consciousness, however, is not straightforwardly determined by the location of those occupations within the labour market. Migrants are not passive victims, without symbolic and other resources to create a social world. In the most materially deprived American ghettos, for example, a rich, sustaining culture with its own integrity is to be found (Hannerz, 1969; 1980). People together create social worlds that accommodate, challenge, sustain, replicate, change and give integrity to their material circumstances. We realise this when, using a range of systematic research methods like participant observation, discursive interviewing and other sensitive ways of collecting data, we engage with people to understand how they view the world. Then, by systematic analysis of those data, we search out unrealised links between what at first sight appear to be discrete meanings of relationships and phenomena; a diversity of interpretations of the world among people sharing the same structural position; a social world created, structured and recreated by human action.[5]

Another consequence of this view of sociology is recognition of different levels of analysis and a need to take account of them in any particular study. If we distinguish 'race' solely as a reified structural feature that limits human action it seems to me that we cannot and should not then also assume that we have analysed clearly the forms in which the phenomenon of 'race' is articulated within organisations, occupational cultures, groups, and so on. These so-called lower levels of analysis create particular contexts within which 'race' becomes more or less salient to relationships and phenomena. 'Race' mingles with cultures, being shaped into different phenomenal forms. Within diverse contexts of human action relations become racialised. The meaning of 'race' is negotiated and attributed to phenomena and relationships that could be connoted or denoted by a host of other meanings. It is more appropriate to refer to racialised relations than 'race' relations.

In the area of race relations research, however, the quest for sameness rather than diversity is often found when it is assumed that the object of study is 'black people' alone, meaning all people whose skin is dark. In this view people of Afro-Caribbean and Asian origin share the one experience of something called 'racism'. The danger here is that 'race' is reified, given a virtual, absolute status that separates off too sharply those people classified as 'black' from all whites.[6] However, within the criminal justice system, no less than any other institution, people of Asian and Afro-Caribbean origin tend to be treated differently and may regard themselves differently (Modood, 1992). The term 'Asian' is similarly misleading because it is heterogeneous, including people from India, Pakistan, Bangladesh, and other regions, members of each group having somewhat different experiences as victims of crime, as offenders, and so on. Skin colour alone is an inadequate criterion for a definition of 'racial classification'. We also need to take other role signs into account: dress, accent, demeanour, spatial location, for example (Banton,

1967). If this was not so we would exclude assaults on Jewish people, which is ridiculous.

When any 'racial' category is given absolute status there is a danger of solidifying an either/or type of analysis. A zero-sum calculation of power is made, white people holding all power in all contexts and a formulation of racism equalling prejudice plus power is developed. This places the Afro-Caribbean and Asian businessperson in the same structural position as the unemployed black youth; the Indian home-worker at one with the office receptionist of Afro-Caribbean origin (Mason, 1992). Sameness is the keynote. Structural criteria like employment status, income and educational qualifications certainly have to be taken into account when life-chances are charted. Attention should, however, also be given to the ways in which organisational structures frame racialised relationships and mediate the meaning of phenomena, as well as ways in which cultures provide symbolic resources to sustain racialised perceptions and related strategies of action.

The prejudice plus power formulation suggests a wholly unsociological notion of power. Power is not a static resource distributed in a zero-sum game but more adequately understood as an aspect of social relationships in which material and symbolic resources are mobilised in interaction. This processual analysis of power requires us to discover the resources that members of 'racialised' groups mobilise and negotiate (Mason, ibid.). Some black police officers in the London Metropolitan Service, for example, have recently formed a representative association, claiming the right to define themselves as officers working within an organisation dominated by policies and practices that have inadequately tackled racialised prejudice and discrimination, and to challenge the ways in which white colleagues have stereotyped them in the work-place. The City of Chicago Police also has a Black Police Officers Association but the processes of negotiation it has been engaged in to ensure that its members' views are represented to the Chief Officer have to vie with and yield to those of the African American, Hispanic, Asian, Jewish, Greek, and other associations. Racialised relations within this police force are highly complex and involve varied alliances around different issues. Once we consider the processual, negotiated form of relationships a zero-sum notion of power is jettisoned. Racialised relations become more dynamic and diverse.

We also need to look carefully at the different contexts within which 'race' becomes salient. Rather than suppose it is all pervasive

– recognising age, gender, and, less often, social class as also important – it is necessary to identify the social contexts in which the idea of 'race' is more or less pertinent. This suggests attention to the particular contexts within which power is negotiated – the police station, public places where people are stopped on suspicion of an offence, the courtroom, private houses, or wherever (Stinchcome, 1963; Ball, 1973; Holdaway, 1977). The 'always and everywhere' type of analysis fails to research adequately the interwoven character of structures and processes of racialised and other phenomena. All life becomes racialised in an absolute form.

Later in this book we will find that there is a strong strand of racialised prejudice in the occupational culture of the police rank-and-file and it is misleading to separate it from other stable characteristics of that culture. In this context 'race' and 'racism' cannot be boxed neatly into analytical categories, separated from other routines of organisations and perceptions of the world. We need to contextualise 'race' as a complex process of interaction (Barth, 1969).

A sociologist's interest is sometimes in the structure of whole societies, maybe colonial relationships so far as they have an effect on contemporary race relations (Rex and Mason, 1986). The interest is sometimes in a smaller scale setting, perhaps relationships between the members of occupational groups like the police (Smith, D. *et al.*, 1986; Holdaway, 1991). Whatever the focus of their work, sociologists should be concerned to collect various types of data which may verify, qualify or challenge as error what other people regard as common sense. This is not to claim for sociology a unique, privileged access to the truth or to contend that sociologists always agree with each other's ideas. In later chapters of this book we will find, for example, that disputes remain about sociological assessments of the extent of the involvement of black youth in crime and about the nature of the police response to this issue (Lea and Young, 1984). Sociological work should nevertheless allow us to return to other peoples' commonsensical accounts of race relations and, at the very least, assess them from the basis of systematically gathered evidence, which has been analysed rationally.

More common sense about race

Here is another nugget of common-sense wisdom, this time from a police officer who worked at the station where I carried out covert, participant observer research about urban policing (Holdaway, 1983). He was standing with a colleague in the yard of his station. The cells backed onto the yard and he could hear some people shouting. He asked his colleague:

'Is it a drunk?'

'No, five in for grievous bodily harm'.

'A coon?'

'No. Irish'.

The assumption that black people commit violent crime was a view I found to be held consistently among the many officers working at the station. On another occasion, after a colleague had been assaulted outside a night club, the officer in charge of the shift explained, '. . . the reason we need dogs for the coloureds is because they are so bloody violent, and that's why you want them' (Holdaway 1983, pp. 66–71). Indeed, police stereotyping of black youth as criminal continues to this day (Keith, 1993).

There is no natural, necessary or actual connection between being black and acting in a violent manner. Some black youths did commit violent crime in the area covered by this station but not to an extent where it could be considered remotely suited to a status of inevitability. In spite of this evidence, officers accepted and propagated the idea that a black skin infers the 'race' of a person and, taking the context of action into account, is a viable criterion for predicting behaviour.

Apart from these particular analyses of the relationship between race and criminality, it should from this early stage be realised that the descriptive and analytical validity of fundamental common-sense terms like 'race' are not based on a firm foundation of scientific evidence. Take the idea of 'race' itself, for example. The notion of 'race' is essentially an attempt to classify and categorise people into distinct biological types, with distinct biological features. Common biological origins and continuing characteristics serve to sustain particular races. There are inherited differences amongst peoples but they are continuous, not a set of separate, distinctive packages of traits. However, despite the wide accepted common sense that there are in reality races and, therefore, groups of people who belong to them, the biological basis of 'race' is refuted by all but a small number of natural scientists. As Professor Michael Banton, a leading scholar of race relations has put it.

As a way of categorising people, race is based upon delusion because popular ideas about racial classification lack scientific validity and are moulded by political pressures rather than by the evidence from biology (Banton, 1975).

The linking of people defined (albeit spuriously) as belonging to races to personal, social and cultural competencies mobilises what sociologists call 'race'. It creates racialised relations. If we go back to my example from Hilton police station, the officer's assumption of a relationship between people arrested for grievous bodily harm and their being black leads us in the direction of 'race' or, more appropriately, the racialisation of policing. Racialised relations are essentially relationships between individuals, groups, institutions and societies based on an assumed biological determinism related to expected and actual action.

The history of the idea of race has documented its various meanings and phenomenal forms. Race has at times been related to lineage; as a series of distinct biological species; as status. In other words, what we accept as the meaning of race may in fact be a highly particular and partial view (Banton, 1977; 1979). There are considerable differences in the ways in which some of these expressions of race have been understood by sociologists. The primary factor is the presumption of a biological determination of action, which can of course be expressed in different ways, perhaps through an assertion of nationalism or citizenship for example. The research task here is very difficult because it is not easy to ascertain if a person is orienting their action towards another on the basis of views about biology or some other explanator and we have very few studies indeed that can help us at this point.

This is not just an esoteric point because any meaning attributed to the idea of race has implications for policy solutions to tackle disadvantage, the restoration of fairness and justice, and so on. Our conceptualisations place limits on options to tackle social problems. If race is biologically based and directly determines certain forms of behaviour – violence, for example – there is frankly little that can be done to change the future situation, other than extermination or a lengthy programme of interracial breeding. If, on the other hand, disadvantages experienced by, say, black British people are more the result of class divisions than biological characteristics you can see that a different line of policy for change is identified (Banton,

1987). Here, economic and social policy reforms might become appropriate.

Social constructions

'Race', then, is not an objective, scientifically identified human property. We cannot be assigned to a 'race' on the basis of phenotypic characteristics. The notion of 'race' is a *social construction*, used to classify people and predict their characteristics, including behaviour (Berger and Luckmann, 1967). So constructed, the idea of 'race' confers a certain orderliness upon the uncertainties and ambiguities of the social world. The orderliness which we impose on the social world, however, is shown to be somewhat insecure when we find that in the recent past in South Africa, for example, a dark-skinned Italian might be classified as coloured, black or white, depending on the particular social context in which the 'race' of such a person is classified (Watson, 1970). Although the constitutional basis for racial classification is very different, it is also the case that a dark-skinned Italian might move between different 'races' in contemporary Britain.[7] Each one would depend on the social context, the nature of interaction taking place and other factors (Barth, 1969). 'Race' should be considered as a social process. Again, we are concerned with the contexts in which relations are racialised.

Some sociologists have argued that because discussions of race relations offer a spurious reality and credibility to a divisive concept we should jettison the notions of 'race' and 'race relations': they are epi-phenomena (Miles, 1982). A discussion of race relations in a book like this one continues to give validity to an essentially misleading categorisation of people and perpetuates existing patterns of domination and subordination. Robert Miles, for example, argues that 'race relations' are essentially class relations, perpetuated by aspects of capitalism. Irrespective of its use in common-sense discourse, 'race' is not a scientific concept and should be rejected (Miles, 1989). The status of 'race' is that of ideology, beliefs sustained in the interests of subordinating a particular population, erroneously identified by stock differences.

'Racism' is an analytically valuable term for Miles because it describes the process of subordinating people from minority ethnic groups. Robert Miles is mostly interested in the labour market but racism could refer to the subordination and exclusion of groups in many different contexts. By historical analysis, periodising the immigration of workers from other societies, Miles analyses how the demands of capital for cheap labour drew people from less powerful societies to our market place, and did so for economic reasons. These relations, basically economic in nature, were racialised, drawing on images of biological inferiority and subordination. By analysing the racialisation of relations we avoid reifying the phenomenon of 'race', while retaining a purchase on how it is constructed and reconstructed as a social phenomenon.

Miles therefore also introduces the notion of 'racialised relations', for him essentially class relations, constructed in periods of labour demand. This means that the attribution of biological determinism related to skill levels, intellectual development and natural ability amongst migrant workers is moulded in a process involving the claim to and use of particular resources. Power is a negotiated phenomenon and migrant labour was not straightforwardly subjected to the domination of whites.

Miles's work is at the macro level of analysis and premised on the Marxist notion that economics, not biology or a range of social factors, frame and, on some readings, determine social structures. This is an essentialist, scientific position. Surface appearances of phenomena, like 'race', shield the essence of economic change and class interest. His work is valuable because it deconstructs the notion of 'race' and introduces us to one possible use of the idea of racialised relations. It is difficult, however, to see how his detailed analysis of migration can deal satisfactorily with third and fourth generations of black and Asian people who are British and form the majority of the minority ethnic population. Further, 'race' may also have an integrity for black people who affirm it as a resource to claim identity and solidarity (Gilroy, 1987; Hall, 1992). We need to go beyond the macro level of analysis to institutional, organisational and cultural contexts within which particular social processes racialise relationships between people, investing them with inferences about behaviour directly related to inherited, phenotypic characteristics. Stephen Small has described the core of the 'racialisation problematic' as a,

> need to move to study of racisms, racialised relations and white people. This looks at how groups not previously defined as 'races' have come to

be defined in this way, and assesses the various factors involved in such processes. The problem is not relations between races but relations which have been racialised; not the physical attributes of blacks or their presumed inferiority, but the motivations of non-blacks, and the obstacles they impose (Small, 1994, p. 30).

Other scholars argue that racialised relations based on an assumed deterministic relationship between biology and behaviour have for various reasons been obscured from public gaze, with no less effect than when more public and visible. The ways in which racial divisions are expressed change over time. An assumed natural 'nationalism' or cultural incompatibility, for example, has replaced but not wholly eradicated notions of biological superiority. The sociologist's task is to analyse changing discourses of 'race' and to probe their cultural forms. The title of Paul Gilroy's book, *There Ain't No Black in the Union Jack*, neatly conveys one of the main themes of those interested in the 'new racism', focusing on nationalism and other phenomena that exclude black people from full citizenship in contemporary Britain (Gilroy, 1987). The new racisms remind us of the different ways in which 'racial exclusion' can be sustained but writers in this vein do not always provide adequate evidence to rule out biological determinism lying behind their surface appearance. Given that 'race' refers to biology, the new racisms would be better conceptualised as forms of ethnocentrism, meaning a tendency to regard the beliefs, standards and code of behaviour of one's own culture or subculture as superior and normative in relation to those found in other societies.

Despite its ambiguity and changing forms as a description of human beings, race as a biological category, commonly identified by skin colour, is a powerful source of commonsensical knowledge for predicting behaviour. This was noted from the words of the police officer I quoted earlier, who made a virtual, natural connection between grievous bodily harm and black people. 'Race' and 'race relations' are real in this sense. Denotations and connotations of 'race' construct, sustain and maintain racialised relations.

But why does race remain a powerful idea if it has no firm biological basis? An important aspect of an answer to this question is that categorisations of race are usually comparative, made with reference to some other racial group. The idea that black British people of Afro-Caribbean descent are violent implies that white

British people or the members of some other group are less so. Notions of 'race' often order patterns of domination and subordination, of superiority and inferiority thereby reconstructing and perpetuating social inequalities (Miles, 1982; Cashmore and Troyna, 1983). In subsequent chapters we will see how some sociologists have found in capitalist societies a need to scapegoat minorities, as a way of deflecting attention and blame from the inequalities caused by a fundamentally prejudicial economy. Some seem to argue that many, if not all societies need an 'Other' to function as an exclusionary scapegoat. Relations of subordination and domination, however, are rarely absolute and it is consistent with the view of power and social structure taken here that we should always conceive of them as negotiated, drawing on material, political and symbolic resources to realise inclusion or exclusion.

Nazi Germany was of course an example of a society that placed the Jewish race in total subordination to the supremacy of the Aryan race.[8] To be Jewish or identified as such was, in a sense, to be criminal, unworthy of any human regard. Here, race is synonymous with a notion of criminality. In the recent past, to be classified as 'coloured' or 'black' in South Africa meant you committed an illegal act if you bathed from beaches reserved for 'whites'. Black people in South Africa were and still are perceived by many whites as morally or, rather, immorally contagious. The law has been used to preserve their separation from white people. South African law and therefore the whole of the South African criminal justice system has been organised to ensure the perpetuation of racial discrimination and a particular social order.

These are highly visible examples of the influence of race on the working of a criminal justice system but of course there are many other less obvious examples. The fact that in Britain, for example, less than 2 per cent of black and Asian people are recruited to the police service, despite their representing about 5 per cent of the whole population, requires us to search beneath the surface appearance of recruitment procedures, personnel practices, and many other features of police organisation to identify and analyse underlying racial categories implicit and explicit within the recruitment process and beyond (Holdaway, 1991).

Importantly, and with particular reference to the example of police ethnic minority recruitment, police officers are not consciously excluding black and Asian people from police employment but, rather, do not take sufficient steps to compensate for their under-representation within the ranks, by monitoring the selection process for bias, clarification of their policy stance on race issues, and so on (Holdaway, ibid). Doing little or nothing in the light of evidence that something needs to be and can be done may be as discriminatory as conscious, active discrimination. It is recognised in law that discrimination can be direct or indirect. Phenomena and relationships can be racialised indirectly, by inaction as well as purposeful motives (Banton, 1994).

Indirect discrimination can be a consequence of policies that inadvertently, systematically disadvantage the members of particular racial groups. This is where institutional discrimination enters the picture. For example, until recently all police forces in England and Wales had a minimum height limit for recruits. This could have disadvantaged some Asian people whose height is usually less than five feet eight inches, the police norm. The height standard was introduced to ensure that officers' physical stature was such that they could be assumed to have sufficient physical force to defend themselves. However, it is now clear that policing is mostly a peaceful occupation and the height restriction is not relevant to the skills and knowledge required by officers. The police had institutionalised a rule that was racially (and sexually) discriminatory.

This is also an example of the interwoven character of racial with other, more mundane, organisational policies and procedures. Race is not neatly boxed for the sociologist to select from the shelf marked 'discriminators'. It is necessary to tease out the reasons for the racialisation of policy and practice, as well as the social processes leading to decisions that solidify and reify 'race'. Institutions only live through human action.

Race and ethnicity

Race tends to be a categorisation ascribed to groups; it refers to 'them' rather than 'us'. Ethnicity is the term more generally used to describe the common, subjective identification of group membership which is focused on any number of criteria – language, religion, custom, a common sense of destiny, for example. Members of a group recognise these common features as bonds that mark them off from others. There may be a coincidence between a perceived racial group and an acceptance of ethnic identity but this need not be so (Eriksen, 1993).

Race is generally ascribed by others and ethnicity is a self designation. The self designation of ethnicity may also be, and usually is, a response to structures of domination and subordination, of superiority and inferiority that form a framework of racialised relations within a society. Ethnic minorities may be the subject of racialised prejudice and discrimination. In my study of ethnic minority police officers, for example, it was found that one of the significant problems they face is racialised prejudice from their colleagues. These same officers, however, did not strongly identify themselves as the members of an ethnic minority: they were members of the population of Britain who happened to be black-or brown-skinned. (Wilson, Holdaway *et al.*, 1984). Remember, however, that all the points about the diversity of identity, of the contextualisation of definitions and about the changing nature of definitions made in relation to 'race' also apply in equal measure to ethnicity.

Prejudice and discrimination

Some sociological explanations of race relations focus on the behaviour of individuals and on racial prejudice. When the police officer who opened this chapter said, 'I call them niggers myself now, but I don't really mean it' she was prompting us to consider the idea of racialised prejudice. Prejudice refers to generalised attitudes based on learned beliefs and values that lead an individual or group of individuals to characterise or stereotype an ethnic group in a particular way that runs counter to objective facts. Prejudice is similar to ignorance but characterised by an inflexible refusal to change when contrary evidence is presented. The idea that black people are intrinsically violent, for example, which we found in an earlier quote from a study of the police, runs counter to research evidence and, indeed, contrary to the day to day working experience of police officers – it is an example of racialised prejudice. In particular, notice how the concentration on prejudice leads to a discussion of racialised relations in terms of the attitudes of individuals.

If ideas about 'race' are powerfully lodged in common sense we need to not only describe their form but also explain why they manifest themselves in the first place? Some researchers have tried to determine if racial prejudice is a personality characteristic of particular people.[9] The officer spoke of some of her colleagues 'who really hate them and will go out of their way to get them.' These officers may be exhibiting personality traits that issue in racialised prejudice.

Theodore Adorno's *The Authoritarian Personality* seeks to identify the characteristics of people who are prone to hold prejudiced attitudes (Adorno, 1950). His explanation is basically that people who have had a particularly disciplined upbringing, especially during early childhood, are likely to be authoritarian, seeking scapegoats who are weak, unable to resist the authoritarianism directed towards them. Their anger is displaced into intolerant, rigid views – into prejudice. There is little evidence to support Adorno's views, which will be considered later along with the idea that people with a particular personality – a 'police personality' – are attracted to join a constabulary. Again, the main point here is that prejudice is an attitude, analysed at the level of the individual.

Racialised prejudice – an attitude – may or may not find its way into discrimination – an action. The Policy Studies Institute (PSI) report about the London Metropolitan Police found considerable evidence of racial prejudice amongst officers but this was mostly confined to conversations between colleagues (Smith, D. *et al.*, 1986). Their language did not necessarily lead to action that discriminated unfairly between black and white people. The PSI authors argued, however, that an analysis of racial prejudice amongst police officers should be more concerned with an understanding of the characteristics of the rank-and-file work group than individuals who might have a prejudiced personality. Any discussion of race relations, they argued, should move from an understanding of individuals to the rather different but related level of analysis concerned with the influence of social groups on members (Smith and Gray, ibid).

Colonial history and immigration

A considerable number of studies of contemporary racialised relations begin from an historical analysis, stressing the ways in which historical antecedents continue to act as constraints on, for example, the employment, housing, education and consciousness of minority ethnic people. After the Second World War Britain's economy began to expand rapidly, requiring a considerably enlarged work-force. Immigration from the West Indies and, later, from the Asian subcontinent was one feature of this expansion, with its benefits to both Britain and, given assumptions about people eventually returning to their homeland with money and new work skills, to the countries of migration (Miles, 1982). Countries from which they emigrated had been 'conquered' during British colonial expansion and were thereafter patterned by relationships of racialised dominance and subordination between the colonial and indigenous populations, relations that were to have a lasting effect as immigrant peoples began to settle in Britain.[10]

When immigrants entered this country in the 1950s they found employment in low status, often menial, work located in our metropolitan centres. They became victims of prejudice and discrimination in housing provision, living within an existing, deprived environment of the inner city, without adequate government or other forms of investment to enchance that environment. Employers wanted to hire immigrants of any colour but they did not have to pay directly for their housing or social services. In the absence of such investment, indigenous residents – 'both those who remain and those who depart – will be encouraged to speak of an area not being what it was and of housing being overcrowded and falling into disrepair' (Miles, ibid, p. 35). Immigration and urban decay became associated as cause and effect (Lambert, 1970). Colonial stereotypes of people were certainly to change but, consistent within the flux and flow, an idea of the inferiority of black and Asian people was pronounced. Ethnic disadvantage was moulded at the material and ideational levels.

The urban areas where settlement originally took place were also high crime areas, with associated blame, irresponsibility and just deserts attached to those who lived there. Immigration into Britain was therefore not just a process of entry into a neutral territory but of people into a complex web of ideas about colonial status – not all of which were lasting or negative – and a particular material context with its own consequences for social disadvantage (Rex and Moore, 1967; Rex, 1973).

These disadvantages continued across generations, at times reinforced by government policy. One consequence of Acts of Parliament to control commonwealth immigration, for example, implied that the status of black and Asian people as citizens was less than that afforded white people (Gordon, 1985). Immigration controls, it has been argued, have created a climate of suspicion about and an erosion of the acceptance of black-and brown-skinned people as less than full citizens. They and only they are permitted to reside in Britain in limited numbers. They have been defined as a problem, as 'trouble', a perception that found its way into the minds of police officers, policy makers and, therefore, into the very fabric of the criminal justice system as an institution.[11]

A racist society

These features of British society have led some commentators to characterise it as a racist society. A constitutionally racist society has formal, legally prescribed boundaries within and between all its institutions. Opportunities afforded groups defined by inherited racial characteristics are used to control these institutional boundaries. A dominant group holds power over a racially inferior group consistently to sustain social inequalities. Individuals working within these institutions act consciously to exclude members of particular 'races' from full or at times partial membership of and participation in activities that lead to material benefits, a strengthened self identity, citizenship. South Africa before reform and Nazi Germany come readily to mind as examples of constitutionally racist societies.

There are, however, many versions of the racist society thesis, ranging from a conspiracy by a powerful ruling class which retains its power and privilege by employing a vulnerable, poorly paid immigrant work force to the view that the unanticipated consequences of a range of actions can inadvertently have a cumulative effect of disadvantage for ethnic minorities (Mason, 1982). At this point there is no need to describe or evaluate all these theories. The point is that a racist society refers to an analysis of the whole of a society and its institutions.

Institutional racism is a similar notion that describes the way in which policies and practices within an institution systematically disadvantage ethnic minorities and thereby perpetuate racial inequalities. The discrimination, which is negative, can be direct or indirect; the conscious aim to discriminate on racial grounds need not be clearly evident to 'prove' institutional discrimination (Banton, 1994). Police stop and search exercises within areas of high minority ethnic settlement, for example, may be accepted as routine practice by officers but nevertheless disproportionately expose people from those minorities to an infringement of their liberty and disadvantage them. If not otherwise justifiable, such operations can become an example of indirect discrimination.

The associated notion of racism is highly contestable, used in many different ways and, in my experience, with a lack of care and clarity. For some it means ideas about inferiority and subordination, irrespective of reasoning based on biological determinism; for others any unequal outcomes of action in criminal justice or any other sphere of policy is evidence of racism – outcomes impute prior motive and intent. A circular argument is invoked; racism is present because racism is the outcome. For others, racism denotes attitudes, beliefs, ideology, social actions and structural locations (Carmichael and Hamilton, 1968). The concept is so expansive that in these forms it is meaningless.

An overriding problem with many versions of the racist society and institutional racism views is that, like all 'isms' they often cannot be falsified; they are an ill-defined (or more like convenient) catch-all. These formulations have tended to make the notion of racism a rhetorical slogan, in itself a linguistic sign that the speaker is opposed to the processes of exclusion on the basis of race that the term is intended to encompass.

A rather more important task is to disentangle the different signs and processes that constitute *racialised relations* and phenomena. This is one of the intentions of the introduction of the term 'racism' into academic discourse but its misappropriation has led some writers to suggest that we should jettison it, save for use in those situations where a clear biological determinism is evident and specification of the particular historical context within which it is identified (Mason, 1994). Again, we need to remember that 'race' is a contextual, processual phenomenon. Descriptions of Britain as a racist society or one of its institutions as institutionally racist can easily neglect the complexities of the different ways in which 'race' is moulded to create racialised relations.

Robert Miles and others have used the concept of 'racism' to analyse ways in which class phenomena have been signified as racial (Miles, 1989). The notion of ideology is central here (Omi and Winant, 1986). A rather more yielding concept, which does not tie us to the epiphenomenal form of 'race' as a class relation, is 'racialised relations' (Smith, 1989). This clearly signals the social construction of 'race' and myriad ways in which relations, ideas and other phenomena become connoted or denoted with the reference of 'race'. The implication is that the world could be constructed in other ways. Racialised relations are not inevitable. Rather than rely on interest-based ideas like ideology, we can direct research to the study of social processes and ideas that in complex and subtle ways construct racialised relations and consequential social exclusion.

Consequences

The historical experience of immigrant peoples has indeed had a continuing effect on their position within British society. Remember that they tended to enter particular sectors of the employment market, lived in particular residential areas and therefore only had access to the already stretched local authority services within existing, deprived, inner city areas. A complex web of disadvantageous material conditions, prejudice and direct and indirect racial discrimination continue to structure the lives of the main ethnic minorities in Britain.

This is not to suggest that the situation remains static or that black British people are passive victims, wholly impotent to change their situation. I am describing a dynamic framework of action. There is evidence of diverse responses to the one situation faced by people from ethnic minorities, created around assimilation, accommodation, rejection and acceptance (Lea and Young, 1984; Field, 1984; Pryce, 1979). There is nevertheless, 'Clear evidence that racialism and direct discrimination continue to have a powerful impact on the lives of black people (Brown, 1984, p. 318).'

All these circumstances, then, have a lasting impact on ethnic minorities' experience of crime, policing, and the working of the whole of what we rather strangely choose to call the criminal justice system. They have an effect on the levels and types of criminal victimisation they endure; the public and police perceptions of their victimisation; on levels of criminality within the minority ethnic population itself; the character of police discretion; the sentencing of the courts; the work of the probation service; and so on. Social structures and processes that have been briefly described are interpreted by and frame common-sense views about race relations in Britain. The focus on Britain in this book, or more precisely England and Wales, is intentional because until we have more detailed research about processes of racialised exclusion in other societies we cannot readily make comparative judgements. In the first instance it is important to document processes of racialised exclusion within their particular societal context and to then ask questions about possible common features that reach across societal boundaries.

I have argued that a sociological perspective might well begin with commonsensical views about race relations weighed in the balance of an evaluation of various types of evidence. The intention so far has been to encourage reflection on some of the central concepts used in the study of racialised relations and on your own use of terms like 'race', racism, discrimination and prejudice.

Those who find themselves at the sharp end of inequality and racialised prejudice understandably often find discussion about appropriate forms of analysis of race relations an academic luxury. Progress in changing racialised disadvantages in Britain has been lamentably slow (Banton, 1987). There is a clear need, however, to reflect on the available evidence, to criticise it where necessary and at times accept its implications, no matter how uncomfortable they may be. Racial prejudice and discrimination are not easily changed by the weight of rational counter argument, but it is necessary to advance such debate. The only alternative seems to be an unhelpful trading of emotions based on a body of completely unverified common sense.

In the rest of his book various manifestations of 'race' within the sphere of the police and policing will be considered to advance such arguments as seem reasonable from the available evidence. The intention is to go further than the usual criminological method of using statistical, usually multi-variate, analysis to discover the extent of discrimination evident at various stages of the criminal justice process. Typically, a study like this begins with the over-representation of black people within prison and then works back from that over-representation eventually to the figures for stop and arrest that form the starting point that could lead to prison (Smith, 1994). I have chosen to emphasise a different but not necessarily contradictory type of analysis because even when a quantified level of racial discrimination has been determined we cannot treat it as an external, powerful force acting upon passive victims. There are many more questions for the criminologist to consider than those about the measurable extent of racialised discrimination. We need to describe and analyse the social processes that have led to the racialisation of the phenomena and processes in question. This means that criminology must retain a sociology and an appreciation of social theory, which is not always in evidence in research studies. While using some statistical data I will therefore try to place statistics representing racialised discrimination within a wider societal context of analysis.

Secondly, where appropriate, I intend to move way beyond the macro level of analysis to consider ways in which 'race' is mediated through oganisational structures and cultures. Our interest is how 'race' is constituted and constructed within relationships between the police and black and Asian people. This can be explored with a focus on whole societies but my preference, where possible and appropriate, is also to consider a smaller scale level of analysis, with attention to the everyday, common-sense worlds of police and people. Although in a very brief compass, I have already tried to explain why I think this is required.

The subjects chosen for particular attention in each chapter are not exhaustive. My interest in this book is the police of England and Wales. Some examples from other societies are used to illustrate the text but part of my argument is that we need to understand each society in its particular before we can move to comparative analysis. I therefore remain with research dealing with the society with which I am most familiar; no bias is intended by this choice. I have been guided by areas where research has tried to concentrate and focus on racialised subjects and contexts of importance to the police during the last two decades or so. These contexts might be called 'sites of racialisation'. The first of these is victimology. Within large scale victimology surveys there has been considerable attention given to the extent to which black and Asian people have been the victims of crime but relatively little adequate discussion of why any additional burden of victimisation exists. I then move to consider patterns of racial attacks and harassment, which focus sharply on the racialisation of relations between black, Asian and white people in contemporary Britain. The victimisation of black and Asian people, and other minorities for that matter, is of importance to the service offered by constabularies and an important 'site' within which officers and the organisation they represent sustain racialised relations in contemporary Britain.

Chapter 4 deals with the ways in which the police occupational culture mediates 'race' into the practice of police work and here some attention is given to the criminalisation of black youth and what has come to be called the 'race and crime debate'. This is followed by discussion of what official publications called the major street disturbances of 1981 and 1985, and the main police responses to them. Race relations within the police, dealing with the recruitment of minority ethnic groups, the occupational experience of serving black and Asian officers and the police response to racialised prejudice and discrimination within their ranks form the subject of the next chapter.

Finally, I try to pull together some strands of recent attempts to reform policing including racialised relations within and without the service, but place most emphasis on the racialisation of identity amongst black and Asian officers. This eventually brings us full circle to the need for an appreciation of the study of racialised relations and for a sociological underpinning to criminology – but not to link-up society, the police and police officers into a neat sociological system!

Chapter Two

Victims of crime in Britain

Settlement in the inner city

As they entered Britain during the 1940s and 1950s, people from the Caribbean and the Asian subcontinent were faced with limited opportunities in employment, housing and many other institutional spheres. In part, this was because most of them arrived without the necessary financial capital or work skills to secure a different, more beneficial niche in the labour market, one that would lead from non-manual employment to the enjoyment of wider financial and other benefits afforded by skilled or professional work. Their settlement was confined to inner city areas where they were disadvantaged by the lack of opportunities to gain better employment, good standard housing, and so on. This continued as their children grew up within British society. Structures of social inequality within our society then shaped, and to some extent continue to have an effect on, the lives of people from these minority ethnic groups, including the experience of being a victim of crime (Brown, 1992).

Such inequalities could have been lessened if Caribbean and Asian migrants had found an adequate measure of mobility within the labour market. Their skill deficit was certainly a disadvantage but their retention in unskilled and semi-skilled employment was also due to exclusionary practices used by employers. Asians were stereotyped as 'slow to learn', West Indians as lazy. It was said by many, though not all, employers that their indigenous work-force would not accept 'coloureds' as fellow workers and certainly not as supervisors. The key point is that a combination of exclusionary practices, including the widespread use of racial stereotypes, excluded Asian and Caribbean workers from advancement in the labour market and adequate financial resources to move from their areas of initial settlement.[1]

Robert Miles, who has written extensively about these exclusionary processes concludes that,

> '...the interrelationship between the racialisation of migrants, racism and exclusionary practices set limits to the parameters of the labour market open to migrants from the Caribbean and Indian sub-continent...This interrelationship between racialisation, racism and exclusionary practice has continued to constitute a structural constraint for people of Asian and Caribbean origins seeking wage labour, thereby maintaining a hierarchy of market (Miles 1989, p. 126–7).

As far as their experience of crime is concerned, these Afro-Caribbean and Asian migrants lived in inner city areas exhibiting conditions of social deprivation, including comparatively high levels of crime and disorder, levels of crime and disorder, it should be repeated, that were present before substantial immigration began from the Caribbean and the Asian subcontinent (Lambert, 1970). These existing patterns of inner city crime and victimisation were therefore woven into the day to day experience of the ethnic minorities. Some important changes should be recognised but the conditions have not been significantly ameliorated, despite the policies of successive governments (Benyon and Solomos, 1987).

Inner cities are of course not the only areas of Britain with high rates of crime and disorder, by which I mean rowdyism, delinquency, disputes and public incivilities. Neither are they uniformly ridden with crime. Disorder occurs in the suburbs, though usually in more private settings, contained within earshot and knowledge of families and, perhaps very occasionally, immediate neighbours, but rarely spilling over onto the streets. Within the inner cities, disorder is more of a public matter, more intrusive, coming to the notice of residents, entering many more lives directly or through a feeling of threat and anxiety about personal safety in public and private places.

There is nothing particularly new about these features of inner city life, though peoples' levels of tolerance to and acceptance of them has changed over the years. Studying the patterns of immigration and gradual dispersal of successive waves of immigrant peoples within the city of Chicago during the 1930s, for example, led some sociologists to delineate an inner circle of the city that exhibited special characteristics. Immigrant peoples settled in this area during their early years in America, a 'zone in transition' that exhibited consistently high levels of crime and delinquency (Shaw and McKay, 1942).

The Chicago School of Urban Sociology identified what seemed to be a natural pattern of movement of immigrant peoples from this zone to areas of lower crime and delinquency, the suburbs, and so on (Park and Burgess, 1925; Hannerz, 1980). Rates of offending became progressively lower as one moved away from the inner city to its outer areas. The Chicago sociologists' explanation of this pattern mostly dwelt on conflicts between the culture of immigrants and their children, whose hopes and aspirations were primarily moulded by the dominant culture of the host society into which they had been born and socialised. Conflicts of culture helped to create and sustain disorder, including criminality.

The Chicago explanation of patterns of delinquency and crime did not take into account the pitfalls of accepting the recorded crime rate for each city area as an accurate measure of the actual extent of crime. Many other criticisms could be levelled at the approach taken (Hannertz, ibid). The main point here is that inner city areas, historically and across societies, have exhibited high rates of crime and delinquency. Immigrants entering Britain during the 1950s settled in our inner cities and, not through some quasi-natural process of population movement but as the consequence of a range of racially exclusionary policies, employers' practices, material circumstances and ideas about race and immigrants, found constraints placed on their ability to move to and work in different areas of the metropolis and, more widely, the country (Rex and Moore, 1967). This was a pattern of exclusion that would have lasting effects on black and Asian peoples' experience of criminal victimisation.

This chapter deals with the continuing effects of the history of social exclusion of black and Asian people from full participation in our society and in particular its consequences for their experience of criminal victimisation. Myriad social processes need to be described and analysed for a complete account of how patterns of and responses to victimisation have been constructed and reconstructed over the years. Most of the published research, however, has been concerned with statistical levels of victimisation amongst different populations rather than the structure and interaction over time of social processes that have led to the outcomes documented by the statisticians. We have an album of research snapshots rather than a cine film.

Although it has been very briefly described, the historical context of Asian and Caribbean immigration into Britain set a structural framework, a framework not a straitjacket, that placed particular meanings of black and Asian people into common currency.[2] Their origins predate the 1940s and 50s but within the metropolitan centres of Britain exclusion was based on meanings about the natural abilities of immigrant people of different races. Their stock attributes fitted them to certain work and a particular social life – to what amounted to particular patterns of social exclusion. Although obscuring processes that have reconstructed these relations, the studies to be reviewed provide a body of evidence, not all of it by any means clear or consistent, to support an argument that racial exclusion has led to a distinctive experience of criminal victimisation amongst minority ethnic groups.

Crime as a social problem

In his study, *Crime, Police and Race Relations*, John Lambert analysed recorded levels of crime in Birmingham during the late 1960s, particularly in areas of high immigrant settlement (Lambert, 1970). Lambert stressed the important role of the housing market in structuring levels of victimisation and perceived criminality amongst minority ethnic groups, or 'coloured immigrants' as they were then more usually called:

> 'It is very apparent that the housing market operates in such a way that immigrants, and particularly coloured immigrants, live in certain typical conditions and areas, one of whose features is high rates of crime and disorder, both in terms of occurrence of crime events and in terms of residence of criminals and delinquents (ibid, p. 122).'

Birmingham's four areas of largest coloured immigrant residence exhibited the highest overall *recorded* crime rates within the city. This had consequences for patterns of criminal victimisation amongst immigrants' and white peoples' perception of their association with criminality, an ill-conceived perception, as Lambert's data demonstrate.

Persistently high rates of crime and associated material and psychological effects on victims remain in inner city areas, identified as a significant problem by residents of all ethnic backgrounds. Evidence of this view comes from a small number of research studies, mostly carried out in London, concerned with levels of criminal victimisation among the ethnic minorities. Some of the studies have documented the seriousness residents ascribe to social problems affecting the area where they live, and crime and disorder have been consistently identified as serious problems that spoil the quality of peoples' lives.

All residents of these areas find crime and disorder a problem and black and Asian people share the common circumstances of all people living in inner city areas; at this point structures of social class and 'race' are related. As part of the first of the Home Office British Crime Surveys a representative sample of the national population was asked to identify the worst things about the area in which they live and rank them in terms of their seriousness (Hough and Mayhew, 1983). Across the country as a whole it was found that crime and vandalism were not cited as the most significant problems of local areas. Shopping facilities and related amenities were cited most frequently, followed by 'Too much traffic'. 13 per cent and 11 per cent respectively of all people taking part in the first British Crime Survey ranked these problems as a priority.

In what they defined as multi-racial areas, which could be called inner city areas, and the poorest housing estates, however, it was found that residents gave a priority to crime and vandalism. 12 per cent of the residents of multi-racial areas and 17 per cent of residents of the poorest housing estates gave a priority to these matters as the worst things about the area in which they lived. The other problems given a priority by the general population, shopping facilities, transport, and so on, were also found to be important but overshadowed by crime and incivilities. The Home Office researchers found that levels of victimisation and fear of crime were highest in these multi-racial areas and housing estates (Hough and Mayhow, 1985, p. 40, 76).

In a study of the multi-racial population of the London Borough of Islington, Jock Young's research team found that 87.1 per cent of a large sample of residents cited unemployment as a major social problem (Jones, Maclean *et al.*, 1986). 71 per cent similarly cited crime and 68 per cent vandalism. A much smaller number of people,

25 per cent, said race relations was a problem in Islington and just 8 per cent that it was a 'big problem' (ibid p. 8). The Islington team of researchers carried out a similar survey on the Broadwater Farm Estate, soon after the riots that occurred there in 1985 (Broadwater, 1986). On that estate 94 per cent found unemployment a big problem and 57 per cent said that crime was a problem.

When the Islington interviewees' replies to questions about social problems were analysed by age, race and gender, it was found that black people were as likely as white people to view crime as a big problem. This was particularly the case among black women in the 25–44 age group. Asian people, on the other hand, did not find crime such a general, pressing problem, which may partly be a reflection of a more secluded style of life (Jones, Maclean *et al.*, 1986, p. 8), itself symptomatic of the extent of racially motivated crimes they faced. The finding may also be a consequence of the small sample of Asian people interviewed in the study. However, other studies, for example, the London Borough of Newham, have shown that Asian men and women rate the seriousness of racially motivated attacks as highly as unemployment and crime in general (London Borough of Newham, 1987).

As long ago as 1980, in a large survey of Londoners conducted by the Policy Studies Institute (Smith, 1986), it was found that when ranking the crimes to which the police should give the highest and lowest priority, racial attacks were rated fifth, after burglary (ibid. p. 46). All the young people interviewed, however, gave a priority to racial attacks. Along with sexual assaults against women, in this study racial attacks were also given a clear priority by black and Asian people, of whom 67 per cent and 76 per cent respectively, as opposed to 37 per cent of all whites, cited an attack as a matter of primary concern (ibid p. 48). Put another way, virtually twice as many black and Asian people as all white people named racial attacks as a priority. This finding is broadly consistent with the Newham study. Furthermore, in the Newham survey Asian people were significantly more concerned about rowdyism in the streets than any other racial group, possibly because they had a greater fear of being victims of crime of violence or abusive behaviour on the streets.

The diverse design of these research studies is almost bound to yield divergent findings and a straightforward combination of their findings leads to misrepresentation. On the one hand the British

Crime Survey is deliberately wide ranging, designed to obtain a national picture. It is not particularly easy to break down figures from this level of analysis to compare and contrast findings from different cities. The smaller city- or borough-wide studies, however, have used different questions to assess residents' perceptions of crime and other problems faced. This means that their findings cannot be usefully compared. All we can strictly say, for example, is that in the London Borough of Newham in 1987 so many residents perceived crime as a serious problem.[3] Despite this imprecision we can nevertheless say that crime remains a clear concern of black and Asian people living in urban areas.

Racial motivation

While black and Asian people living in urban areas share a some-what common experience of crime with their white neighbours, there are also more distinct, racial elements that should be taken into account. In the last two British Crime Surveys ethnic minority respondents who had experienced a crime or threat in the last year were asked whether they thought what had happened was racially motivated (Mayhew, Elliott *et al.*, 1989; Mayhew, Maung *et al.*, 1993). As Table 1 shows, 14 per cent of Afro-Caribbean and 24 per cent of Asian people said they thought this was the case. In particular, assaults, threats, vandalism and thefts of personal property were thought to have included a racial motivation. There are nevertheless differences between the groups in these and other categories of crime and it makes little analytical sense to talk uniformly of 'black people' in relation to this and other areas of criminal victimisation. Asian people, for example, perceive a higher proportion of assaults, threats and acts of vandalism to be motivated by a racial element than Afro-Caribbeans.

When the category of assaults is broken down into different types of attack, more Afro-Caribbeans than Asians cited a racial element in incidents in the work-place and in pubs. As far as pubs are concerned, it is likely to be a cultural factor – the large proportion of the Asian population who for religious reasons abstain from alcohol and do not therefore visit public houses – that explains most of the difference. The difference between the groups for acts of vandalism is partly explained by the higher level of property ownership amongst

Table 1   Proportion of incidents involving racial motivation: 1988 and 1992 BCS

| | Afro-Caribbean | | Asian | |
	Yes	Don't know	Yes	Don't know
Assault	30	4	44	5
Threats	35	3	57	8
Vandalism	22	7	30	22
Robbery/theft from the person	2	11	8	2
Theft from motor vehicle	2	13	2	12
Burglary	4	14	4	18
Theft of motor vehicle	–	6	2	15
Other household theft	1	8	4	11
Other personal theft	13	2	3	8
All BCS offences	14	8	24	12

Source: 1988 and 1992 BCS care and ethnic minority booster samples (weighted data). From Maung and Mirlees-Black, 1994.

Asians. As far as robbery and theft from the person is concerned, fear of attack may curtail the frequency of movement within and location of public places Asians frequent. Racialised factors are predominant here.

Different facets of an explanation of perceived racial motivation should therefore be considered. Some will focus more sharply on cultural, some on more directly racialised and some on material factors. A combination of these factors leads to a distinct perception of criminal victimisation, constructing a reality of 'race relations' for black and Asian people in contemporary Britain. There are differences between ethnic groups; within the same groups there are differences based on gender, socio-economic class, age and other factors. A full analysis of perceived criminal motivation no less than any other phenomenon requires careful analysis involving these and other elements, for example, organisational and policy related elements.

Perceptions of motivation may of course be exaggerated and needlessly pessimistic. When we find black and Asian people perceiving crime against them to be racially motivated, however, there is a sense in which it matters little whether or not their perception is wholly accurate. If their judgements were wildly at variance with real levels of crime I would not argue in this vein but, given the distinct experience of black and Asian people, it is important to recognise the souring effect perceptions of levels of crime and disorder have on their routine lives. This finds its way into everyday life in mundane ways – 'I must take care as I walk down this street'; 'who is this person walking towards me, will they insult me?'; 'I will go home this way, it is longer but seems safer'. Feelings like these become routine, even taken for granted, yet they spoil, aggravate and sour the quality of life, more perhaps for women than men, more for older people than the young, but they despoil nevertheless.

Crime and associated incivilities, then, are perceived as a significant problem by black and Asian people, affecting their views about and satisfaction with the area in which they live; their feelings of personal safety; and views about levels of crime in their locality. Here they share a good deal with other people. The structure and content of the views documented by the various research studies discussed are nevertheless significantly related to the racialised status of the victim.

Victim surveys

The assessment of actual rather than perceived levels of crime has become a topic of increasing interest to criminologists. If the incidence of crime in a locality is documented more precisely it becomes possible to test the accuracy of common-sense perceptions and formulate appropriate policies to both allay worry and fear, as well as tackle crime itself.

Researchers have tried to document the real figure of reported crime by asking a representative sample of people if they have been the victim of a crime during a recall period of time and if they reported that crime to the police. Their replies, it is argued, inform us more precisely about real crime rates. Crime or victim surveys, as they are called, including the four national surveys conducted by the Home Office, have recently become a regular feature of criminological research in Britain (Hough and Mayhew, 1983; Hough and Mayhew, 1985; Mayhew, Elliott *et al.*, 1989; Mayhew, Maung *et al.*, 1993).[4]

Problems of research design and method

According to the 1991 census, people of Afro-Caribbean and Asian origin make up 3.8 per cent of the national population aged 16 or over, being concentrated, we know, in urban areas. If a crime survey wants to include within its research design a representative sample of people from, say, Afro-Caribbean and Asian backgrounds, a random, national sample will not yield sufficient numbers of them to assess the statistical significance of the research findings. A solution to this problem is to include a booster sample of black and Asian people in a study ensuring the overall sample is more accurately representative of the population as a whole, and to form a sub-sample of data for detailed analysis. This is what the last two British Crime Surveys (BCS) have done, including in the 1988 survey 733 Afr-Caribbeans and 996 Asians and in 1992 1043 Afro-Caribbeans and 980 Asians. For further discussion see Maung and Mirlees-Black, 1994; Zedner, 1994.

An alternative, less accurate, means of assessing levels of victimisation among black and Asian people is through a classification of the types of residential areas in which they live – multi-racial, for example – and then by comparison with findings for people living in different areas. The BCS researchers have used what is called the Acorn classification, an area type classification system, to carry out precisely this type of analysis. A problem with the BCS use of this system, however, is that it relies on the 1981 census data, which included a question about the country in which people were born (but not about ethnic status), the answers to which were related to areas of residence.

One consequence of relying on these census data is the risk that the areas classified as multi-racial within the Acorn classification do not adequately describe the diverse range of areas in which people from ethnic minorities live. This is partly because people of Afro-Caribbean and Asian descent who were born in Britain were not counted in the 1981 census as belonging to an ethnic minority.[5] They may live in areas that are rather different from those where people born outside Britain reside.

When the Acorn classification is used we therefore cannot be clear about the spatial spread of representation of the various ethnic groups within and between areas described as, 'multi-racial', 'poor council estates', 'older housing of intermediate status' or other areas of ethnic concentration. It seems, for example, that Broadwater Farm Estate, where a significant number of black people live and the site of serious riots in 1985, would not be rated as 'multi-racial' within the Acorn classification and could therefore not be matched with BCS data about criminal victimisation. Broadwater Farm Estate would be partly classified as part of a 'poor council estate'. Problems like this limit the potential of the Acorn classification when differences in crime levels are analysed in what are described as 'multi-racial' and other types of areas.

Problems of attrition can also affect the scope of crime surveys, especially the potential value of booster samples. In the Islington crime survey interviewers and interviewees were matched by gender and ethnic background because it was thought that such an arrangement would encourage the fullest disclosure of information about victimisation. In fact, many ethnic minority interviewees were suspicious of their interviewer and declined to give any information. A number of interviewers from ethnic minorities resigned because of the abuse they received at the hands of white respondents (Jones, Maclean *et al.*, 1986, p. 246). The size of the minority ethnic sample in the Islington survey was eventually considerably diminished and its findings should be read appropriately. In what the researchers call their black sample there were just 14 men and 15 women aged between 25 and 44 years; 11 men and 12 women over 45; 27 Asian women between 16 and 24 years, and so on. Further, taking account of the hostility towards interviewers which was a continuing problem, we need to be somewhat wary about the accuracy of some replies to questions about crime and victimisation? Exaggeration or, equally feasible, a straightforward aim to get an interview completed as quickly as possible by giving minimal information could have distorted the data gathered.

The 1988 British Crime Survey also found a less serious but nevertheless notable problem within its sample of Asians interviewed. 60 per cent of Asians interviewed were men, which is an over-representation that may be due to the reluctance of Asian women to be interviewed, itself related to a somewhat sheltered style of life. There could of course also be a 'racial' factor working here because exclusion from public places may have been partly increased by apprehension or fear of victimisation in the streets. Cultural factors and the roles women play within minority groups can nevertheless restrict the scope of a research study like a victim survey.

A further methodological issue to take into account when conside-ring the findings of crime surveys is the problem of comparing data for one group with that for another; for white and Afro-Caribbean origin youth, for example. Basically, to be accurate, comparisons of groups of people must ensure that like is being compared with like. Take the example of assault and for the moment hypo-thesise that members of an ethnic minority are more likely to be victims of assault than white people. Unless we ensure that the ethnic minority population is not skewed in terms of its profile of sex, age, area of residence and other factors that could have an effect on victimisation levels, comparative studies are pretty meaningless. Men aged between 18 and 24, we know, are more likely to be the victims of assault than the members of any other group. If the age structure of the black population is skewed towards that range it is reasonable to anticipate that they are likely to be disproportionately represented as victims of assault. An expla-nation of this situation is therefore more concerned with age than it is with ethnicity. Controls for age and other factors within both white and black populations therefore need to be included in a research design. Remember, however, that it is not possible to control all relevant variables and that multi-variate analysis, in which statistical techniques are used to isolate relevant variables to measure the extent to which 'race' explains patterns of victimisation, is always limited.

Finally, the British Crime Surveys conducted so far have used the categories of Afro-Caribbean, Asian and White. In an important paper, Marian Fitzgerald, a Home Office researcher with principal responsibility for the race relations research programme, points out that this categorisation obscures real differences within the Asian category.

'At one extreme, it comprises Indians who in socio-economic terms, are not dissimilar to whites; and, at the other, it includes Pakistanis and Bangladeshis who occupy a still more disadvantaged position than Afro-Caribbeans. We found some evidence that it was the Indians who suffered higher rates of crime; but the Pakistanis and Bangladeshis were more likely to say that crime against them was racially motivated. This suggests, although it does nothing to explain, a pattern which is distinc-tive from that for whites, but one in which the most important distinction is that between ethnic minorities themselves (op. cit. 49).

Patterns of victimisation

In general terms, the available research on differential patterns of victimisation indicates moderately higher levels amongst ethnic minorities than among white people. The evidence on this issue, however, has not been gathered in a straight forward way and is not unequivocal.

A 1980 Home Office study of a police division that included the Moss-Side area of Manchester concluded that there were no significant differences between the victimisation rates for Afro-Caribbeans and whites (Tuck and Southgate, 1981). Significant differences, however, were found when housing types and areas of residence were controlled. These variables rather than ethnicity seemed more significant. People living in purpose-built flats were more liable to suffer break-in, attempted break-in, assault, theft from the pocket or a bag than those who lived in houses. But this of course was a very small study, not intended to infer wider patterns of victimisation. It did demonstrate, however, that a range of variables other than ethnicity, such as housing type, need to be taken into account when differential rates of victimisation are assessed.

This Manchester study may on the other hand also indicate the importance of small scale studies. In detailed research in small areas of Leeds, for example, Jefferson and Walker found that fewer blacks than whites had been victims of crime and fewer had reported criminal incidents to the police (Jefferson and Walker, 1993). Asians had been victims virtually to the same extent as white people and more than blacks. National surveys miss these variations that exist at the local level, and smaller scale research will always be required, not just to unravel the differences within and between minority ethnic groups but, crucially, for the development of policies to deal with particular problems of victimisation faced by ethnic minorities.

As explained earlier, the 1988 and 1992 British Crime Surveys included a booster sample of people of Afro-Caribbean and Asian origin and it is now possible to begin to compare these groups' risks of victimisation with those of white people. In a recent Home Office report that presents the findings of an analysis of the victimisation risks of Afro-Caribbeans and Asians interviewed during the 1988 and 1992 surveys, it is pointed out that after taking social and demographic factors into account, particularly area of residence, their higher rates of victimisation are greatly reduced in terms of statistical

Table 2   Differential risks of victimisation: percent victimised once or more, by ethnic origin: 1988 and 1992 BCS

	White	Afro-Caribbean	Asian
Household	4.3	3.5	6.2**
Vandalism Burglary	5.8	11.1**	7.8**
Attempts and no loss	3.1	5.4**	3.7
With loss	3.0	6.7**	4.6**
Vehicle crime (owners)			
Vandalism	9.1	10.00	11.6**
All thefts	19.1	27.3**	21.0
Bicycle thefts (owners)	5.0	9.1**	4.7
Other household theft	9.4	8.4	8.8
All household offences	30.8	34.8**	36.2**
Assaults	3.4	5.9**	4.0
Threats	2.5	3.3	4.5**
Assault/Threat	5.5	8.5**	7.9**
Robbery/theft from person	1.3	3.2**	3.1**
Other personal theft	3.9	4.5	3.1
All personal offences	9.7	13.9**	13.0**
Unweighted N	19 294	1 776	1 976

Notes:
**Indicates a significant difference from whites at the 5% level.
Source: Maung and Mirlees-Black 1994, p. 7.

significance. Some differences nevertheless remain after such an analysis. Both groups (see Table 2 below) are, in statistical terms, significantly more at risk of burglary, assaults/threats, robbery and theft from the person. Asians are particularly at risk of vandalism, both household and vehicle vandalism, robbery and theft from the person, having higher risks than Afro-Caribbeans and whites. Afro-Caribbeans are more at risk of domestic assaults than whites or Asians and of vehicle theft.

A further, rather different, comparative factor is the immediate context within which black and Asian people become victims. The 1988 BCS, for example, found Asians more vulnerable to victimisation by groups of strangers: 28 per cent of their incidents involved four or more offenders (19 per cent for whites and 10 per cent for

Afro-Caribbeans). Offenders were also much less likely to be known; if they were known it was by sight (p. 46). Similar findings are also apparent from the 1992 survey (p. 90). Although it is different for various offences, the 1988 and 1992 BCSs indicate that as far as what are called 'home based offences' are concerned (offences of violence in and immediately around the home, excluding those by partners, ex-partners and relatives), 88 per cent of white victims said their attacker was white, 24 per cent of Afro-Caribbean and 76 per cent of Asian victims said the same. 2 per cent of white, 32 per cent of Afro-Caribbean and 5 per cent of Asian victims said their attacker was black and 1 per cent of white, 41 per cent of Afro-Caribbeans and 22 per cent of Asians said their attacker was Asian. Victims' perceptions can be inaccurate but these data show that Asians in particular are more at risk of assault by white people whom they do not know, in groups of four or more perpetrators committing offences in and immediately around their home, than white or Afro-Caribbean victims (Maung and Mirlees-Black, 1994, p. 91–2).

Some 'real' differences of risks of victimisation therefore remain when 'extra racial' variables are taken into account and it is evident that a racialised factor is structuring these patterns of victimisation. The pattern is sometimes similar and sometimes different for Afro-Caribbeans and Asians. If the Asian group was further divided into Bangladeshis, Pakistanis and Indians, further differences are likely to become apparent.

Considerably more detailed empirical and theoretical research is needed to explain how racialised, cultural and other factors fashion the structure of victimisation discovered by the large scale British Crime Survey. If we take the offence of criminal damage, for example, which is a term summarising a large number of different forms of damage, we find that much of it is concerned with damage to motor vehicles. A 1982 Policy Studies Institute study concerned with this crime found that levels of criminal damage to motor cars owned by what they defined as ethnic minorities were lower than those for whites (Brown, 1984). They also experienced less damage to the area surrounding their house and garden. A difference was, however, found in the incidence of damage to houses and flats. Here, there was a comparable level of victimisation among whites and Afro-Caribbeans but a significantly higher level among Asians – 5 per cent as opposed to 2 per cent. Asian households were therefore found to be around three times as likely as whites to experience criminal damage to their dwelling, which could be explained in part by the higher level of home ownership amongst some groups of Asians or Afro-Caribbeans; by the purely racial element of vandalism directed towards Asians; and other factors.

From Table 2 on page 38 we can also see that distinct patterns of victimisation for minority ethnic groups are revealed as far as the whole of England and Wales is concerned. Small scale, local area studies are likely to reveal another range of patterns of victimisation, which would not just assist our understanding of how racialised relations are structured in contemporary Britain but, crucially, would also be invaluable for the development of a strategy to intervene in and prevent further victimisation, as well as the provision of more finely-tuned support services for victims. In the first Islington crime survey, for example, much higher overall rates of vandalism were found than those documented in the PSI study. Black women in particular were found to have high risks of victimisation of criminal damage.[6] Elderly Asian men were also frequent victims, being three times as much at risk as black men. Furthermore, wide variations in patterns of victimisation of criminal damage were found in different electoral wards and it may be that groups experiencing high rates of criminal damage lived in these areas (Jones, Maclean *et al.*, 1986). Other studies, for example, the London Borough of Newham study, found a different pattern of victimisation, and so we could go on (London Borough of Newham, 1987).

Unfortunately, the results of different studies cannot be adequately compared because they have all used different sampling techniques, research strategies and questions (Fitzgerald and Ellis, 1989). Despite this problem, the point about the local area effect on patterns of victimisation amongst minority ethnic groups is an important one. Aggregate figures of victimisation, within and between the different minority ethnic groups can obscure significant differences, not only between offences but also between areas.

The context of 'race'

Methodological and other problems mean that it is not easy to identify the racialised element of victimisation within the complex documentation of statistical variations between different groups, localities and offences. However, even when they are overcome within the victim surveys the criminal victimisation experienced by minority ethnic groups is still not adequately described or analysed. This is mainly because the criminological traditions of quantitative research that have informed many research studies dealing with racialised discrimination tend to fail, sometimes completely, to place what are presented as discrete findings about victimisation, and other social phenomena for that matter, within a wider context of social relations (for a recent example of this completely atheoretical stance see Smith, 1994). The notion of the construction of racialised relations, or any other conceptual framework for that matter, is neglected in too many victimisation studies and within criminology generally.

Tony Jefferson has recently described the over-empirical and under-sociological type of research so frequent within criminology like straining variables through a sieve until a residue of 'race discrimination' remains (Jefferson, 1993). Area of residence, for example, is one variable that seems to be of relevance to the extent of victimisation amongst Afro-Caribbeans and Asians, as does form of housing tenure and type of property inhabited. In much research these are variables that would pass through the statistical sieve and be discarded until the real 'racial factor' remained as a residue. Once isolated, 'the race factor' is conceptualised as a stand-alone feature of our society, acting independently.

Quantitative analysis is certainly a part, an important part, of an explanation of rates of victimisation but an incomplete view of the ways in which apparently essential social phenomena are reconstructed in different forms. Area of residence, type of housing owned, type of tenure, and so on cannot be straightforwardly regarded as extra-racial variables and should be related to the history and racialised segregation of black and Asian people in Britain (Rex and Moore, 1967; Smith, 1989). If inner city areas have consistently high crime rates and this is where largish numbers of black and Asian people live, it follows that their presence in a high crime area is of relevance to the rates of criminal victimisation they experience. If we then go on to ask why they settled there in the first place and probe the historical processes that have led to such a pattern of residence we are faced with constraints related to the racialisation of the residential and employment prospects of black and Asian people? These, at first sight disparate but, under the sociological eye, interrelated factors frame relationships between groups defined by racialised criteria. They reconstruct and sustain the structure of racialised relations within contemporary Britain.

'Race' cannot therefore be simply isolated as a discrete statistical variable. Its relevance to victimisation and any other subject of research should be demonstrated by systematic and rigorous research methods: there is no argument about that. However, the tendency of much criminological research to deal with racialised discrimination as a discrete variable within the criminal justice system fails to take adequate account of the historical and continuing social structural, cultural and other constraints that sustain racialised relations related to risks of victimisation.

This does not mean that patterns of victimisation for Afro-Caribbeans, Asians or any other group are static; neither is it meaningful to describe all of their experience of criminal victimisation, housing, residence, employment, and so on as the outcome of systematic racism needed by the economic system. This collapses cause and effect into one and the same, spiralling us into a tautological argument (Mason, 1992). Diversity and similarity characterise the relationships we have discovered.

A final point about the ways in which criminological research based on statistical analyses of victimisation are potentially incomplete follows from this discussion. Typically, rates of victimisation for particular offences and for crime in general are analysed and results presented as if they are a unit of analysis in themselves. Risk of burglary is this much, risk of criminal damage that much, and so on. A series of snap shots, linked in album format by a research report, describes patterns of risk of victimisation for black, Asian, white and other groups.

This description of victimisation risks is misleading because it fragments the social world, compartmentalising it into moments rather than a stream of lived, reflected upon, enduring consciousness (Bowling, 1993). Individuals who have experienced an offence do not place their concerns and worry about what has and in the future might happen to them into neatly packaged parcels of experience. They relate their victimisation to other spheres of their lived experience, to other misfortunes they have suffered, to any sense of unfairness they might harbour; they discuss their experience with family, friends, colleagues at work; they mention it in various forums and listen to the experiences, explanations and, no doubt, frustrations of others who may have also been victims or heard about the same or similar events at first or second hand.

An individual's experience of victimisation is but one aspect of their consciousness of crime, of their personal safety and fate within a locality and within a society. Individual experience flows back and forth, perhaps creating dis-ease and misapprehension, even fear of similar happenings in the future. From this perspective the experience of victimisation amongst black and Asian people is a thread running through other social contexts within which 'race' is articulated.

We need to learn much more about the ways in which the personal experience of being a victim of crime and the general victimisation of black and Asian people is relevant to personal and collective identities, and to action. This does not necessarily mean that the black and Asian experience is either uniform or wholly distinct from that of white victims. Research in this area, however, would help us to understand how racialised relations structure and provide meaning for, in Schutz's terms, a 'life world' and, therefore, how processes of exclusion draw contours of racialised relations in contemporary Britain (Schutz, 1967).

Recognising the racialised nature of many relationships that have led numerous individuals and, by implication, groups to an experience of disadvantage, hurt and frustration, it is not surprising to find that fears of victimisation are amplified; the racial element of a victim's account of one or more crimes is heightened, perhaps even constructed from minimal evidence. This does not mean that, as one famed paper about the use of drugs suggested, 'fantasy can become reality' (Young, 1971). It does suggest that the experience of victimisation lived by the members of minority ethnic groups coheres around a greater number of reference points than the single crime to which they have been subjected (Walklate, 1992). Immediate, more distant, rumour-based and many other types of information and knowledge are relevant to the encapsulation of criminal victimisation within experience.

This wider context of racialised relations is the one faced by the police as they deal with minority ethnic victims of crime. Officers are not called to deal with a discrete crime, separated from a victim's stream of human experience. The wider social context that becomes personal when a crime is committed has particular connotations for black and Asian people. They may immediately relate their experience to other misfortunes; to their 'racial' origins; to experience of employment; and so on.[7]

Public issues, as C. Wright Mills called them, that are understood by individuals as personal problems, cannot be wholly ameliorated by police action (Mills, 1959). However, once aware of the distinct social context and 'life world' of minority ethnic groups, resources need to be, allocated appropriately, training programmes undertaken and supervision practised to ensure that the context of racialised relations within which victimisation occurs is not sustained through neglect, ignorance, or inadequate police attention. Unless they are aware of this context, appropriate police services will not be provided for minority ethnic groups, which is an important matter in itself. Further, and of equal importance, without sensitive police attention to the victim, racialised relations of exclusion from full membership of our society, access to its services and the opportunities provided for personal safety will be sustained by the police. Just as Wright-Mills argues that personal problems have wider, social structural reference points so the personal attention a police officer gives to a black or Asian victim partially reconstructs their personal reality and the reality of 'race' within the wider societal terrain.

Crime and other events with a clear racialised connotation or denotation are of particular importance to members of minority ethnic groups. In particular, the prevalence of racial attack and harassment raises in sharp focus the risks faced by the members of these groups, symbolising their possible victimisation, the attitudes of white peers, the police and, maybe, the society within which they live. Racial attacks and harassment denote the exclusion and marginalisation of minority ethnic groups. They are the subject of the next chapter.

Chapter Three

Racial attack in Britain

'A crime is a crime is a crime' was how Dame Jill Knight MP, member of the House of Commons Home Affairs Select Committee, responded to Michael Howard, the Home Secretary, when he argued that racial attacks should not be made a specific offence in law. Proof of racial motivation is too difficult a criterion for successful prosecution and, so he argued, it is better to deal with violence and criminal damage as just that, taking any evidence of racial motivation into account when sentence is passed. Racial attack and harassment are in essence like any other crime – for Michael Howard 'a crime is a crime is a crime' (House of Commons, 1994, p. 66).

In one sense Michael Howard is right(!), racial attacks and harassment are often breaches of existing law. But the question of how far a racial motive changes the nature of an assault or act of criminal damage brings to the fore wider issues about the social context within which people from minority ethnic groups live and the appropriate response of legislators and policy.

'Racial attack and harassment' summarises a very wide range of offences and incivilities ranging from murderous assault, damage to property, including the daubing of racist slogans, to verbal and other forms of personal abuse of an isolated or persistent nature. The apparent minor nature of some acts of racial harassment is immaterial. Their cutting edge is a pervasive or partial racial motive. In their 1986 report about race relations, the House of Commons Select Committee on Home Affairs described racial attacks as, 'the most shameful and dispiriting aspect of race relations in Britain (Home Affairs Committee, 1986), and in their evidence to an earlier enquiry by the committee the Association of Chief Police Officers (ACPO) described racial attacks as 'the most wicked additional burden faced by ethnic groups resident within already high crime areas (Home Affairs Committee, 1982)'.[1] The committee returned to the subject in 1994 but were unable to report real progress in curbing attacks and harassment, 'Racism, in whatever form, is an evil and destructive force in our undeniably multi-racial society. We are in no doubt that racial attacks and racial harassment, and the spread of literature that preaches racial hatred, are increasing and must be stopped.' They ended their report on a note of urgency, 'As racism is spreading so rapidly, time is short (House of Commons, 1994, p. xxxvii).'

In some areas of the country, particularly in London, harassment and attacks are very frequent. A representative from the Bangladeshi community living in the London Borough of Tower Hamlets told the 1986 Home Affairs Select Committee, 'the daily walk to and from work and school becomes a never ending nightmare.' Six years later a Home Office study found Bangladeshi families in Tower Hamlets still facing repeated victimisation, often from groups of small white children (Sampson and Phillips, 1992). Another witness to the committee described a situation in which, 'women live like prisoners. They do not go out to the doctor's surgery or to do shopping on their own. Children are often not allowed to play outside because of abuse and attacks (House of Commons, 1994, p. ii.).'

These features of racialised relations in our society can so easily go unnoticed by the majority of white people. Incidents of racial attack and harassment that do attract media coverage, serious assaults and murders for example, are reported in most newspapers and occasionally on the main television news. But the bulk of racial attacks and harassment – physical violence, verbal abuse, daubing of property, the pushing of excreta through letterboxes, damage to property, and so on – do not receive the same level of media attention, being articulated in a threatening subterrain of British society. If not reported to the police, as is often the case, these incidents straightforwardly erode the quality of life for victims, their family and friends because fear, insecurity and intimidation become stable features of everyday life, adding to the burden of racialised discrimination already experienced.

Apart from the immediate physical and mental harm done by the offence, racial attacks and harassment have a wider significance because they challenge the right of ethnic minorities to live in Britain at all. They are amongst the most pervasive public expressions of racial inequality and distinction. Racial abuse and violence not only often result in injury and damage to the dignity of the person attacked; and not only create a climate of fear and intimidation; also, they communicate the message that distinctions of 'race' are distinctions of dignity, respect and citizenship. Both victims and offenders learn from the messages contained in the attack and from the nature and quality of legal and policy responses by institutions.

Most attacks are committed on Asian and black people but certainly not limited to that group. A study in Glasgow identified Chinese people victimised by attacks; in Strathclyde, Vietnamese and Chileans were found to be victims; and there is much evidence of Jewish people being the target of incidents. The Metropolitan Police recorded 239 out of a national total of 281 cases of anti-semitism during 1992 (McFarland and Walsh, 1987; Walsh, 1987; *The Independent*, 1993). Indeed, the wide range of groups subjected to harassment is probably not appreciated, in part because research has tended to focus on the main minority ethnic communities (Fitzgerald and Ellis, 1989).

Attacks and harassment are not confined to urban areas or places with a high minority ethnic population. People living in isolated communities may be the subject of harassment. The owners of Asian restaurants, Chinese take-away shops, the relatively small number of black and Asian people living in white suburbia and small towns are also likely to be victims, without the support of a community living around them. Some incidents are particularly prevalent on council housing estates, where 'welcoming groups' have abused new tenants, but are by no means confined to these areas (CRE, 1988). In his *Racial Violence and Harassment*, Paul Gordon describes incidents that have occurred in suburban and rural Britain and he regards the situation as sufficiently serious to call them acts of 'racial terrorism' (Gordon, 1986). The seriousness of racial attacks and harassment cannot be denied or neglected and in their 1986 report the Home Affairs Select Committee advised all police forces to make them a priority area of work, a view endorsed by the Home Office.

This contemporary situation has distinct features but it is not wholly new. Racial attacks were perpetrated against Jews during the 11th century; against black people in London, Cardiff, Bristol, Glasgow and Liverpool during the early part of this century; in

Notting Hill in 1958; in London's Brick Lane area and in other places of Pakistani settlement throughout the 1960s to the present day (Pearson, 1976; Gordon, 1986; Lawrence, 1987). Over many years right-wing fascist and racist political organisations and parties have advocated repatriation and other measures to curb the rights of people from minority ethnic groups. In the East End of London, for example, a long and complex history of racialised politics has played its part in the rise of the British National Party (BNP) as a contender at local elections and, in 1994, election to a seat on the local council (Hobbs, 1988).

In Welling, south London, the BNP has opened a 'book shop' and headquarters. There has been a noticeable increase in the number of racial attacks in the area since the opening of the shop, including the murderous stabbing of Stephen Lawrence, a black youth simply waiting at a bus stop. One of the BNP's main activities is the publication and dissemination of racist literature, not least in areas where black and Asian people live. Other groups, especially Jews, have also been particularly affected by the BNP. Since 1984 the Board of Deputies of British Jews has encouraged people subjected to racial harassment or assault to inform not only the police about their victimisation but also to send them details. Their methodology is by no means sound but it reveals the desecration of tombstones and synagogues, as well as the distribution of derogatory leaflets to houses in established Jewish communities, and a range of assault and other acts that amount to concerted harassment.

Far Right groups are able to concentrate their use of propaganda and other activities in particular geographical areas, creating fear and insecurity amongst populations already facing considerable difficulties. There may be a relationship between the activity of the BNP in localities and increases in the number of racial attacks in the same places. Again, the methods of data collection are unstated but it was reported in *The Observer* on 13 February 1994, that during January 1993, 17 racial attacks occurring on the Isle of Dogs were reported to the police; following the election of a BNP councillor in September 1993 the figure rose to 57 attacks during January 1994.

All the activities of Far Right groups in Britain echo the recent rise of nationalism within Europe and, in some European countries, Germany in particular, there has been a horrendous increase in racial violence by neo-Nazi and other extreme right-wing groups

(Oakley, 1993). Jewish people living in Britain find their history of persecution under Nazism to be interpreted as a subject for glorification by active political movements in Europe and, by implication, within their own society. Their personal and collective security is brought into doubt.

The Far Right also represent the immediate possibility of abuse and assaults on black and Asian people if direct political activity is focused in their locality. Racially motivated murders of black and Asian people – nine in 1992 and a further three in the early months of 1993 were cited in the evidence of the Churches' Commission for Racial Justice Evidence to the Home Affairs Committee – symbolise for black and Asian people the possibility of death and therefore the risk, no matter how small, of a serious offence committed on oneself or one's children in public and private places. White people rarely face this situation.

A thread of murderous and serious, racially motivated assaults is now woven into the history of black British and Asian people. These are not discrete events, sporadically reported in the press, but constituents of a living history linking myriad incidents of many different kinds. They are all of a piece as far as the lives of black and Asian people are concerned. Many white people live at risk in high crime areas; any criminal victimisation is a potential shock, bringing emotional and physical consequences. The added burden for people from minority ethnic groups is a victimisation based on their 'race' and a questioning of their right to citizenship itself. People who perpetrate racial attacks and harassment try to extinguish hope and security from the lives of their fellow citizens because, *and only because*, they happen to be defined as belonging to the wrong 'race'. Their lives are racialised.

Within this context Michael Howard's view that it is not necessary to create a new statute to cover racial attack begins to appear less secure. Legislation has a symbolic as well as an instrumental function, declaring that racial attacks and harassment are not just discrete offences but interwoven with historical themes of racialised prejudice and discrimination that erode and challenge claims to citizenship. Although important within their own sphere, on their own, arguments about the pertinence of legal measures to deal with racial attacks and harassment fall short of adequacy, failing to take account of the social context within which they occur.

Definitions

Although there is a long history of racial attacks occurring in Britain and it is acknowledged that they are a pernicious feature of race relations, contention has surrounded attempts to define clearly just what amounts to an attack. In part, these disputes have arisen because racial attack is not a criminal offence defined in statute. At another level, disputes about this definition resonate academic debate about the definition of 'race relations' as distinct from other relations, especially to what extent is it necessary to include a consciousness of 'race' within such a definition?

A key feature of a racial attack is the racial motive of the attacker and it is ultimately only the attacker who has full knowledge of motive. People whose work brings them into contact with victims of racial attacks have to interpret what might be ambiguous or contradictory evidence about motives. Or maybe we can liken relationships between white, black and Asian people to a zero-sum power game and thereby confidently define any attack or act of harassment on a black, Asian or perhaps any person from a minority ethnic group as a racial attack *per se*? Who is then the best judge – the victim or the police officer recording the incident; the race relations worker or the local authority housing officer? Who is to judge whether or not a racialised motive lies behind an action?

This is not just an academic issue because the problem of finding an appropriate definition has substantial implications for policy and practice to deal with racial attacks and harassment. It is necessary in this area, which is fraught with misunderstanding, to know what we are talking about; to know what is and what is not to be defined and accepted as a racial attack or act of racial harassment and, therefore, when law enforcement and other agencies should or should not take action. Equally important, the reporting and official recording of more or less racial attacks and harassment will be directly related to the definition accepted. A broadly based definition may include many more incidents than a tightly drawn one and this will lead to different policy responses, requiring different types and levels of resources.

Following the presentation of sustained evidence from various organisations representing ethnic minorities, in 1981 the Home Office conducted research into the extent of racial attacks or, rather, what they then called 'inter-racial incidents'. The Home Office definition of an inter-racial incident used in this study was, 'an incident or alleged offence by a person or persons of one racial group against another or property of another racial group, where there are indications of a racial motive' (Home Office, 1981).

This definition was to become the target of considerable criticism, some of which seems contradictory. It was argued that the definition was too inclusive and the specifically racial context of attacks was watered down by the broadly defined framework of 'racial incidents' (Klug, 1982). There was also unease about defining situations as racial incidents where white people fall victim to offences committed by members of ethnic minorities. Structures of social inequality and institutional racism framed by imbalances of power between majority and minority ethnic groups are neglected and virtually denied by the notion of a 'racial incident'.

On the other hand, an exclusive aspect of the definition was also criticised. The vague wording of the Home Office definition meant that when it was put into operation by the police and other officials, many incidents with a racial motive could slip through the net, through ignorance, error, prejudice or discrimination. For these and many other reasons police officers and other officials should not be the ultimate assessors of whether or not a person acts with a racial motive. The upshot of this definition is neglect of the victim's crucial assessment of what has happened, which should always be in the ascendancy.

Of course, the only final arbiter of the motive for an assault, act of criminal damage or whatever is the offender. Second best is the view of the victim and it is the victim's perception of the motive leading to an incident that is now more fully taken into account. Since 1985, at the suggestion of ACPO, the following definition should be put into operation by all police forces, 'any incident in which it appears to the reporting or investigating officer that involves an element of racial motivation; or any incident which includes an allegation of racial motivation made by any person.' The intention here is to introduce a number of checks and balances into the definition to ensure racial incidents are adequately identified. The reporting and investigating officer and any person making an allegation has an opportunity – in theory if not in practice – to define the incident as racially motivated. Further, it is possible for any person, irrespective of ethnic origin, to be the victim or perpetrator of an attack.

In theory this definition should capture the vast majority of racial attacks and acts of harassment and, although its limitations were debated during the most recent Home Affairs Committee hearings, it remains official policy to this day. But if arguments about responses to racial attacks are based solely on the adequacy of written definitions, a crucial feature of the process of policy making and implementation will be neglected because no distinction will be made between written policy and practice (Holdaway, 1978). The inconsistent translation of policy, including definitions of racial attack and harassment, into the routine, operational practice of the ranks has persistently dogged policing. An officer recording an incident may perceive no difficulties if a clearly articulated and persistent expression of racial motivation is conveyed by 'any other person'. The difficulty comes when the person alleging that a racial motivation influenced an incident puts the allegation in muted or uncertain terms. For many different reasons – wanting to avoid 'paper work', a lack of interest, as well as racialised prejudice and discrimination – an officer might fail to record the incident as racially motivated. Despite the authoritative status of the ACPO/Home Office definition, both police policy and practice have to be taken into account if we are to understand how rank-and-file officers sustain the racialised nature of many crimes and acts of disorder.

Policy and practice – research

Formal definitions of racial attack, then, are important but not necessarily the primary guiding principle for rank-and-file officers dealing with an allegation. There may be a gap between police policy and practice, between the formal and working rules guiding police action. The success of the ACPO definition ultimately depends on the police rank-and-file acceptance of victims' accusations about racial motivation.

One of the continuing criticisms made of police officers' perceptions of and action to deal with racial attacks is precisely that they do not take victims' and others' allegations of racial motive sufficiently seriously, and therefore do not appreciate how the impact of what, from an observer's perspective, might seem a rather minor incident is transposed when committed in a context of racial prejudice and discrimination. Minor damage to property is no longer minor when a racial motive is perceived to lie behind it. If the full extent of racial incidents are to be recorded by the police and an appropriate response made, it is crucial for police officers to favour the victim's account when recording an incident as a racial attack.

Research about the extent of racial attack has not been particularly helpful in this regard. It has often depended on official police records and therefore incidents defined by police officers as having a racial element. Studies of racial attack and harassment have unfortunately used different definitions, complicating and negating the calculation of meaningful estimates of their extent within contemporary Britain (Fitzgerald and Ellis, 1989). The evidence is therefore fragmented and often based on diverse, incompatible research designs.

The first research to measure the extent of attacks and harassment was carried out by Home Office researchers in 1981 (Home Office, 1981). All racial attacks, racial incidents in Home Office terms, were studied, which meant the analysis of police data, with its definitional problems. From this slippery base it was estimated that about 7000 racial incidents occurred each year; 51.2 per 100 000 West Indians and 69.7 per 100 000 Asians.

A more reliable research strategy which was not so dependent on official police records was used in a Policy Studies Institute project about race relations in Britain published the following year (Brown, 1984). This was in effect a type of victim survey in which a matched number of white and minority ethnic respondents were asked if they had been the victim of a racial incident during a recall period of time. All attacks on Asians and West Indians by white people and all incidents where a victim specifically mentioned a racial motive, a racialist organisation or obvious hostility and unprovoked attack were included in the analysis. On the basis of these data it was assessed that the Home Office figure was a gross underestimate and should be multiplied by a factor of ten to provide a more accurate indicator of the extent of racial attacks in Britain. Little wonder, then, that the research also found that minority ethnic people felt the situation was worsening.

Since this PSI research was completed, a number of studies have looked at the levels of racial attack in localities but, as I have suggested, it is unfortunate that they cannot be satisfactorily compared because the ethnic groups interviewed were defined differently: distinctions have not been made between important sub-groups within broad categories like 'Asian'; different sampling techniques have been used, sometimes including or excluding a white control group; different definitions of racial attack have been employed and attacks committed by members of one minority ethnic community on the member of another have been defined out of some studies; and different questions have been asked to respondents comprising very different sizes of sample (Fitzgerald and Ellis, 1989).

This lack of attention to co-ordinated research and policy makers' need of consistent data has, according to Marian Fitzgerald and Tom Ellis, frustrated the planning of effective intervention. Civil servants have been faced with a very complex and disparate array of findings suggesting many different and sometimes competing types of policy developments. Neither national or local policy-making has therefore been assisted by this diverse approach to research.

Local studies

The 1987 London Borough of Newham study, that included questions about racial attacks and harassment (but with no white control group for this part of the study), indicated that one in four of the borough's minority ethnic residents who live in council owned property had been the victim of racial harassment in the previous 12 months (London Borough of Newham, 1987). Given the relative under-representation of Asian people living in council housing this estimate is perhaps on the low side. Men and women were found to be equally likely to be victims and victimisation was extended fairly evenly across all age groups. Attacks were said to be committed overwhelmingly by white people on Asians and black people but no attention was given in this survey to whether or not, for example, victims thought that acts similar to the 'muggings' and offences of violence committed on Asians by black people – the extent of which was reported in the 1992 British Crime Survey and other Home Office studies – were perceived as racially motivated (p. 92; Sampson and Phillips, 1992).

In 1989 another survey was conducted in one part of the borough of Newham, this time by the Home Office. This study included some features that partially corrected the inadequacies of previous research. Ethnically matched interviewers were used and 1150 respondents took part, including a booster sample of Asian people

(Saulsbury and Bowling, 1991). It was found that one in five Afro-Caribbean and one in six Asian men and women suffered a racial attack in the preceding 18 month period. Women were no more likely than men to have experienced an attack but women mentioned a greater number of incidents, which suggested a greater likelihood of multiple-victimisation. The majority of victims clustered around the 25–44 age group. Two thirds of the incidents mentioned in the survey by Asian respondents involved white perpetrators, one fifth involved Afro-Caribbeans and one tenth involved a 'mixed' group. All the incidents mentioned by Afro-Caribbeans involved white perpetrators. Of the incidents mentioned by white respondents half involved Afro-Caribbeans and 12 per cent involved other white people. The motive here was frequently thought to be 'racial vengeance, getting back at white people'.

Although the findings from the Newham 1987 study may have been restricted because only council tenants were interviewed, the later 1989 study gave some credence to the view that Asian council house tenants are more at risk of victimisation than those living in other types of property. 38 per cent of the incidents mentioned by Asians were cited by those living in council housing and since just 14 per cent of the Asian respondents in the survey lived in council housing it seems that they had been more frequent victims than those living in other property. However, it is possible that this finding is in part the result of police officers who work permanently on council estates and local authority council officials recording more racial attacks and harassment than those working elsewhere. Council tenants regularly meet officials to pay rent and are then able to report victimisation, and so on. If a report is recorded by the housing department it is likely to be passed to the police and recorded in their files. Recording policies and practices in a range of agencies then boost the established levels of attack.

Different levels of victimisation were experienced by the different gender groups interviewed. 18 per cent and 21 per cent respectively of Asian and African/Afro-Caribbean women had suffered an incident during the previous 18 months. Most of these occurred near to their home but many of the incidents reported by African and Afro-Caribbean women were said to have occurred at their place of work. Asian women, who as a category did not have the highest rate of harassment, were found to be the group upon whom racial harassment had the greatest impact. Of those who were victimised,

60 per cent became fearful as a result of their experience, one in three of whom said that the worst effects were still continuing. Only one in ten Asian women interviewed said they did not worry at all about being racially attacked or harassed. Nearly seven out of ten Asian women, whether or not victims, said they worried either 'a great deal' or a 'fair amount' about themselves or a member of their family being victimised.

A further aspect of this 1989 study is the inclusion of evidence about attacks on white women and 'mixed race' families. These mostly occurred near their home and involved abusive language, in these respects being similar to the incidents reported by women from other groups. However, white women were twice as likely to mention a racial incident involving 'theft' than Asian women, and four times more likely than Afro-Caribbean women.

White perpetrators were involved in many of the incidents reported. In three out of ten incidents all the perpetrators were white and in a further 12 per cent of cases people involved were mainly white. More generally, white perpetrators were involved in more than four out of ten incidents directed against white women. The survey did not fully clarify the reasons for these incidents but it seems that they are concerned with women who are members of mixed-race families; who associate with black people; or, members of minority ethnic groups who are white, for example, Irish or Jewish people.

The vast majority of perpetrators were said to be young men between the ages of 16 and 25. This is a slightly wider age range than that for the majority of all perpetrators of assaults, and victims of assault for that matter. It is not always easy for victims to judge the age of youths and many of them could have been younger. In fact when police records were analysed it was found that 57 per cent of perpetrators arrested were between 11 and 15, which could indicate a very poor prognosis. One of the arguments about the way in which young men should be dealt with by the courts has been influenced by evidence that most of them grow out of offending during their early twenties. Such an argument presents real difficulties in the light of this evidence of 11 to 15 year olds committing racial attacks and harassment, because it is simply not possible to allow them to grow out of this type of offending behaviour. In this sense too 'a crime is not a crime.' The harm caused to black and Asian people is far too great.

We can now perhaps more clearly picture the setting of some of Newham's council house estates with groups of youths directing racial abuse at Asian and black residents walking to and from their homes, adding to the other difficulties of living in those areas. It is significant that 'rubbish and litter' (51 per cent) and crime (44 per cent) were most frequently mentioned as significant problems by people living in the estates where research was conducted. An unpleasant physical environment is simply further personalised by racial harassment and attacks. Add to this situation harassment in schools, in recreation grounds, around one's home, at work and the utterly dispiriting environment within which many of Newham's black and Asian residents live – and by implication those in many other areas of Britain – strikes home.

The 1987 Newham survey further indicated that just under 5 per cent of incidents of racial harassment were reported to the police, whose clear-up rate was small. One reason for this level of under-reporting was that most of the incidents of harassment involved insulting behaviour and did not attract police action (ibid p. 35). Indeed, Newham's ethnic minority residents placed a low priority on police action against this type of harassment, perhaps indicating the invidious way in which racial prejudice and discrimination had eroded the quality of their lives to become a routine, virtually taken-for-granted occurrence (ibid p. 39). Priority was given to physical assaults and attacks on homes.

Overall, in the case of the 'most important incidents', one in three were reported to the police. Of those not reported, in 50 per cent of incidents it was thought that the police would do nothing and in 37 per cent it was felt that the matter was not sufficiently serious to warrant a report to the police – a pattern that is consistent with the general reasons for non-reporting found in victim surveys covering all types of offences.

The 1989 Newham research included an assessment of levels of reporting against levels of recording in police and local authority housing department records. Respective rates of just over 2 per cent and 5 per cent were found. Remembering that racial harassment is not a specific offence and the majority of incidents are of verbal abuse, it is not surprising to find such a low reporting rate. Two thirds of victims thought that the police could or, more disappointingly, would do nothing if an incident was reported. This is an accurate assessment in strictly legal terms but indicative of a serious lapse in perceptions of the help officers can offer and, perhaps, also officers' perceptions of appropriate police work because a visit from a home beat officer, a referral to Victim Support or to some other source of potential help could have been given (Kimber and Cooper, 1990).

Many respondents said that they felt they had not been informed adequately about the progress of their case. Half of the incidents recorded had been relayed by the police to the housing department, whose workers would have repaired damaged property, erased graffiti and so on. But this did not seem to assuage the feeling revealed by the research that Newham's police rank-and-file are not particularly interested in or understanding about the impact of racial harassment.

History and persistent neglect

Public dissatisfaction with police service is not new. As long ago as 1979, in their evidence to the Royal Commission on Criminal Procedure, the Institute of Race Relations argued that 'the failure of the police to protect the black community leaves it exposed to racial violence. At its worst police practice reinforces that violence (Institute of Race Relations, 1978, p. 20).[1] The report claimed that police officers have frequently failed to recognise the racial dimension of attacks; that there has often been a significant time delay in response to calls for assistance; an unwillingness to investigate or prosecute offenders; the provision of inadequate advice; and general hostility towards victims. The institute concluded that reform should include police training which acknowledges the reality and pervasive nature of racism in Britain and its manifestation in racial violence. Clear procedures are required to record and investigate racial violence as a specific crime; and foot patrol – under-used in 1979 – is likely to be more successful a police strategy than the deployment of specialist units.

These themes of criticism have persisted, again apparent in 1989 when the House of Commons, Home Affairs Select Committee returned to the subject of racial attacks and harassment, to conduct an enquiry into how far the Home Office had implemented recommendations made in their 1986 report.[2] In general terms the committee thought inadequate progress had been made, though they recognised some important developments. First, they were concerned that the level and types of police record keeping for racial attacks were inadequate. It was not possible for the committee or, more importantly, the police, to know: if attacks were in any sense increasing or decreasing; if consistent record keeping systems were in place throughout the 43 constabularies of England and Wales; or what level of priority chief constables were affording the subject.

Jayne Seagrave, a Home Office researcher, in a paper made available to the committee, argued that serious racial attacks were decreasing but less serious incidents seemed to be increasing (Seagrave, 1989). This situation could of course have been influenced by police record keeping practices and changes in reporting behaviour. Importantly, Seagrave found that of the incidents she documented, in one in six cases, there was a difference of opinion between the victim and the investigating officer when recording the incident as a racially motivated offence. Three out of four cases were those where the victim thought there was a racial motive but the police officer had apparently not accepted this view.

Other statistics, rather more striking ones presented to the committee by the Association of Chief Police Officers, indicated the historic basis of uncertainty and confusion from which the police were assessing their response and undertaking future planning.

In 1986, when the number of police forces recording incidents increased from 20 to 28, the number of racial attacks recorded nearly trebled. The following two years saw an increase of a further 12 forces recording attacks but a gradual drop of attacks to just over

Table 3   Recorded racial incidents in provincial forces in England and Wales 1984–8

Year	Recorded Incidents	No of Forces recording incidents
1984	1329	15
1985	1626	20
1986	4519	28
1987	2965	38
1988	2366	40

Source: Home Affairs Committee, 1989

half the 1986 level. The more forces recording, the less attacks recorded! Since 1988, 6359 and 7734 racial incidents were reported and recorded in 1990 and 1992 respectively.

Remembering that there seems to be a tendency for racial attacks and harassment to be under-reported and therefore under-repre-sented in official statistics, these figures indicate the insecure basis of information from which police policy and practice has been planned. The Association of Chief Police Officers suggested to the 1989 Home Affairs Committee that the Home Office should undertake a national study similar in design to the British Crime Survey but focusing more clearly on racial incidents. This would at least set a base level of evidence about the extent of racial attacks. The committee agreed but did not also mention that local studies are equally if not more important, providing much more finely tuned data for policy deve-lopment. The Home Office response was the inclusion of an in-creased booster sample of black and Asian people in the 1992 British Crime Survey, which was discussed in the last chapter. In the report of that survey it is suggested that between 130 000 and 140 000 racial incidents were recorded by the police, implying that only one in 16 were reported.

When in 1994 members of the Home Affairs Committee returned once again to the issue and questioned Peter Lloyd, a Home Office minister, and other witnesses about the extent of racial attacks and harassment they seem to have been tipped off about the inadequacy of the statistics produced by the Home Office. The minister was asked for the figures for different 'racial groups', for different localities, different types of acts, and other detail but he could not answer. The statistics are not available and the upshot was sharp criticism about the limited Home Office action taken in response to the Committee's last 1989 recommendation about research. A strong recommendation was made that the Home Office should go much further than its inclusion of a booster sample in the British Crime Survey and conduct frequent research to discover the specific extent and nature of racial attacks and harassment. It was also argued that the proposed survey might help to raise an awareness of the sustained priority every constabulary must give to dealing with racial attacks.

In addition to placing emphasis on national research, in their 1994 report the committee also expressed strong support for local moni-toring projects. They argued that government funding should be made available to these projects established to gather information for the development of local policies.

All these and other recommendations depend on chief constables giving a clear priority to racial attacks within their local policing plans. Recommendations by the Home Affairs Committee to the Home Office cannot be assumed to translate directly into chief constables' priorities. The right to autonomous decision-making is jealously protected by chief officers. There have been occasions when Home Office directives have led to immediate police action but prediction of any response is risky. Such is the relationship between the Home Office and chief constables. In their evidence to the 1989 Committee the Home Office said they could identify just four forces where a stated priority had been given to dealing with racial attacks. Other forces might have had a less public and therefore visible commitment but it was not possible to be sure. A Home Office circular about the need for all chief constables to give a priority to racial attacks had been published and circulated but their response had been patchy, a point acknowledged by ACPO's representative who appeared as a witness before the 1994 Committee hearing.

Much more needs to be done to encourage victims to report harassment and attacks. The figures of under-reporting reveal a less than adequate response by the police and the Home Office has again been asked by the Home Affairs Committee to issue guidance to chief constables about the need to give a priority to racial attacks and harassment. A new offence of attack or harassment might help here but the initial task is for chief constables – all chief constables because attacks and harassment occur throughout the country – and their senior staff to establish work in this area as a priority. When that initial commitment is placed within policy and publicised, it is hoped that victims will be more encouraged to begin reporting incidents and the needed police response develop.

There certainly needs to be every encouragement and opportunity for victims to report to the police the attacks and harassment to which they have been subjected. Here, the general level of confidence in which the police are held by people from minority ethnic communities is all important. By the publication of leaflets, local surgeries, the provision of panic buttons, household alarms and other devices, confidence and a sense of personal safety can be enhanced, as well as encouragement given to report further incidents to the police. It is, however, no use reporting racial incidents to police ears that are hard of hearing. A force priority expressed by chief officers is vitally important as the basis of policy but insufficient if the same level of priority is to be afforded to attacks and harassment by the lower ranks, who deal with incidents on the ground.

One police response to this problem is to set up a special squad of officers who deal exclusively with racial attacks and harassment. There are not a great number of these squads but where they have been established they have demonstrated some benefits. In 1990, for example, a Racial Incident Unit was established at Plumstead police station in south east London. The officers staffing the unit deal with all cases of attack and harassment in the area, providing continuity for the victim. They build up relationships with the local minority ethnic community, encourage the reporting of incidents and try to establish trust. Adequate statistics to assess the impact of the unit are not available but it seems that many more racial incidents are reported to Plumstead police than to officers at nearby stations. Their clear-up rate for attacks is also higher than the average in London (House of Commons, 1994, p. xiii).

Special dedicated units have their place and if the 1994 Select Committee has its way they will become a regular feature of policing in areas with large minority ethnic populations. Specialisation, however, also brings problems, not least a perception among officers working on routine shift duty that racial incidents are not their concern. Racial attacks and harassment are dealt with by a specialist squad and therefore not a priority within the routines of daily patrol work. Some constabularies, Kent for example, have deliberately turned away from a policy of specialisation for this reason.

In the 1989 Plaistow research project the lack of interest in and awareness of the nature and extent of racial attack amongst the police rank-and-file became apparent. During interviews with police officers it was clear that many of them had little or no knowledge of patterns of harassment in the area for which they held a responsibility. Many had little experience and, presumably, expertise to deal with the incidents when they arose. Without adequate knowledge and sensitivity there was a tendency to deny both the problem of racial harassment itself and the limitations of the police response.

Some other officers, those who patrolled home beats and the members of a special squad, Newham Organised Racial Incident

Squad (sic), were much more aware but they were not, as it were, the front-line police response to allegations of harassment that led to emergency calls for police assistance. They shared a perception of colleagues working on reliefs as unaware of the dimensions of the problems faced by the victims of harassment. Racial incidents had become the province of specialists.

The question for the police is now surely one of balance, not an exclusive choice between one or other stance. Specialist units will have their role in many areas and where very high levels of racial attacks and harassment are apparent they are appropriate. One of their functions, however, is gradually to transfer their work to patrol officers, preparing the ground as a transitional phase. It is crucial for the rank-and-file to be generally aware of the priority to be afforded and specific attention to be given to incidents of racial attack and harassment.

Inter-agency strategies – problems of organisational structure and culture

Whatever the police balance between specialist and generic approaches to racial attacks and harassment, the incidents themselves often include damage to local authority housing, occur in or near schools, involve youth and create the need for support services for victims. If, for example, the same children who have been abusing black children at school are members of families who also abuse their black housing estate neighbours, it is obviously helpful for cross-referenced records to be kept about such perpetrators and, at best, the introduction of a joint strategy of action based on commonly shared principles.

Realising that a number of local agencies are involved in dealing with racial attacks and harassment, the Home Office has stressed the need for an inter-agency approach (Home Office, 1989). At the level of central government an Inter-Departmental Racial Attacks Group, with a membership of civil servants from all relevant ministries, has been established. The group was originally meant to gather examples of good practice, monitor developments and retain a collaborative impetus for policy development. Although it published two substantial reports the group ceased meeting regularly and the Home Affairs Committee has again strongly recommended that it should be reconvened to meet on a regular basis, not least to monitor the extent to which its recommendations find fruition in local projects.

The Racial Attacks Group has suggested a wide range of inter-agency activities for development at local level. Local authority housing departments, for example, can include clauses about racial harassment in letting agreements and implement eviction orders as part of a preventive strategy (CRE, 1981; Fitzgerald, 1990). They can implement a flexible housing allocations policy in which ethnic minorities at risk are not allocated to properties in areas prone to racial violence; improve the security of properties too readily accessible to attack; publish leaflets about action that will be taken against perpetrators; make interpreting facilities available at estate offices; install immediate response alarms in the homes and shops of the most frequently victimised; and take a vigorous approach to an integrated, inter-agency policy (Sampson and Phillips, 1992; The Runnymede Trust, 1993).

Schools are able to focus on the peer-group pressure and aspects of teenage-culture that stress the acceptability of racial abuse and harassment. In a recent publication by the Runnymede Trust it is suggested that, among other initiatives, pupils should be made thoroughly aware of school rules prohibiting racial harassment, abuse, graffiti, name-calling anywhere in the school and on journeys to and from school; all staff – teaching and support staff – should be aware of the policy and not prohibited from using formal procedures for recording and dealing with bullying and racial incidents; parents' awareness of and involvement in agreeing principles and procedures for dealing with bullying and harassment should be fostered (The Runnymede Trust, 1993).

Victim support schemes, tenants' associations, cleansing departments, transport authorities and many other local agencies can together formulate a coherent and concerted range of policies to deal with racial harassment, linking with the police, who will probably always take the lead when planning is required. In the Metropolitan Police area, for example, a number of Racial Incident Panels have been set up, bringing together police, local authority officers and representatives of community groups, to monitor and develop policy and practice. Reports of harassment and violence can be collated by these groups, information pooled and discussion sustained. Other more recent police initiatives have included the distribution of multi-lingual leaflets to community centres and places of worship (in Bedfordshire), the compilation of a database to measure the problems of racial harassment (in Greater Manchester), and work with Asian women support groups, to encourage the reporting of offences against women and children (in West Yorkshire) (Home Office, 1993).

Inter-agency approaches to racial attack and harassment require clear communication between agencies, a tolerance to each other's styles of work, determination to co-ordinate best practices for the benefit of victims and a humility to consider new ideas. Although evidence of the working of inter-agency forums and racial incident panels is sparse, there is a growing body of knowledge to suggest that many stumbling blocks have impeded their development. Conflict and misunderstanding seem to have often prevented the co-operative partnership required.

The Legal Action Group, in 1990, surveyed local authority use of the law against perpetrators of racial harassment and found that one of the reasons for what they considered · an under use of legal proceedings was a lack of communication between housing and legal officials working *within* local authorities (Legal Action Group, 1990). We have other evidence of the lack of communication about racial attacks between police officers working in special squads and their colleagues working on routine shifts. If there is a lack of agreement and co-ordination about the nature of racial harassment within participating organisations it is surely more than likely that confusion will be compounded when inter-agency forums are convened.

During a research study of police consultative group meetings in different cities it was found that police officers participating in them were confused about the meaning and extent of racial harassment (Pearson, Sampson *et al.*, 1989). These were not inter-agency forums strictly speaking but they did include members from local community associations, the probation service, local authorities and the police. A rather different arrangement for consultation was found within each city but this did not lead to better or worse co-ordination of policy within any of them. The basic issue identified was an interplay between different definitions and perceptions of race relations and racial attacks, which led to different priorities for policy. These views lay under the surface of discussion but apparently had a real effect on the response of the different parties involved. Race issues were constructed within a sometimes unstated vying and yielding of ideas, in which some members argued that the basic issue was the over-policing of black people; that the police do not adequately respond to racial incidents, they are under-policed; that racism within the police ranks needs to be tackled; and that systems of community representation tend to exclude the members of the range of locally based minority ethnic groups from discussion within the inter-agency forums. Attention should therefore be directed to exclusion within local systems of representation.

This research suggests that participants in the consultation process have difficulty tying down the ways in which these different understandings frame particular discussions and, importantly, lead to a neglect of the wider context of racialised relations that restricted their appreciation of limits of intervention. In particular, the police individualised 'racism within their ranks', blaming a few bad apples who did not taint the whole police barrel and isolated racial attack and harassment as one-off incidents rather than parts of a wider pattern. The wider pattern of incidents was thereby prohibited from reaching the surface, not least because the police had power to frame discussion and sustain their own agenda within the consultative forums.

It is unfortunate that it is less than clear from this research what might be done in practical terms to deal with the difficulties found. They nevertheless point to some of the problems of the inter-agency approach advocated by the Home Office and many chief officers of police.

A more detailed appraisal of a multi-agency project to deal with racial attacks in Plaistow, east London also found confusion and a lack of consensus about fundamental issues of policy planning and implementation (Saulsbury and Bowling, 1991). Differences of perspective among workers from the participating agencies were found from the outset and it was necessary for the organisers 'to confront very real ideological differences, a history of mistrust and surprisingly deep misunderstandings of the operational and political constraints affecting the groups involved (p. 13).'

Even when differences were acknowledged about very basic issues, like the definition of racial attack to be used during the project, underlying conflicts were not neutralised. The local council wanted to adopt a definition that included the word 'racism'; other parties were content with the ACPO definition. Agreement was reached but, 'This resulted in failure to come to grips with the fact that rather different organisations understood racial attacks and harassment in fundamentally different ways. This tension remained unresolved throughout the life of the project (ibid, p. 21).'

Differences like these remained as the project developed but its fate did not just rest on the extent to which, as Pearson and his colleagues have argued, members of the agencies involved understood the relationship between wider structures of race relations and the dynamics of group discussion. Other impediments not so directly related to race issues *per se* were placed in the way of the development and implementation of consistent policy. The key point from the Plaistow study is that race relations are mediated through organisational structures and cultures, which affect the extent to which it becomes possible to develop policy approaches to phenomena like racial attack and harassment. Perceptions of 'race' play their part but are by no means the only factors that need to be understood. An adequate analysis and, it follows, related policy solutions also need to take account of organisational structures and cultures that enhance or distract from innovation.

Within the small group formed to write an action plan for the Plaistow project, new ideas of how to tackle racial attacks and harassment created uncertainty, frustration and feelings of threat that extended to the members' agencies. Marginal departures from accepted practices were developed but more basic changes proved extremely difficult. There was uncertainty about the level of resources available to underpin initiatives and a failure to follow through their implications and consequences.

Project members did not adequately communicate the action plan to colleagues working in their agencies, as far the police were concerned, especially to shift inspectors and sergeants. Participating departments within the one local authority were inadequately organised to work in partnership or with co-operation. It was incredibly difficult to sustain a commitment to organisational change and a frequent complaint claimed that effort thought to be beyond the call of duty was required. Indeed, the participating organisations were not adequately able to undertake the basic step of gathering data about the extent and nature of attacks and harassment because research was a new or existing but rather marginal activity for them.

Crucially, it has to be realised that the early stages of negotiation that aim to establish an inter-agency project do not lead to the definitive act of policy implementation. Unexplicated, different definitions of what amounts to racial attack and harassment; assumptions about the appropriate boundaries for social work, housing department or probation service involvement in racial attacks and harassment; ideas about the role of each others' responsibilities that are occasionally hinted at but never fully articulated are all framing the implementation of policy. Policy development and implementation are not two separate parts of a wholly rational, means/ends focused series of decisions. They are interwoven as a mish-mash of ideas and unspoken, usually unrealised, assumptions that construct what for all practical purposes amounts to inter-agency work.

Changes of procedure do not occur overnight within organisations. Organisations based on divisions of rank or status, like the police and local authority departments, are particularly prone to inertia. The ethos and related culture of organisations affect the speed of innovation. The police, for example, are used to acting quickly when they have a particular project to develop, often too quickly, but longer term planning is rare within constabularies. Social services can be incredibly deliberative and their staff unappreciative of the possibility of working with the police, whilst using a different language about 'race'. Criticism and self-reflection are not easy within most organisations. Outside the organisation, agencies not included in the participating core group can have an unrealised but critical effect on policy implementation. The Crown Prosecution Service, for example, can fail to recommend prosecutions of perpetrators. If prosecuted, courts can find perpetrators not guilty, and so on.

Local projects require particular approaches to work from their members and the management staff who support them with resources. They could benefit from an 'independent' chair who has professional credibility and can bring attention to real and apparent differences of ideas; sit lightly on the primacy of assumptions made by the representatives of the different agencies involved; and draw together strands of collaboration that can gradually be strengthened. From the available evidence inter-agency initiatives offer a range of potentially helpful responses to victims. The professionals just need to get out of each other's way and focus more sharply on the needs of victims!

The future

The latest Home Affairs Committee report about racial attacks and harassment includes a comprehensive review of the subject and 38 recommendations for change. In addition to the reforms already mentioned, they also argue that new laws dealing with racial attack and harassment should be put on the statute books. Peter Lloyd, the Home Office minister who appeared before the committee and Michael Howard, the Home Secretary, argued that adding a burden of proof of racial motivation to an attack would mean failed prosecutions because the motive had not been satisfactorily demonstrated to a court. The importance of a racial motive should be taken into account when the judge passes sentence, not as a matter of proof.

The committee responded by arguing that in the case of a physical assault, for example, a defendant should be charged with both (ordinary) assault and racially motivated assault. The court would decide the appropriate offence after hearing the evidence. Michael Howard thought this was an unnecessary complication and not advisable but his point failed to convince the committee. He also failed to recognise the ways in which law can symbolise a measure of intended protection to vulnerable minorities facing particular forms of victimisation, irrespective of the difficulties of proof which were overestimated by the Home Secretary in this instance.

After a split vote on the proposition, the committee agreed to recommend the introduction of new offences of racial attack and harassment and Sir Ivan Lawrence, it's chair, proposed the creation of the new laws by tabling an amendment at the Report Stage of the debate on the Criminal Justice and Public Order Bill. The amendment failed, challenged by the same arguments that the ministers put before the Home Affairs Committee. However, in time it seems likely that the law will be reformed and specific statutes to deal with racially motivated violence and racially motivated harassment will be introduced. Further, in Lawrence's amendment more technical changes were proposed to the laws concerned with incitement to racial hatred, and the committee thought that it was worth giving further consideration to a new law dealing with group defamation, where, for example, literature is directed to Jewish people in general but no individual in particular.

Law in action

Whatever legal provisions are introduced, laws are mediated through the organisational cultures of the institutions that enforce them.

Research about the ways in which organisational structures and culture have an impact on the development of law and policies concerned with aspects of race relations is much neglected. It would simply be wide of the mark to argue that racial prejudice and or discrimination, or a variant of institutional racism are sufficient explanators. Studies of the introduction of crime prevention initiatives, new technology to assist police patrol, new systems of patrol, and many other aspects of police work have demonstrated that virtually all the organisational features identified in the Plaistow Racial Attacks Project impede innovation and organisational change (Hough, 1980; Chatterton and Rogers, 1989). Studies of local authorities and social service departments could be added to this literature (Young and Connelly, 1981; Connelly, 1989; Connelly, 1990).

Racial attacks and harassment are, as many of the documents and other material reviewed in this chapter indicate, acts that powerfully subordinate and racialise the status of members of minority ethnic groups. They are a barium test for the adequacy of government responses to questions of racialised relations in contemporary Britain and the ability of the police and other agencies to co-ordinate a range of strategies to deal with local needs.

These, however, are not just administrative measures of varying adequacy to deal with an objective problem. They are certainly related to social change, however small scale it might seem, but they also articulate a wider structure of relationships defined around the notion of 'race'. 'Race' is not a static phenomenon but continually recreated by human action. Racialised relations are constructed from the different understandings and actions of victims and the members of organisations and institutions dealing with attacks and harassment. All of the ideas and actions described and analysed here, and those of relevance neglected or undocumented, are part of that wider whole sociologists call social structure; social relationships that are accorded with some sedimented and more fragile meanings connoting and denoting 'race'.

Crucially, the occupational culture of the police rank-and-file moulds all policy and practice to accord with what is regarded by officers as their common-sense ideas and actions. Numerous studies have identified this as one, if not the main impediment to change within the police service (Skolnick, 1966; Bittner, 1967; Manning, 1977; James, 1978). Ideas about 'race' have a powerful and often central place within the occupational culture but are intertwined with its other features. Specialist squads of officers given the task of dealing with racial attacks may well be separated from their colleagues assumptions about 'race' and its relevance to police work. This of course does relatively little to change the ways in which a call for police assistance is answered by an officer on routine patrol. Here, the dominant assumptions of police common sense come into play. It is crucial to understand this culture if policing is to be analysed and reformed and, equally important, the ways in which police action sustains racialised relations.

Chapter Four

The cultural mediation of 'race' – occupational cultures, crime and arrests

Malkjitt Natt was arrested near his home in Manor Park, east London in January 1992. Two officers had attended an incident during which Natt was alleged to be threatening his wife, from whom he was separated. This was one of a succession of calls requiring police officers to attend similar incidents. Natt was arrested but fled from the arresting officers and, it was said, attacked a woman constable. On this occasion Natt was carrying a tape recorder because when previously stopped by officers he had been verbally abused. The following is a transcript of the recorded conversation that took place after his arrest.

Natt: Why am I being arrested?
PC: You're just a pain in the arse, ain't yer?
Natt: Oh God.
PC: Why don't you go and set fire to yourself or something?
Natt: You carry on arresting me without reason. Why?
PC: Because you are a shit
Later:
Natt: You are going to arrest me?
PC: It often happens in your country, don't it? It happens at home – where your lot come from.
Natt: What happens over there, it would never happen like that.
PC: Yes, it does. Worse than that.
Natt: What?
PC: They try and beat you up, don't they. They just go out and beat you up or shoot yer.
Natt: What?

PC: That's what we should do, fucking shoot yer.

Natt: You shoot me?

PC: Yes, I would.

Natt: What for?

PC: Well, (inaudible), wanker.

Natt: That's no good for a police officer doing that thing.

PC: Why don't you go home?

Natt: What's go home?

PC: Go home – you know – to India or Pakistan, or wherever you fucking come from.

Shortly afterwards:

PC: It's not your fucking country.

Later:

Natt: Why beat me? Why?

PC: Because I like it.

Natt: You like to beat me?

PC: I got no respect for someone like you.

If you are familiar with the occupational culture of the police rank-and-file this incident will be unremarkable and the relevance of 'race' within its analysis less than clear. From the officers' point of view, repeated calls to a 'domestic' are a waste of time and not 'real police work'. Resisting arrest for any offence is a sign of a lack of respect for officers. To hit a police officer is to breach the rank-and-file assumption that the uniform and physical body of an officer are virtually sacred; to hit a female officer is a grave breach of an occupational cultural rule. Profanation of the sacred requires redress by the offering of physical force. To ask why you have been arrested is to answer your own question (Manning, 1977; Chatterton, 1979; Holdaway, 1983; Reiner, 1985).

Many features of this incident are therefore commonplace as far as routine policing is concerned. An analysis of it would focus on a primary value of the rank-and-file culture associated with a police ideal of absolute control of territory and the people with whom officers come into contact (Holdaway, 1983). Peace keeping might have been initiated when the officers arrived at the incident but, as they perceived Natt's refusal to assent to their control and his disrespect for their advice, they moved towards a law enforcement style of policing and eventually arrested him (Bittner, 1967). Associated notions of 'real police work'; of respect for authority; and of women officers' vulnerability follow. The basic orientation for the officers' action is the rules and associated actions lodged in the occupational culture. However, there is another aspect of this incident that has to be taken into account, its racial dimensions.

So far the police response to Natt's behaviour has not taken racialisation into account. My argument is that very similar action would have been taken if the person arrested had been the member of any ethnic group. Yet 'race' seems to enter into the situation through the officers' invocation of an outsider status for Natt. Their consciousness of 'race' and its relevance to Natt's behaviour, however, does not appear to be a primary factor in the way they deal with the incident before and after his arrest. Indeed, it is not surprising that he was arrested given that other officers had been called to deal with Natt's troublesome behaviour towards his wife on four previous occasions. We should not disregard the possibility that his arrest was precipitated by positive action that placed the protection of Natt's wife as the officer's primary objective.

There nevertheless seem to be references to 'race' and ethnicity in the officers' account of their action and we need to understand how they mingle with other features of the occupational culture, constructing a framework of possible action and understanding around this and other incidents. The officers' conversation with Natt does not reveal clear references to biology as an explanation of his behaviour. A full analysis of the text would have to satisfy an argument that, though clearly exclusionary, their comments about him going home to India or Pakistan and that England is not his country carry 'racial' connotations and denotations. The forms in which individuals describe and act on notions of 'race' will of course change across time and within space. We would not expect to find clear references to biology and inheritance in data gathered in formal research interviews and they are by no means always clear and direct in data from more naturally documented contexts, like the one here.

It seems to me that it is nevertheless reasonable to argue that the officers dealing with Natt are working within a context where 'race' is relevant to their words and actions. They understand Natt as someone who is not in his 'home' country; who is given undeserved preferential treatment in England; and who should 'go home'. These are exclusionary notions, related to place of birth, membership of a nation and, by implication, of not belonging to our nation. When placed within a slightly wider context of the occupational culture of policing, with its documented characteristics of racialised prejudice and discrimination, it seems fair to argue that there are racial connotations here and an explanation of the officers' actions should take 'race' in account.[1]

It remains essential, however, to place an analysis of 'race' within the complex of values, norms and actions, together conceptualised as the police rank-and-file occupational culture. 'Race' is not an objective phenomenon that drives a clear, deterministic path through organisations to individual action; it is not a constant of a capitalist or any other type of economic system and therefore an ever present personification of an 'Other' awaiting its scripting on the stage of social structure when its role needs to be played. Racialised relations are cast in a particular structure with a somewhat distinct content related to the organisational context within which they are constructed. 'Race' is constructed and reconstructed within the meandering of the day to day work that takes place in organisations. An explanation of the Natt incident must therefore be derived from the context of the occupational culture of the police lower ranks.

The occupational culture of policing

When they began their research in the London Metropolitan Police, David Smith and Jeremy Gray quickly gained the impression that among police officers working in areas of substantial minority ethnic population,

'racialist language and racial prejudice were prominent and pervasive and many individual officers and also whole groups were preoccupied with ethnic differences (Smith, D. *et al.*, 1986)'

Some might interpret this as evidence of a racist police but Smith and Gray were more cautious because,

'At the same time, on accompanying these officers as they went about their work we found that their relations with black and brown people were often relaxed or friendly and that the degree of tension between them and black people from day to day was much less than might have been expected either from their own conversation or from accounts in the newspapers and on television (ibid, p. 388).'

Following a well drawn academic distinction, officers' attitudes and actions are separated in the PSI research – racial prejudice and discrimination are retained as distinct aspects of the police world. This is a valid perspective but in my view an inadequate conceptual scheme to analyse the ways in which the rank-and-file occupational culture mediates 'race' within routine police work or to contextualise 'race' within the structures and values of the occupational culture itself.

The basic problem is that Smith and Gray conceptualise 'race' as a discrete aspect of the social world of the rank-and-file, rather than one that is intertwined with other features, perhaps not at first sight of immediate relevance to police work with black or Asian people but, when viewed under a closer analytical eye, found to have a particular effect on routine police relationships. Police ideas and actions about black and Asian people are not, as Smith and Gray argue, wholly distinct from their ideas and actions about the policing of other people. The way officers dealt with Natt illustrates the point. Our analytical task is to both separate those features of routine police work that centre on 'race' *and* to relate them to other features of the occupational culture that are not explicitly racialised but nevertheless relevant to understanding the continuing racialisation of relations between police officers and black and Asian people.

Using illustrations from Smith and Gray's research and my own work, I want to emphasise the integrated structure of the occupational culture. Although the degree of integration is tenuous at times, it is nevertheless important if we want to understand ways in which notions of 'race' are mediated through the occupational culture to police action on the street. One implication of this view is that some features of what the police ranks regard as routine policing may cause no conflict when white people are policed but create tension when black and/or Asian people are policed. The manner in which people are routinely stopped in the street or dealt with in the charge room of a police station, for example, might be particularly insensitive to black and Asian people but accepted uncritically by those from other groups. Police officers do not switch on a separate compartment of their mind labelled 'blacks' and associate it with another compartment called 'race' when they see a youth behaving

suspiciously. They assimilate particular and general ideas and practices about routine policing into their work, including the policing of
black people.

Another implication of the view is that the occupational culture is
related to wider social structures of racialised relations and associated
ideas about ethnic minorities. An explanation solely based on structural determinism is unsatisfactory but this does not negate the
notion of a framework of constraint related to sedimented meanings
of 'race'. If unemployment falls differentially on black youths, for
example, and in some inner city areas these youths find themselves
spending a great deal of time on the streets, an unthinking use of a
police stop and search policy will bear more heavily on black than
white youth. Here, the internal structures of the occupational culture
– in particular, assumptions of virtual absolute control over people
and of interpreting demeanour in particular ways – are related to
over-arching structures of unequal, racialised relations.

If this argument is accepted, we can identify racial prejudice and
associated discrimination which are unrealised and unintended but
nevertheless powerfully lodged in the minds and actions of officers;
in the dynamics of relationships within the working group of officers;
and in the police as an organisation with mundane policies that
re-construct 'race' when put into practice. These 'normal' aspects of
policing are institutionalised and an example of what the law knows
as indirect discrimination (Mason, 1982).

One important caveat is necessary before the occupational culture
is discussed in more detail. Do not regard police officers as clones!
There are different styles of policing and police specialisms that issue
in different practices (Fielding, 1988). My discussion is concerned
with core elements of the occupational culture from which different
styles of policing have developed. To retain credibility, however,
these styles have to be pitted against the normative values and
actions of the occupational culture.

Ideas about 'blacks'

In her study of a city police force during the early 1960s, Maureen
Cain found officers divided the population into categories of 'roughs'
and 'respectables'. In addition, people were further differentiated by
gender and race. Coloured 'immigrants', the term used by officers to

characterise all minority ethnic groups, were typified as disorderly, potentially violent and permanently under suspicion. Asians were regarded as devious, liars and potential illegal immigrants (Cain, 1973, pp. 117–9). Similar ideas were found by John Lambert in his study of the Birmingham police (Lambert, 1970).

More recent research has confirmed the themes of racial prejudice within the culture of the lower ranks but this is not a static situation. There now seems to be less stress on the idea that black and Asian people are immigrants. During my study of an inner city station in a large metropolitan force I found that 'blacks' were viewed negatively; 'coon', 'nig-nog', 'spade' and 'nigger' were common verbal currency among the lower ranks. Derogatory terms like these were part and parcel of wide-ranging attitudes of racial prejudice which, as some officers recognised, were shared by the people who lived near them and in the area they patrolled. This is an officer talking about selling his house.

> 'You might call me a racist bastard and I know I haven't got a logical argument but I'm not going to live next door to them . . . People on the other side of the road, racist bastards, are leaving their cars out the front of the neighbour's house and so on and are really trying to upset them. Well, I'm not racist. It's just that I think they're very nice people but I don't want to live next door to them. I know you can say that I'm wrong but that's the way I feel (Holdaway, 1983, p. 67).

There was a widely shared view among officers at Hilton, the station I researched covertly as I worked as a police sergeant, that you could not trust black people. Whilst patrolling with an inspector during the early hours of the morning we passed a black youth apparently walking home. The inspector driving the patrol car slowed, 'These coloured people certainly ask for trouble from us. They seem to hang about and look suspicious (ibid, p. 68).' 'Blacks' were typified as not liking the police; as disorderly; as having a predisposition to crime; as violent; and as a complaining, untrustworthy group.

David Smith's evidence from his 1980s PSI study in London is similar, although he includes criticism of racial prejudice from within the ranks. A woman officer working in the special patrol unit remarked that '. . . racial prejudice in this job is dreadful. I've got a lot of young coloured friends. How can I explain to them why a PC calls them spades? (op. cit. p. 398).' He also found more extreme views expressed, here by a CID officer, 'Well, they're used to running around in the jungle plucking what they want from the trees and off the floor and killing someone for it. When they get here it's all different. They don't know how to behave (ibid, p. 392).'

There have not been many substantial participant observation studies of the police since the 1980s but other data from a variety of sources confirm that the evidence gathered over 20 years of research remains sound.[2] The Police Complaints Authority Annual Report for 1993, for example, describes a large number of allegations of racial discrimination by officers. Cases of racial discrimination in employment brought against chief officers by constables also strongly confirm the continuing ascendancy of the themes of the police occupational culture identified over many years.

Prejudiced officers

One possible explanation for this situation is that an overwhelmingly large number of people who join the police are basically prejudiced, the fault lies in their personality. The men and women who are recruited are authoritarian, dogmatic, conservative – all ingredients of a racially prejudiced individual. If racial prejudice is the problem it follows that the effective monitoring of recruits by the use of personality tests might be the best weapon available to senior officers keen to change their organisation. If prejudiced applicants are screened out during the recruitment process, rotten apples will be removed from the police barrel, which will become clean.

Researchers have tested some of these ideas. For example, in one study a battery of psychological tests to measure dogmatism, authoritarianism and conservatism, and open-ended questions about race relations, were completed by samples of police recruits in training school, probationary constables in their first two years of training and a control group of equal number not employed in the police. The conclusion was that 'the police force attracts conservative and authoritarian personalities, that basic training has a temporarily liberalising effect, and that continued police service results in increasingly illiberal/intolerant attitudes towards coloured immigrants (Colman and Gorman, 1982).'

Social scientists who relish this type of quasi-scientific study paw over the ways in which samples of interviewees have been constructed and statistics computed. In response to the Colman and Gorman paper, Dr Tony Butler, now a chief constable, who has a PhD in psychology, homed in on its research design and particularly the use of a control group with a markedly higher level of educational qualifications than the police group. He argued that like had not been compared with like and the more liberal attitudes of the control group were related to their higher educational attainment than personality characteristics of authoritarianism, conservatism and so on.

Other studies in this vein have combined psychological and social variables. An excessive concern with status and a tendency to identify scapegoats to explain one's restricted opportunities in life, for example, has been argued as typical of the strivings of the lower middle class from whom the police tend to recruit. These traits will therefore find their way into the police and the fostering of racial prejudice (Brown and Willis, 1985).

The basic criticism of these studies is that they individualise racial prejudice and discrimination. There may be a small number of officers who hold consistently extreme attitudes of racial prejudice but there is no clear evidence that an explanation in terms of their personality characteristics is sufficient. Colman and Gorman's point that 'continued police service results in increasingly illiberal/intolerant attitudes towards coloured immigrants' suggests that if we want to describe the development of a 'police personality' we should look to the continuing experience of police employment and the ways in which peers influence recruits (Fielding, 1988). This returns us directly to the occupational culture.

A little culture

During my research at Hilton police station, a special crime squad was established to deal with a rise in the number of street robberies and offences of pickpocketing reported by victims who described their assailants as black youths (James, 1978). The squad, staffed by officers seconded from the uniform branch, was established to deal with a spate of reported offences and its members were told to observe particular streets where they had been committed, gathering evidence before making arrests. This meant long periods of quiet observation for the officers involved, often from a nondescript van.

They had to wait for their evidence to materialise before their eyes. By a slow build-up of evidence the *post-hoc* technique of arresting a person on suspicion and then obtaining evidence during a police station interview was to be avoided. This meant that the officers working at observation points had to relinquish control over the area they patrolled because they could not arrest suspects, hoping to secure a confession during an interview session held in the privacy of custody. The offences continued and from reports recorded at the station it looked as if they were escalating.

Members of the squad had a clear brief from their supervisors but it was soon apparent that it did not harmonise with their ideas about how policing should be practised. The basic question was whether the recipes for policing contained in the occupational culture could supplant those detailed in the squad's senior officers' brief? Before long the conflict was settled. The nondescript van, supposedly used for long periods of observation, began to arrive at routine 999 calls and officers left their observation points to travel to emergency calls at high speed, even when it was blatantly obvious that their assistance was not required. The centrality of action and hedonism, which we know to be at the heart of the occupational culture, subverted the more discerning approach to police work required of the squad. The creation of action and excitement, especially a fight or scuffle, are prized and what better than a police vehicle equipped with a radio broadcasting 999 calls, ready to rush to the scene of imaginary, exciting incidents to relieve the boredom of observation?

Another implication of the emphasis the squad placed on action and fun was that the rather slow building of trustworthy and confident relationships between officers and members of the public, which could have been a spin-off from their unobtrusive strategy of evidence collection, was not particularly valued among the rank-and-file. They much preferred to charge to the scene of a trivial incident, milking it of drama and excitement, giving the impression to youths that the full weight of an aggressive police was heaped upon them.

A similar theme can be found in the PSI report, researched some ten years later. A black youth and his friends who are in a mini-cab were suspected of carrying drugs.

'One policeman tried to search them and they all refused to allow him to feel in their pockets. The policeman radioed for reinforcements and a number of transit vans and cars with sirens sounding and lights bleeping arrived and parked on four sides of the mini-cab, which was searched thoroughly . . . the incident has clearly increased their tendency to see police action as selective harassment and victimisation. If they are stopped again in future they are more likely to be hostile and unco-operative than they were last time (Small, 1983, p. 117).

The call for reinforcements is understandable in these circumstances but it is the uncontrolled, though for officers routine, manner in which they arrived at this incident that clearly soured relationships and had broader implications for the racialisation of relations between police and black people. The incident also demonstrates how another feature of the occupational culture can affect and damage existing racialised relationships. The rank-and-file have a firm view that the geographical territory they patrol is their territory, it belongs to them and they have a prior right to control it. This notion of control extends to the situation of a stop and search in the street, where the demeanour of a suspect, particularly a black youth, can be interpreted as a denial or rejection of police control. We see this in another incident recorded in the PSI study.

Clifton, a Rastafarian, was walking out of a tube station at 7.45 am on his way to work when he was stopped by two uniformed officers. He was carrying his working clothes and lunch box. Clifton refused to be searched and pointed out that he was on his way to his workplace, which was a couple of hundred yards down the road. This was an inadequate justification for the refusal to be searched and the officers . . .

. . . proceeded to search him, taking off his hat, going through his dreadlocks and through his bag. Though he protested, they did not respond in any way; he became furious when they took out his sandwiches and looked at the contents: 'Then dem just lef me and go 'long like nothing happened. No apology, no nothing! Dem just walk away (Small, 1983; p. 114).'

Again it is possible, but only just conceivable, that this was reasonable police action, carried out in a thoroughly insensitive manner, leading to Clifton's feeling that, 'Dem don't treat we like humans. Dem treat we like animals, dem a insult we and intimidate we and harass we and shame we and all in public me tell yuh (ibid, p. 115).' The indication is nevertheless that although the officers' actions were discriminatory the key feature of the episode was Clifton's refusal to be searched and the interpretation of his action as a refusal to accept police control. The officers would not apologise when, from their perspective, Clifton was at fault. He should have deferred to their authority.

The assumption of control over people who indicate their acceptance of police authority by adopting an appropriate demeanour can aggravate relationships between officers and black and Asian people (Holdaway, 1978). The souring of relationships between the police and black and Asian people, however, stems from stock features of the occupational culture that structure encounters between all members of the public, irrespective of their perceived 'race'. Though clearly including distinct ideas about 'blacks' and thereby defined as 'racial', they are not ideas that are wholly separate from the ideas that influence the manner in which everybody is policed.

'Race' is therefore significantly constructed and re-constructed through the rank-and-file occupational culture. A 'racial' element is evident and in Clifton's case it seems very likely that he was stopped in the first place because of an association in the officer's mind between Rastafarians and the use of cannabis. In the Natt case the racial element is less clear but seems present nonetheless. 'Race' mingles with other characteristics of incidents officers identify as signs and symbols that some kind of intervention is required. 'Race' will sometimes be at the forefront of an officer's mind when a black or Asian person is stopped. Values and related ideas and actions found in the occupational culture will, however, also be relevant and probably in the ascendant.

The PSI view that the occupational culture is best understood as a realm of rhetoric that somehow separates word from action does not allow us to make this connection between core features of the occupational culture and the manner in which black and Asian people are policed. Racialised relations have to be contextualised and analysed within the occupational culture of the rank-and-file, which refracts it in intended and unintended directions. The fact that officers seem preoccupied with 'racial' differences when talking about black and Asian people but have friendly relations with them does not mean that racialised discrimination can be straightforwardly separated from prejudice. This is to separate discrete aspects of the social world that should always be related to each other and would be a thoroughly unsociological approach to the study of the police.

Once contextualised within the occupational culture, it is possible to find complex but nevertheless 'real' links between word and action, between its racialising and normative elements. Just as 'race' is not a pure biological phenomenon so within the occupational culture it is not always manifested with formal clarity. Police officers regard themselves as acting in commonsensical ways but, to the sociologist who places their commonsense under the microscope of analysis, that which is commonplace and apparently discrete becomes problematic, a facet of the construction of 'race' within the routine world of policing.

Race and crime: stops and arrests

Glib statements that straightforwardly describe the police as racist and therefore likely to arrest every black (but not Asian) youth in sight too often obscure the complex questions we have begun to tackle when discussing the occupational culture. They avoid questioning the relationship between ideas and action; problems about normative and distinct structures of policing; police assumptions about normal policing and the policing of the various minority ethnic groups; between structured inequalities and police policy and action; and about responses of members of minority ethnic groups to police action. All these factors come together in what has at times been a highly contested debate about the extent to which black youths are involved in crime. This has been both a public and academic debate, not only illuminating for its political character but also because it demonstrates different approaches to the study of relations identified by 'race' and, of course, to the relationship, if there be any, between 'race' and crime (Wolfgang and Cohen, 1970).

A public argument about race and crime came to a head in 1976, when in evidence to the All Party Select Committee on Race and Immigration, the Metropolitan Police argued that there was a significant involvement of black youth in crime (Newing and Crump, 1974). This view raised the counter-argument than any police evidence of a disproportionate involvement in offending by black people was an indication of discriminatory policing, not black criminal activity. Qualifications about ethnic disadvantage leading to crime and so on then entered the discussion.

Much of the debate about the extent of black criminality has centred on the problem of the reliability of official statistics. There is also concern about the exploitation of any research findings by groups wanting to stimulate fear and stigma through the criminalisation of black youth. A neglect of the wider social context of offending in many studies, requiring more of the researcher than an analysis of dependent and independent variables, has not helped matters. This requirement, however, does not mean that we can dismiss the statistics entirely, as some of the 'new racism' theorists have done. Both theory and evidence have to be carefully weighed.

Stops

Stopping a person in the street is a routine matter for police officers but one of the utmost importance. It is the point at which the rule of law makes a personal impact and from which public perceptions of police fairness are moulded. Before the introduction of the Police and Criminal Evidence Act in 1984, there was a specific power to stop and search people in the London Metropolitan Police area and various, similar powers contained in by-laws used in other parts of the country. The 1984 Act regularised the situation but the available research evidence deals with the earlier period and almost exclusively with London.

Carole Willis studied the use of police powers to stop people in the street by researching records from four police stations, some within and some beyond the boundaries of Greater London (Willis, 1983). Rates of stopping people were found to be higher for black people than for the population as a whole and in the Kensington area of London to be three times higher among black men aged 16 and 24 than for other men in this group. The overriding problem with this research, however, was its reliance on official records and therefore on decisions by officers to document their activity formally. Many stops may not be recorded and the record of police stops in the street may therefore not be a comprehensive and accurate record of the total number and type that have been carried out.

One research strategy to circumvent reliance on police records is to ask a representative sample of people if they have been stopped by a police officer during a preceding period of time. This is similar to the design of a victim or crime survey, which seeks to look behind the officially recorded statistics of offences. The Policy Studies Institute's London study did just this and found that 16 per cent of

Londoners had been stopped once or twice by the police in the previous 12 months. 12 per cent had been stopped just once and the remaining 4 per cent more than once, leading to the conclusion that,

> People who are stopped repeatedly are a small proportion of the whole population, but account for a substantial proportion of all stops: for example, those who have been stopped four or more times are 1 per cent of the population, 7 per cent of those who have been stopped at all, and account for 30 per cent of stops (Smith, D. *et al.*, 1986).

These figures therefore indicate that there are characteristics of people which form the implicit criteria officers take into account when making a decision to use their stop and search powers. In particular, age, sex, ethnic group and ownership or use of a motor vehicle must have been used as criteria, whether or not the police were immediately conscious of them. As far as 'ethnic group' is concerned, black people were found to have been stopped more than white people, who were stopped more than Asians, a finding, incidentally, tending to confirm Carole Willis's earlier research results. When on foot, blacks were four times more likely to be stopped than people from other ethnic groups; 49 per cent of West Indians who owned or had the regular use of a vehicle said they had been stopped by the police (ibid, pp. 249–55).

These facts seem to indicate clear discrimination. But if we argue this case from an analysis of statistical data it is necessary to be sure that when the stop rates for the different minority ethnic groups are compared, adequate weight is given to any characteristics causing their members to be stopped more frequently. The age range of the black population in Britain is skewed towards the younger end and this means that in relative terms more stops of black people can be expected. Males aged 15–24 commit more crime than those from other age groups and it is reasonable to expect men who come within this age range, including those from minority ethnic groups, to be stopped more frequently than those outside it. Age may therefore be a more important criterion than ethnicity for the use of stop powers. Other factors were also important. In the PSI research, when black and white car owners and users were compared within the same age range, the proportion of people stopped was found to be very similar and the stop rate for Asians significantly lower than for the other ethnic groups. Car ownership and use are seemingly other important factors to take into account when assessing the differential use of stop and search powers.

More significant differences appeared in the PSI project when the repetitive use of stops was considered. Among young people – and therefore especially among black youth – the average number of stops per year was much higher for black youth than for their white peers, with an average of 5.06 stops for the former compared with 1.94 for the latter (ibid, pp. 87 ff). The important point here is that black youth, though not generally the subject of over-policing, were on the receiving end of repeated police intervention, with a police 'strike rate' of an arrest from stops of one in 12. The PSI researchers argue that if viewed simply in terms of the constant result from stops, the higher rate for black youth can be 'justified in the sense than an equal proportion of stops of the two groups produce a result (ibid, p. 106).'

The extent to which this judgement is reasonable, however, is questionable and seems more like a comment on the efficacy of what Michael Banton has called 'statistical discrimination' than a justifiable use of police discretion (Banton, 1983). Banton argues that a distinction should be made between 'categorical' and 'statistical' discrimination, the former concerned with differential treatment of members of a group purely on the basis of membership of a particular social category, the latter with differential treatment resulting from beliefs that members of a group are likely to have particular characteristics, without regard for the specific behaviour of individuals. A belief that you get a 'result' when stopping a black youth, not least when the strike rate is a rather long shot of 12:1, illustrates statistical rather than categorical discrimination.

Findings that tend to present a more complex pattern of police stops come from a study in Leeds that included the analysis of records for stops under the provisions of the Police and Criminal Evidence Act (Jefferson and Walker, 1992; Walker, 1992; Jefferson, 1993). A review of previous research about stops and arrest rates led the researchers in this study to analyse data related to census enumeration districts in which 10 per cent or more of households were estimated to be non-white. This meant that within the very small areas where research was completed it was possible to analyse the stop rates for a sample of black, Asian and white people living in close proximity. To their surprise the researchers found that the black rate was highest only in areas with low concentrations of blacks and Asians. Younger whites had the highest rates in the poorer areas, where the majority of blacks and Asians lived.

Tony Jefferson has speculated that this pattern could mean that, 'blacks are less willing to report and/or police to record black offenders in black neighbourhoods, which might explain the lower black rate in the areas where they tended to live; that such neighbourhood 'protections' do not apply in the white suburbs; and/or black offenders in such areas will be concentrated in isolated pockets of poorer housing which might explain their higher rate in the 'whiter' areas (Jefferson, 1993; p. 33). As far as the white rate is concerned, he argues that this confirms the long-standing relation-ship between social class and differential police activity and a somewhat direct correspondence between police action and social structural factors. This relationship, however, is somehow mediated to roughly attune officers' actions to the characteristics of small geographical areas but of course the research design did not allow them to describe or analyse any mediating processes. Statistical analysis alone cannot do that.

David Smith interprets this evidence rather differently, placing emphasis on the unusual characteristics of white people living in the 'multi-racial' enumeration districts. They had lived in the area in privately rented accommodation for less than three years and, by inference, were transients with unsettled life styles which might attract police attention. But Smith does not relate this interpretation to any wider range of organisational or social structural factors, which could be consistent with Jefferson's point that social class is the relevant variable that mingles with 'race' and other factors, notably age and gender, (Smith, 1994).

We are therefore left with research evidence that has moved from a view that black people are generally stopped more frequently than white people, to consider the effects of factors like area of residence and housing type that seem to mediate the impact of 'racial factors'. We have also found differential stop rates for the different minority ethnic groups. No definitive studies are available. More questions need to be asked about why, as far as Leeds is concerned, for example, police seem to differentiate their use of powers within different spatial areas? We also need to further explore whether or not police definitions of and interest in people living in 'rough' areas are consistent with social science definitions of social class member-ship. Further studies designed to document social processes directly related to the use of stop powers and the construction of racialised relations are required in Leeds and, indeed, other cities.

Crime and arrests

Debate about the relationship, if any, between crime and race has been contentious and at times acrimonious.[3] Paul Gilroy, for example, has argued that such questioning gives, 'intellectual support to racist stereotypes of the black community as socially and politically disadvantaged', dismissing methods of research that involve the manipulation of quantitative data as, 'empiricist haggling over official statistics' (Gilroy, 1982; 1983; p. 147). Part of Gilroy's objection is the dubious criminological pursuit of filtering-out erroneous variables to leave a statistically measured residue of pure discrimination – the racial factor. He is also concerned to contextualise 'race', especially the criminalisation of black youth, but his assumptions about such contextualisation are very different from those made by the criminological statisticians (Gilroy, 1987).

Gilroy wrote about this subject with commitment, which drew equally committed replies. Peter Waddington, for example, has found Gilroy's view a strident negation of any rational basis for an assessment of the extent of the involvement of black and Asian people in crime. He suggests that the arrest rate for black youth reflects a rise in the number of offences they have committed rather than or as well as police discrimination or other features of a racist society. This view was rejected and the boxing match continued (Waddington, 1984). In this section we will review key points of debate in the recent race and crime debate, which illustrates ways of analysing 'race' as well as charting the evidence.

A starting point for the debate in England is the police evidence submitted to the 1971 and 1976 House of Commons Select Committee on Race Relations and Immigration enquiry into the subject (Select Committee, 1971–2; 1976–7). Here we have official statistics of crime rates presented as fact-like, clearly indicative of the behaviour of black youth.

In 1971 various police forces, the Metropolitan Police among them, placed evidence about the 'race' of people arrested before the Select Committee, arguing that crime rates for the ethnic minorities were no higher than might be expected and in some areas of Britain were running at lower than average levels. This evidence harmonised with research conducted by people like John Lambert, whose study of Birmingham included the finding that in the 1960s people of West Indian and Asian descent were represented in the arrest statistics in lower numbers than white people (Lambert, 1970).

Although the police evidence was not entirely consistent (Benyon, 1986, p. 28), the general consensus in 1971 was that ethnic minorities were not involved in a disproportionate level of crime. This, however, was a view that would change within five years, surfacing at the 1976 hearings of the committee, when the London Metropolitan Police claimed 'our experience has taught us the (falsity) of the assertion that crime rates among those of West Indian origin are no higher than those of the population at large (Select Committee, 1976–7; p. 182).' The police evidence did not in fact claim a causal link between race and criminality; neither did it deny the social disadvantages faced by black people, which may have an impact on levels of offending. The Met's concern seems to have been to draw attention to new statistics of differential offending rates, especially for street crime – and presumably to accept the consequences of doing so.

The basis of the Met's evidence was a paper written in 1974 by two of their officers working in the community relations branch, who claimed to find a correlation between the size of the minority ethnic population living in various London boroughs and rates of robbery committed within them. Indeed, they argued that the larger the minority ethnic population the higher the rate of robbery (Newing and Crump, 1974). An updated version of this analysis was presented in evidence to the 1976 Select Committee, making the case that about 12 per cent of all arrests for indictable offences in London during 1975 were of people of West Indian/African background, who made up 4.3 per cent of the population. These percentages increased when the crime categories of robbery and violent theft were considered: 28 per cent and 37 per cent of people arrested for these offences were West Indian/African. Aware of some of the pitfalls of the use of arrest statistics, the police also analysed the evidence of witnesses to the crimes, who indicated that 32 per cent of robbers and 41 per cent of thieves were from the same ethnic groups. As far as the police were concerned, there was a growing trend of criminal activity amongst West Indian/African people which indicated a marked contrast to the situation in 1971.

Criticism of the evidence quickly followed from a number of quarters. On behalf of the Commission for Racial Equality, Professor Terence Morris tackled the methodology and analysis of the statistics used by the police (Morris, 1976). He pointed out that the 12 per cent arrest rate was compatible with social class indicators and that the ethnic origin of offenders may therefore be irrelevant. Secondly, arrest rates could not be equated with crime rates. Police discrimination and the prevalence of particular patrol strategies, the use of a special patrol group for example, could lead to the creation of an *appearance* of increasing crime amongst the West Indian population. Further, many arrests do not lead to a conviction and it is unsafe to infer the proportions of crime committed by members of different minority ethnic groups from arrest figures alone.

The statistical category of 'robbery and other violent theft' summarises many different types of acts, with vastly different levels of seriousness. It is therefore unreasonable to assume, for example, that 'mugging', which is not a specific offence defined in law, is on the increase from an analysis of the Metropolitan Police figures. Neither can it be straightforwardly inferred from the statistics that local people are responsible for the offences recorded. Finally, Morris argued that the eye-testimony of the 'race' of offenders is not wholly reliable. Expectations based on rumour, media images and other sources can promote error.

The Select Committee noted the Metropolitan Police evidence but did not fully accept it. Their primary concern, which drew on Home Office advice, was that the police statistics used were not controlled for sex and age. Further research taking this and other factors into account was suggested and later pursued by Philip Stevens and Carole Willis from the Home Office Research and Planning Unit (Stevens and Willis, 1979).

There were two parts to the Stevens and Willis research, each taking a steer from the themes of the Metropolitan Police evidence. The first part was an analysis of levels of recorded crime in the major conurbations, with an objective to test if there was any consistent relationship between areas of high minority ethnic population, defined in both general and police divisional areas terms, and corresponding levels of crime. This was similar to the Metropolitan Police study but, in contrast, it found no correlation between the selected factors.

A basic problem with this part of the Home Office study is that it used official statistics and aggregated figures of arrests. Aggregate figures obscure different levels of crime amongst different ethnic groups and for different categories of crime (Lea and Young, 1984, pp. 148 ff). One ethnic group might have a very low rate of offending and another a much higher rate. An area, for example, might have a large minority ethnic elderly population and a smaller but more criminally active younger one. Once aggregated, the figures for both groups cancel each other out and real comparisons are lost.

The second part of this study was concerned with trying to unravel the various factors that might explain any relatively high rates of offending, if they exist, among the ethnic minorities. Age, unemployment rates, household tenure and social class were controlled. The single control for age left black youth considerably over-represented in most categories of indictable crime, especially robbery, other violent theft and assault. Asian youth, though slightly over-represented in arrests for assault, were found to be arrested less frequently than might be expected given their number in the population.

Controls for socio-economic factors were then introduced and an association was found between social deprivation and levels of arrest but the particular features of social deprivation differed when the figures for each ethnic group were considered.

'For both the black and Asian arrest rates no single indicator emerged as strongly as the white employment rate for white arrests; but the best indicator of high arrest rates for blacks (for violent crime) appeared to be a low rate of home ownership whilst that for Asian arrest rates appeared to be a high proportion of Asians in the lowest socio-economic group (ibid; p. 41).'

These findings indicate that there are particular social characteristics that refract the impact of social deprivation on ethnic minorities *or* the activity of the police is a strong factor in constructing an arrest rate *or* both are important. The age structure of the minority ethnic populations surveyed and other socio-economic factors explain some of the higher arrest rates, but not all.

Stevens and Willis then considered the explanation that all the remaining differential arrest rate was the result of an extrinsic factor, in particular police activity that leads to the greater number of arrests of black people. This marks a slight move away from the statistical analysis of variables, to consider whether or not police action has constructed an appearance of reality in which black youth commit more street crime than white youth. But,

'To explain the 1975 arrest figures in terms of differential success in clearing up black and white crime, it would have been necessary for police to arrest 66 per cent of all black offenders but only 21 per cent of white offenders. Such an imbalance is implausible, given that the ethnic identity of offenders is unknown at the outset (ibid, p. 34).'

Furthermore,

'It can be calculated that if 75 per cent of all black arrests and only 19 per cent of white arrests in 1975 had been mistaken ones, it would be possible to reconcile the 1975 arrest rate with the hypothesis that rates of underlying black and white crime were identical . . . mistaken arrests alone do not look a plausible explanation of the difference between black and white arrest rates, although they might of course explain some part of it (ibid, p. 34).

These arrest statistics seem to indicate that when population, socio-economic factors and aspects of police discrimination are taken into account, some of the differential arrest rates and assumed crime rate is explained. High levels of assault, robbery and other violent theft remain but, as Stevens and Willis construe, it is also the case that these are offences incorporating many different types of acts which are open to some degree of police discrimination (also see Walker, 1987 for similar calculations).

This Home Office research clarified rather than settled any final answer to the question raised by the 1976 Metropolitan Police evidence to the Select Committee. The methods of research used demonstrate some of the benefits and drawbacks of statistical analysis. Researchers are able to point to differential rates of offending and to separate variables that together form a cluster of factors leading to crime but, whilst valuable, the identification of these variables – age, gender, social class, and so on – does not amount to an explanation of why, as seems to be the case, young black men are arrested more often than expected from their number in the population. They indicate and clarify in quantitative terms that some structural phenomena have an impact on police action and on people from minority ethnic groups but do not explain their relationship to the action of the police or to people from minority ethnic groups, young black men for example. Neither do they describe or analyse social processes that reconstruct and sustain racialised relations and, it follows, the phenomenon we conceptualise as 'society'.

Criminological realism

The finding that black youth is over-represented in some offence categories forms the starting point of John Lea's and Jock Young's contribution to the race and crime debate (Lea and Young, 1982; Lea and Young, 1984). Working within a framework of 'realist criminology' they progress beyond the statistical analysis of variables to include a wider study of social structural factors. The key elements of realism Lea and Young have brought to the discussion are, first, that offending is not a form of political action or a knee-jerk reaction to absolute deprivation. It is a serious issue for the poor, who are frequently disadvantaged by being victims of crime. Secondly, and related, it is necessary within an analysis of crime to understand how structural inequalities frame both victimisation and offending.

Realism therefore rejects the type of analysis founded on a given logic of the inevitable economic constraints of capitalism that generate the 'need' for a scapegoat, found in black youth. It rejects the view that crime committed by second generation black youth is a political activity, at times understood as a residue of resistance to colonialism, now expressed within the colonised metropolis (Gilroy, 1983). Police action is equally political within this scenario, the response of a state needing to create a diversion from economic crisis by the construction of moral panic about black youth (Hall *et al.*, 1978). For realists, crime, whether committed by black or white youth, is a 'real' phenomenon that can be understood in its own right. We may misunderstand or misperceive the form crime takes but it is real nevertheless, not a contrivance or managed illusion through the anthropomorphic behaviour of the political state.[4]

Lea and Young argue that it is a gross simplification to describe black youth as a homogenous group with a common heritage. At the heart of their argument is the view that too little attention has been given to human creativity; to the richness and diversity of cultural forms created by minority groups; and for sociology to be as much concerned with heterogeneity as with homogeneity.[5] An explanation of offending rates should take into account both the ways in which structures of social inequality have made an impact on minority ethnic groups and the diverse responses found within those groups. The diverse, widely drawn cultures of the country from which migration originates, the more specific sub-cultures of those who migrate, and sub-cultures that develop within Britain are all integral to understanding the situation of black youth (Lea and Young, 1984; p. 125). The material conditions of British society are woven within these cultural adaptions forming.

> '... a complex entity involving assimilation to native British culture, the received cultural adaptations of the first generation of immigrants and a process of innovation and cultural construction attempting to make sense of and survive in the harsh conditions of racist Britain (ibid, p. 134).'

There is no straightforward transfer of a monochrome culture from one generation to another, just as there is no single response which can be characterised as 'black culture' or 'Asian culture'. Within the black population, for example, various responses to settling and being born in Britain have been identified, some oriented around religion, some around status and some around hustling (Pryce, 1979; Rex, 1982). This seems an obvious point but if you read some of the 'anti-racism' literature, the different responses of people belonging to the one ethnic group are completely neglected (Dominelli, 1988; Central Council for Training and Education in Social Work, 1991). Too much sociology has been fixated by a conceptualisation of a society as a Flatland (Holdaway, 1987). The social terrain is moulded by an undifferentiated white population, whose zero-sum hold of power is clamped upon a uniformly oppressed black people, who resist or accommodate through the single available resource of a monochrome black culture. However, if we take into account the diversity and creativity within and between different minority ethnic groups as well as an understanding of the common effect of structural factors, including ways in which social deprivation can lead to crime, it is not surprising that an element of criminal activity is *one* adaptation amongst a small number of the members of *one* minority ethnic group (Pryce, 1979; Rex, 1982).

A challenge to this explanation is that there is no significant adaptation by black youth to the racialised context of British society. The gift of creativity is owned and crafted by police officers, whose discriminatory strategies construct the appearance of a higher rate of offending amongst black youths (Lea and Young, 1982). Lea and Young have replied to this saying that it assumes, on the basis of the police evidence to the 1971 Select Committee, that a type of positive discrimination was and continues to be expressed by the police towards Asians since the late 1950s, with an even-handedness towards West Indian immigrants and whites. The stance towards black, but not white, youth has changed. Why? Were the police acting within a framework of positive discrimination in the early 1970s or has crime by some black youth increased? And the critique has to account for police action increasing in relation to a small number of crimes, especially street robbery, not crime and criminality *per se*. Further, if police discrimination is the sole explanatory factor to explain arrest rates it is necessary to assume that all ethnic minorities have identical crime rates, which seems very unlikely. As far as the political character of crime is concerned, Lea and Young, along with other commentators, point out that most crime is intra rather than inter-racial, which may be political by sociological fiat but in reality is a contrivance hardly worth consideration.

The conclusion of Lea and Young's work is that a perception of relative deprivation leads some black youths to commit more crime than white youths. Police prejudice and discrimination responds to this real rise in crime – to be associated with economic circumstances – in inappropriate ways, including arrests of black youths who have not committed offences, partly leading to a construction of higher crime rates.

> 'The notion that increasing youth unemployment, coupled with a high young population in the black community, and the effects of massive, well-documented, racial discrimination and the denial of legitimate opportunity, did not result in a rising rate of real offences is hardly credible (ibid, pp. 167–8).'

This argument needs more empirical evidence to make it finally persuasive but its implications for consideration of the 'race' and crime debate are important. It is not *either* structural factors *or* police discrimination that lead to high crime rates for black youth but both. An analysis of the race and crime question should deal with both social structures and processes that sustain them. The ways in which relations are racialised are central.

New racism

Although not directly pitched to challenge Lea and Young's analysis of race and crime, a rather different critique of 'race', with direct implications for the realist stance, has emerged during the last decade or so. The 'new racism' rejects a realist understanding of phenomena, being based on the premise that reality is constructed by discourse alone, or some variant of the theme, with primary attention given to the ways in which, for example, images of black youth, sometimes connotative and sometimes denotative, have constituted the apparently factual (Cohen, 1993 Gilroy, 1987; Goldberg, 1988;).

Methods of social research are not concerned here with the multi-variate type of analysis relating to the extent to which the ethnic origin of an offender rather than, say, age and other variables is a proportionate part of an explanation. 'Race' and 'crime' have no status other than discourse, the meaning of which may lie beneath its surface. Gilroy, for example, has presented what he calls 'an archaeology of representations of black law-breaking (ibid, p. 73)', which in the first instance deconstructs the related notions of law and legality that express and represent the idea of a nation state and national unity.

> 'The subject of the law is also the subject of the nation. Law is primarily a national institution and adherence to its rules symbolises the imagined community of the nation and expresses the fundamental unity and equality of its citizens ... The changing patterns of their portrayal as law-breakers and criminals, as a dangerous class or underclass, offer an opportunity to trace the development of the new racism for which the link between crime and blackness has now become absolutely integral (ibid, p. 74).'

In the immediate post-war period the notion of 'race' did not symbolise lawlessness. The self-created, squalid living conditions of immigrants and their sexual pretentiousness, which promoted miscegenation, were the focus of public attention. Where criminality was an issue, illegal immigration, living off immoral earnings and the forgery of state benefit claims and immigration documents were presented as typical. Street crime, 'mugging' as it came to be known, was no part of the public imagery of black youth. Public attention, expressed through the speeches of politicians and government action, was more concerned with the quantitative rather than subsequent qualitative distortions imposed by immigrants on a cohesive British culture. The number of immigrants placing demands on the health and welfare services was and in the future would increasingly cause problems in a Britain striving to retain its national culture intact.

Numbers and the threat of swamping remained an emphasis but this picture of Britain was to change during the 1970s, initially through the interventions of Enoch Powell. His 'rivers of blood' speech claimed in powerful rhetoric the notion of black people forming an alien wedge that would change the 'natural' quality of English culture. This qualitative transformation was ably supported by the laws against racial discrimination, placing white people in jeopardy for the 'natural' defence of their culture,

> 'The innocent are to be consigned to prison for being found guilty of racialism while the really guilty one – the blacks who push excreta through letter boxes and know just one word of English – are left free to roam . . . Legality is the pre-eminent symbol of national culture and it is the capacity of black settlement to transform it which alarms Powell rather than the criminal acts which the blacks commit (ibid, p. 86).'

Immigrants were no longer potential returners. They are here to stay, forming a distortion of British culture that for Enoch Powell was well nigh impossible to curtail or assimilate. Law, usually the guarantor of citizenship for English people, was now brought to the specific protection of the alien. By implication, to resist the alien is to fall outside the warrant of freedom assured by the law. In the public mind, Gilroy argues, a radical separation had been placed between the notion of a British way of life and the presence of immigrants. There could be no more English an institution to strengthen the idea than the law.

In the 1970s the object of these 'discourses of race' changed as black youth became an icon of threat and disorder that symbolised the presence of an alien people. We have already seen from evidence submitted to the Home Affairs Select Committee that in the early 1970s black people were not perceived as criminal by the police or government. By the middle of the decade this situation had changed and black youth had become closely associated, if not quite synonymous, with 'mugging'. Gilroy interprets this as evidence of an imagery of lone criminals rather than a collective, cultural motif of black criminality.

In 1976 the Notting Hill carnival with its large scale disorder and media references to temporary no-go areas, for example, suggested that black youth were in coalition. Together they offered each other help to resist the arrest of criminals (also see Jackson, 1989). The idea of the lone mugger was becoming one strand of a more threatening culture of black youth. 'Culture secures the link between the criminal minority and the mob who spring to their defence. Thus attacks on the police are also gradually seen to be expressive of black culture (ibid, p. 94).' And from 1976 until 1981, when the Brixton disturbances erupted, this perception of a collective or cultural disorder among black youth was strengthened by localised if periodic conflict with the police.

The 1981 Brixton disturbances set the tone of the 1980s but it was the more virulent Broadwater Farm Estate riot of 1985 that led the then Commissioner of the Metropolitan Police, Sir Kenneth Newman, to describe 'symbolic locations' in the capital city, 'where police authority and power is challenged in a way that is counterproductive to an ethos in society which makes crime unacceptable.' Black youth and the British ethos are incompatible.

Symbols powerfully extend contentious meanings beyond the immediate context to which they refer and Gilroy's argument is that on the one hand a bricolage of 'race' has effectively excluded blacks from inclusion in the common definition of British society – 'there ain't no black in the Union Jack.' The other and for Gilroy, crucial aspect of this analysis is that within the space between exclusion and response black youth has created a cultural solution to secure a collective identity with the potential to sustain a 'politically' conscious community. 'Collective identities spoken through 'race', community and locality are, for all their spontaneity, powerful means to co-ordinate action and create solidarity (ibid, pp. 246–7).'

There is far more to Gilroy's argument than I have been able to present here. At the heart of his work is a critique of Marxist notions of class as the base of black communities and consciousness. Culture is not a direct reflection of a material base – the base\superstructure relationship as Marxists put it – or in the last instance determined by class conflict (Althusser, 1971). 'Race' may have no biological base but it is nevertheless the 'material' to construct a dynamic culture with its own integrity.

As far as the discussion of race and crime is concerned, Gilroy turns us away from the statistical analysis of dependent and independent variables, 'empiricist haggling' as he calls it elsewhere, to consider a very different and, for him, contrasting analysis. Both crime and race are socially constructed and should not be reified, as in the realist criminology of Jock Young and the positivists' assumption that phenomena can be measured as if this contextualises 'the social'. 'Race' is complexly constructed, significantly through the discourse of public figures and, though there is no close analysis of this relationship in Gilroy's work, its impact on the common sense of white people. A 'new racism' therefore appears in many different cultural forms, mediated through political rhetoric, law, notions of nation, community and national identity from which black people are implicitly excluded.

A central sociological task of the new racism is to identify – excavate is Gilroy's archaeological metaphor – the varied meanings through which 'race' is expressed and their reference points in others' action. The numerical extent of black youths' offending is not relevant to this project; there is no evaluation of discourse in relation to a centre point of truth. To suppose there is another reality lying behind and in some way in the first or last instance orchestrating these cultural variations, other than a socially constructed history of 'race', is to work within a different paradigm, a framework of research with different starting and ending points.

A significant influence on the development of Gilroy's ideas has been the work of Birmingham University's Centre for Contemporary Cultural Studies, especially their *Policing the Crisis* (Hall *et al.*, 1978). In some ways this was the forerunner of his theoretical writings because they too sought to understand why, in the middle of the 1970s, there had been the presentation of black youth as criminal and associated with mugging.

At root the thesis of *Policing the Crisis* is that during the 1970s Britain faced an economic recession. A scapegoat was required to divert public attention from the economic crisis facing the country. Ideas about black youth as criminals, as 'muggers' provided the diversion required. An explanation of the economic crisis would be distracted from its real cause, which was capitalism itself, to black youth. *Policing in Crisis* therefore placed the documentation of the meaning of black youth within a wider framework that included the question 'Why at this particular time were black youths presented as 'muggers?' Their answer is that in the final instance, and at the particular time of crisis documented, the economy provided a framework within which it was necessary for a scapegoat to be found, which was black youth.

Although its authors would probably strongly dissent from my interpretation, there seems little daylight between this analysis and any other postulating a clear continuity between economic structure and dominant, pervasive ideas. System needs are constantly in the ascendancy and ideas about 'race' are orchestrated accordingly. This is why Stuart Hall and his colleagues have been open to criticism from others who have carefully combed their evidence and found it inadequate, inappropriate or wrongly interpreted (for example, James, 1978; Waddington, 1986).

If we ask Gilroy why the ideas about black youth and black culture changed in the periods he has analysed, a less certain answer is given, partly because he is not interested in a quasi-causal analysis, resisting any reification (in the jargon) of phenomena. The idea of an economic system which orchestrates discourse is anathema. There is, however, the glimmer of an answer signalled by his rather strange capitalisation of the writing of 'the Other'. Here he follows other erstwhile members of the Birmingham group, Phil Cohen, for example, who has in turn been followed by Tony Jefferson (Cohen, 1993; Jefferson, 1993). Jefferson's argument is that an 'Other', in the shape of a scapegoat for class division and inequality, is constructed around the empirically verifiable but nonetheless contrived categories of 'young', 'male', 'working class' and 'black'. 'The Other' is needed if the structure of power is to hold within its necessary boundaries. This is essentially a variant of the *Policing the Crisis* thesis.

Phil Cohen has also looked at the history of black youth and crime, finding resonance between material and ideational factors but he is especially keen to emphasise the almost infinite ways in which 'race' can be expressed through notions of nation, community, and so on (Cohen, 1993). In relation to Jefferson and Cohen, Gilroy can be placed further along a continuum reaching from economic determinism to his preferred relative spontaneity of discourse. He seems to have moved from an economistic analysis of considerable stridency to an implicit analysis of 'the Other' as a silent yet powerful presence to which categories can be compared.

Symbols, with their rich and simultaneous multitude of meanings, lead to comparison. They are at one inclusive and exclusive, defining incorporation and exclusion. The notion of being British, for example, calls out the connotation of being white, being a member of a nation, and so on. Without 'the Other' we have no point of comparison. 'The Other', a construction without a realist base, excludes black people from the discourse of Britishness; it incorporates white people under the flag and in so doing excludes black people.

Critique

The 'new racism' research is centrally concerned with forms in which presentations of difference between people belonging to minority groups are constructed and articulated in myriad ways. The biological basis of racialised social relations need not be directly articulated as those relations are constructed. Social exclusion based on explicit or implicit racialised criteria may be articulated through notions of nationalism and the nation, community membership, legality and citizenship, and many other cultural processes and forms.

Methods of research used to study this subject tend to be rather difficult to grasp in the sense that they are not as programmatic as those used in, for example, the collection of qualitative data by interview, systematic observation, unobtrusive measures, and so on. Discourse analysis, sometimes akin to the archaeological excavation of meanings that Paul Gilroy describes as his research strategy, decodes, extrapolates and represents the implicit and, occasionally, explicit meanings of texts. These are more often than not formal political speeches, public statements by senior police officers and others in positions of power, rather than examples of everyday discourse. There is a rationale for using these texts in that they are presumably well considered by their author and for obvious reasons exclude any direct references to biological differences as social differences. If notions of racialisation are in the mind of the speaker they are almost bound to be hidden beneath the surface of the text.

Formal texts present a host of interpretative problems for research and the evidence of whether or not references to nation and nationalism in Margaret Thatcher's speeches, for example, amount to racial exclusion or ethnocentrism is a matter of interpretation (Barker, 1981). This is not just a matter of semantics because it is important to know what we are talking about and analysing for a number of reasons: to enable research studies to be adequately compared; to identify the continuity and discontinuity of ideas within and between different social contexts; to understand what is the precise subject of research; and, not least, to develop appropriate policy responses.

There is also a significant gap between the apparent meanings contained in speeches, and other formal discourses analysed, and the everyday, common-sense discourse of various publics. We cannot assume that because a leading politician of influence articulates ideas of racial differentiation in the guise of nationalism they are somehow directly routed into the consciousness of newspaper readers, television viewers, or through rumour, mundane conversations or any other form of communication.

In studies that have suggested a more generic basis to the new racism, literary criticism and hermeneutics are used (for example, Cohen 1993). The exclusionary devices of the written text and other cultural forms may reveal meanings that connote 'racial exclusion'. This does not mean, however, that the new racism can be said to be in the ascendancy. Within some forums, the political and literary, it may be. But within the common conversation of everyday life biological rather than cultural reference points of differentiation and exclusion may remain. We don't know. The question of how far the new racism is related to what might be called the old racism is an empirical one that awaits sufficient evidence to support it (Mason, 1992; 1994).

This type of criticism does not mean that we revert to multivariate statistical analysis and a form of essentialism that seeks to isolate 'race' in the process of empiricist haggling Gilroy has dismissed. Neither does it wholly release us from it. Too much sociology is concerned with either essentialism *or* phenomenalism when the intellectual quest should be to combine both (Rock, 1979; Mason, ibid). Social processes of many different types constitute the practices that lead to the construction of racial difference like police stop rates, arrest rates and other relationships between the police and the members of minority ethnic groups. Arrest rates, for example, imperfectly measure the extent of known criminal activity of some youth, including black youth. These data are meaningful and for all practical purposes reliable as indicators of the extent to which something defined as 'race' is a variable *to take into account* when trying to calculate the extent of discrimination.

We also have to look much closer at the social processes leading police officers to construct ideas about crime and its relationship to black youth, and black youths' ideas about the police. We have to understand the ways in which organisational and cultural factors lead to particular racialised outcomes, mediating wider structural factors within the specific context of police work. Both types of analysis should be combined, placing an emphasis on both the phenomenal and essential features of racialised relations between the police and minority ethnic groups.

Chapter Five

British police responses to riots

'The police have to thank the West Indians for doing us a favour in making us think again about our authority (*The Guardian*, 1973).'

This was Sir Kenneth Newman's view, expressed over 20 years ago, when he was head of the Metropolitan Police Community Relations Branch. Since then, not least during his incumbency of the commissionership of his force, the authority of the police has been tested to the limit by black youths demonstrating on the streets. During the 1980s place names like St Pauls, Brixton, Toxteth, Moss Side, Handsworth and Broadwater Farm Estate have become symbols harmonising a litany of discontent, prompting Newman in 1987, the year of his retirement as commissioner of the Met, to speak of police 'no-go' areas in inner London.

Although they also involved a considerable number of white youths and, within a wider sweep of history, were not new, the disturbances during the 80s brought specific questions about the policing of black people·to the fore, and in many ways marked a turning point for discussion of the wider role of the police in our society. In this chapter perspectives on minority ethnic groups that have been implicit or explicit in police theory will be analysed. The riots of 1981 and 1985 will later form a focus for discussion about recent changes in this area of policing. The starting point is the 1960s and a police awareness of our increasingly heterogeneous society.

Policing across cultural boundaries

The initial and to a considerable extent continuing theme of police race or, as it is more usually described, community relations policy and practice has been concerned with understanding the cultures of immigrant peoples. During the 1950s, 60s and 70s there was the visible presence of various immigrant groups within urban Britain and, so far as it was noticed, a police problem of communicating with them. This was perhaps more relevant to Asian people but it included black people and there was an awareness of the difficulty of dealing with young West Indians, as they were then called. 'Paki-bashing' was a frequent occurrence in the East End of London and northern towns but, despite the serious nature of what was happening, neither police nor public attention was suddenly ignited by or slowly drawn to an issue called 'police race relations' – it was not perceived as a problem urgently requiring a solution (Pearson, 1976; Hunte, 1966). Knowledge of and comment about the working reality and impact of existing police relations with immigrant people was therefore sparse. The puzzle of policing a culturally diverse society could be solved in good time as immigrants assimilated into our increasingly pluriform society.

The main perspective on police race relations is well articulated by the Parliamentary Select Committee on Race Relations and Immigration, which examined what they called 'police/immigrant relations' during the early 1970s (House of Commons Select Committee on Race Relations and Immigration, 1972). Most of the long list of recommendations contained in the report cluster around the view that improved relations would be secured if immigrants were informed and educated about the role of the police in British society. More adequate communication across cultural boundaries would be enhanced by changes in a number of areas of police work, especially: in training; the provision of multi-lingual publicity about the police; recruitment of officers from minority ethnic groups to the regular and special constabularies; work in schools; sensitive attention to the small amount of crime committed by people from the various immigrant groups; and the appointment of police community liaison officers. All these recommendations would assist a wider process of assimilation.

There were some signs that during the early years of the 1970s a small number of senior police officers were willing to give attention to the problems which they and the Select Committee identified. In 1972, for example, Geoffrey Dear, former Chief Constable, of the West Midlands Police and now an inspector of constabulary, published an article, *Coloured Immigrant Communities and the Police*, in which he described patterns of immigration into Britain, the problems of settlement and of the second generation of settlers caught between two cultures, those of their host society and of the society of ethnic origin to which their parents were primarily committed (Dear, 1972). Dear found the remedy for 'culture conflict' in what he called a social role for the police, embracing police, community relations and many of the tasks identified by the Select Committee. A perception of a cultural gap between the British police and various immigrant peoples nevertheless remained. Training and the creation of specialist community relations departments were needed to enable communication across this cultural gap and to bridge it within the historic framework of policing by public consent. Policing is undertaken on behalf of the people and as immigrants assimilate into British society so the police will be accepted as their guardians of law and order. Dear put the argument clearly,

> Most of my proposals have had two central themes. The first has been the education of police officers concerning immigrants and there is room for gainful work in this respect. The second has been the education of immigrants into the role and responsibility of the British police, and there is room for even more profit to be made here (ibid, p. 149).

Specialisation develops

One organisational consequence of these ideas was the establishment of specialist police community relations departments, staffed by personnel holding middle rank. These officers were to possess the knowledge to understand minority ethnic communities and so be a first point of contact when difficulties were experienced on either side of the cultural divide. Alternatives could have been considered, for example: a form of regular accounting within every police division, requiring clear plans for the working evaluation of police race relations; training for constables and supervisors; programmes of policy development dealing with patrol work; and so on. Specialisation nevertheless became a keynote of change and in a 1976 Home Office survey of all 43 police forces in England and Wales, 29 said they undertook community relations work, although the substance of this was not clarified (Pope, 1976). In organisational terms, specialist community and race relations departments created a managerial line that descended from senior ranks to constables working as specialist community or home beat officers in local areas.

This perception of police race relations as conflicts of different cultures was in tune with the multi-cultural perspectives developed in education and other institutional spheres during the 1970s (Allan and Macey, 1988). Specialisation within constabularies, however, also harmonised with wider change within the British police, not least the development of an image of police professionalism.

During the 1970s the idea of the police as a profession was carefully fostered and tended. Part of this process of professionalisation was the creation of a cadre of graduate officers, many seconded to university to study a range of subjects, mostly law but including the social sciences (Holdaway, 1977). Knowledge of race relations was an appropriate subject to enhance the career profile of a professional police officer who, in time, could be employed in a specialist race and community relations department and liaise with people working in various race relations organisations and 'community leaders'. The basis of consultation and liaison was a parity of professional status. A particular problem of dealing with people from particular cultures was perceived as a task for specialist police officers working in specialist departments.

Some of the general limitations of the multi-cultural perspective limited the ways in which the police responded to race issues. Racial divisions, it is now realised, are not simply sustained by cultural difference and problems of police race relations are not straightforwardly sustained by police policy. The notion of a homogeneous Asian or black (or white) English culture is problematic – cultures are not transported by the first generation of immigrants and preserved as an artefact passed from generation to generation. They are dynamic, with diverse strands that orientate the identity and action of those who recognise them. Account also needs to be taken of the wider framework of social structure as a context for immigration and the organisation and practice of policing. The reduction of police race relations to ignorance about ethnic cultures has clear limitations.

When a process of assimilation forms the principal element of a race relations policy, a considerable onus for change is placed on minority ethnic people. The worth of minority ethnic cultures may be placed in doubt and the problem of 'race' is perceived as primarily one of people who are different to the English. They, the immigrants, present the main problem and need to change, not the majority population. Implicit notions of exclusion from an imagined, majority community are established (Anderson, 1991). The integrity of minority cultures is diminished and perhaps threatened. The status and identity of minority ethnic people are placed in doubt.

Frustrated opportunities in employment, education and other institutional spheres help sustain an imbalance of power and therefore unequal opportunities for advancement between minority and majority ethnic groups. Irregular distributions of power are not given adequate, if any, weight in the cultural conflict perspective. Processes of exclusion in the labour market, for example, have not been sustained through ignorance of cultures but through the direct exercise of discrimination, indirect discrimination through a lack of attention to the consequences of employment practices that are taken for granted as fair and, more widely, patterns of opportunity in education and other institutional spheres that lead to differential employment opportunities (Jenkins, 1986; Jenkins and Solomos, 1987).

The idea that the aggressive use of stop and search powers by police officers, the use of excessive force and of racist banter can be solved by educating them about ethnic cultures is more than wide of the mark. Educating police about the different cultures of 'immigrants' may have the opposite effect of reinforcing a view that such people are really very different from 'our own' and should indeed be treated differently.

At the institutional level, the police policy of specialisation created and to a considerable extent still creates a situation where problems of race relations are understood as the province of particular officers who possess the professional skills required to deal with them. Specialisation within the police and their work in the area of 'race' and community relations nevertheless remains a feature of many constabularies.

In a survey of all forces in England and Wales completed in 1989 I found that over 90 per cent had a specialist race or community relations branch at headquarters and some other level of their organisation (Holdaway, 1991). This form of organisation tended to separate race relations issues from routine police work, defining them as a specialism to be dealt with by particular officers. Routine patrol and other work continued, unaffected by the specialists. Attention was deflected from an understanding of how patrol strategies or any other aspects of routine policing might have a detrimental effect on relationships between officers and black and Asian people (Holdaway, 1978). The question of whether or not complaints about the policing of ethnic minorities, for example, are essentially different from those made about the policing of members of other groups is an important and obvious one but it has rarely been asked. If it had been asked during the early years of the 1970s, race relations may not have presented themselves to the police with the urgency and stridency they later assumed. 'Race relations' would have been placed within the wider organisational framework of policing and the routines of police work itself.

The disintegration of cultural barriers

During the 1970s many constabularies continued to develop their community relations work. Cultural difference remained the cornerstone of policy but in one respect the problem of race relations was being redefined, as an emphasis on high crime rates in areas of large black population was introduced. Rather different perceptions of the police were also developing among black people. The police policy of specialisation was interpreted by groups representing the ethnic minorities as an intention to separate the policing of black people from the policing of the rest of the population.

There is no clearer representation of this perspective than the Institute of Race Relation's (IRR) evidence to the Royal Commission on Criminal Procedure, *The Police Against Black People* (Institute of Race Relations, 1978). The IRR argued that there is a fundamental difference between the policing of black and white people. Separate police community relations departments deal with black people while white people are policed by generic policies and practices, which amounts to an extension of the historical, colonised status of black people to contemporary Britain.

> 'In effect this means that police accountability to the black community is relegated to and institutionalised in a particular officer, thereby absolving the rest of the division from the type of 'identification' considered so essential for policing the general population (ibid, p. 67).'

Conflicts between cultures play no part in this view – black people are the subject of a discriminatory, racist form of policing and the

IRR's message to the Royal Commission was that it would increase. Their questions were about the use of police powers and the discriminatory treatment of black people, which an understanding of different cultures could not overcome. By the turn of the decade a relationship between crime and black people, especially young black people, had developed in the police mind; an association between the police and illegality grew in the minds of black people. The now reformed 'Sus Law';[1] the over-policing of events where black people gather; the manner in which black people are treated in police stations after arrest, and the lack of police attention to allegations of racial attacks were interwoven to sustain the IRR evidence to the Royal Commission.

At this time, evidence of racialised inequalities in Britain was available but there was still a lack of systematically researched data about the policing of ethnic minorities. Academics were generally uninterested in the police; there was virtually no discussion about how the problems of gaining access to carry out research studies could be overcome (Holdaway, 1979). Clear evidence, however, is not always the guiding light of police race relations, which is why attention to perceptions is crucial. By 1981, for example, the members of a police–community liaison group in the London Borough of Lambeth were at loggerheads and had stopped meeting. The 'community' side of the committee published an utterly condemnatory report about the police, based on data capable of equal condemnation for its unsystematic character (London Borough of Lambeth, 1981). In London and, though less obvious, other major cities relationships reached tension and then boiling point. By 1980 Kenneth Newman's argument that West Indians (meaning second generation black British youth) had caused the police to think about their authority was soon to be subjected to the most severe test.

Riot – a testing of police authority

Preceded by confrontation between police and black people in the St Paul's area of Bristol, the serious public disorder that occurred in Brixton during 10–12 April 1981 and subsequently in Toxteth, Liverpool, Moss Side, Manchester and Handsworth, Birmingham marked a turning point for police race relations. As street disturbances, looting and burning of property took place, the idea that problems of police relations with members of minority ethnic groups were essentially misunderstandings about different cultures were laid to rest as ashes.

In his report about the disturbances, Lord Scarman spent little time praising any semblance of police policy (Scarman, 1981).[2] There was sufficient evidence for him to call the London Metropolitan Police and, by implication, the other 42 constabularies of England and Wales to account. Whatever our opinion of Scarman's analysis of events or recommendations for reform, without doubt he set in train an important questioning of police authority.

Scarman's report is based on an implicit sociology. He did not try to analyse the riots as discrete events but viewed them as part of a larger pattern. The immediate symptoms of disorder – violence against the police, arson and theft by looting – have to be placed within a broader perspective on the whole of British society. Here is the basis of his analysis:

> Many of the young people of Brixton are therefore born and raised in insecure social and economic conditions and in an impoverished physical environment. They share the desires and expectations which our materialist society encourages. At the same time, many of them fail to achieve educational success and on leaving school face the stark prospect of unemployment (ibid, p. 11) . . . Being unemployed, some youths find they spend much time on the streets. There he meets criminals, who appear to have no difficulty in obtaining the benefits of a materialist society . . . Many young black people do not of course resort to crime, nor, recent research has suggested, would it be correct to conclude that young black people are wholly alienated from British society as a result of the deprivations they suffer. But it would be surprising if they did not feel a sense of frustration and deprivation (ibid, p. 11) . . . The accumulation of these anxieties and frustrations and the limited opportunities of airing their grievances at national level in British society encourage them to protest on the streets . . . and to crime (ibid, p. 16). Scarman then concludes . . . these circumstances are not causes but a 'set of social conditions which create a disposition towards violent protest (ibid, p. 16).

Scarman is quoted at some length because I want to explore how far there is evidence to support his key assumption that young black people, 'share the desires and expectations which our materialist society encourages' but find they are frustrated when trying to realise them. He begs the question of the riots as a rejection of the values and institutions of British society and, maybe, the embryonic proclamation of some alternative or, a symptom of the frustration of the rioters who wish to achieve what they find has been denied them. This is very similar to Robert Merton's theory of deviance in which the strategy of 'adaptation' is a form of action prompted by a sharing of central societal values frustrated by institutions which fail to provide paths for their realisation and 'rebellion', a rejection of those values (Merton, 1938).

We have evidence to demonstrate the differential levels of unemployment, educational achievement and poverty amongst black people in the areas of Britain where the riots took place (Brown, 1984). There is not space here to discuss their complexity but they do generally indicate inequalities of the type Scarman highlights. The main point is that they are relative rather than absolute levels and that institutions with the objective of providing knowledge, skills, income, and so on, had for many reasons not granted large numbers of black people (and white people, though in somewhat different measure) with the resources to realise their material aspirations (Lea and Young, 1982). In Scarman's terms 'insecure social and economic conditions' were without doubt the wider context for the riots, to which were added the strident policies of Margaret Thatcher's government, which heightened a consciousness of material aspirations, unrealised achievements and therefore of frustration. 'Frustrated achievement', the first condition for testing Scarman's sociology, and Merton's come to that, was therefore present in Brixton.

Statistics of arrest in Brixton and other parts of London – and taking their inaccuracies and inadequacies into account – reveal the involvement of both white and black people in the riots. We are not describing a straightforward conflict between black and white people, a race riot. Neither were the Brixton or any other disturbances of 1981 a new historical phenomenon. They broke a lengthy period of relative public tranquillity and economic growth which had dipped sharply, leading to high levels of unemployment. The riots therefore stood out from this terrain and seemed novel but they were part of a more lengthy history of social disorder of considerable pedigree.

It seems, then, that all the conditions for straightforward 'rebellion' amongst black youth were in place. But, as Simon Field argues in his review of the literature about public disorder,

The violence and apparent chaos of riots is a fertile ground for myth. It is therefore no surprise that the explanations put forward to account for riots reflects as much the wishes and anxieties of the authors of the explanations as the riots themselves (Field, 1982).

At first sight the riots might well seem like a wholesale rejection of British society. The scale of damage to property, of injury to police officers and of general disorder suggests such a view is credible. Any idea that black youth living in areas of considerable material deprivation holds positive views about British society seems unlikely, to say the least. But this is the second element of Scarman's sociology – whether or not the riots were a rejection or accommodation to the inequalities of British society?

By far the most adequate research in this area is by Dr. George Gaskell, a social psychologist. (Gaskell and Smith, 1981; 1985). Gaskell researched a sample of black and white youths aged 16 to 25 living in several London boroughs with high minority ethnic populations. The sample was divided into five groups: those attending a self help group for usually unregistered, unemployed youth; black youth registered as unemployed; black youth in manual and skilled/unskilled occupations; and white youth matched to the unemployed and employed groups. The members of the self help and unemployed groups were very deprived, all had four to five jobs since leaving school, little money to hand and less than minimal educational qualifications. The suggestion – a reasonable one because we know that most youths involved in the riots lived near to their location – is that these youths shared the same social characteristics of those who took to the streets of Brixton during 1981.

Having assembled a sample reflecting personal characteristics continuous with known social inequalities, Gaskell asked about the youths' attitudes to particular aspects of British society. They were asked about their 'worst/best state of life' and attitudes to some of the central institutions of our society. Surprisingly, the black youths expressed positive attitudes towards job centres, careers offices, schools, further education, the media and British people in general. Negative attitudes were expressed about politics in Britain. White youths' views were altogether more negative that those of their black peers, indeed, the more materially deprived black youths held more positive views than their white peers. The lives to which they aspired were those of parenthood and family, material accumulation and success.

The reason for introducing these findings is not to suggest that we can sit back and be satisfied that black youths basically accept a British way of life or some other imagined notion of community but to gain a handle on the motives that fed the riots of 1981 and, therefore, to take the perspective of those who were on the streets into account when considering remedial policies. The point is that rioting seems to occur because:

> ... certain groups have lost faith in the capacity and will of established institutions to take their interests into account and to provide them with the means of achieving social acceptance and material success (Field, ibid, p. 33).

Gaskell makes a similar point but goes on to draw out its policy implications,

> they view society positively and wish to succeed in it: but they find that they have little chance of realising their aspirations ... the onus is on policy makers to allow young blacks to fulfil their realistic aspirations and not on the blacks to fit their aspirations to unjust social conditions (Gaskell and Smith, 1985).

The ferment of anger and frustration unleashed in 1981 seems to have been formed mainly by the experience of people who wished to participate more fully in their society. Gaskell's evidence tends to support Scarman's implicit sociology (Holdaway, 1988). Black youth is not wholly alienated from British society if by that we mean it favours a wholesale rejection of dominant institutions and preferred goals and objectives. Whilst retaining their aspirations through those dominant institutions, they nevertheless both want to succeed *and* retain their distinctive identity as black. The notion of 'assimilation' as a process of change that is wholly inclusive is misleading and understandably offensive. There are distinctive identities and perceptions of our society amongst black youths, as well as common goals shared with their white peers (Small, 1983).

This research puts arguments like those made out by Cashmore and Troyna in which it is 'reasoned' that the riots were an expression of frustration linked to a 'penchant for violence within the West Indian culture possibly stemming from the days of slavery when the only method of retaliation was doing physical damage to the overseer' seem more like wishful academic thinking from the 'radical' distance of the university than any engagement with black youth themselves (Cashmore and Troyna, 1982). And it renders Marcus Howe's idea that the riots were an embryonic form of revolt that 'must necessarily develop into full blown manifestations in the not too distant future' to a fantasy (Howe, 1981).

There is much more to be said about the motives of people involved in the Brixton disturbances but for the moment we can dismiss teleological sociology and analyses based on a straightforward assumption that because people challenged the police, looted and engaged in public disorder their stance can be described, in Mertonian terms, as one of rebellion. Gaskell's research indicates that the riots were an instance of the adaptation of means to secure more widely desired social ends rather than an upturning of the ends in themselves, which beg new means to achieve them.

Scarman and the police

Motivation to begin and continue engagement in a riot is not uniform, neither is it based on a single, all-pervasive reasoning. If riots are symbolic of a more widely drawn grievance they are likely to have a number of foci. Symbols are multi-faceted. Gaskell's finding that black youths have more positive than negative views towards major institutions could mean that the police, who without doubt were a main target for the aggression of the people on the streets, symbolise the whole of British society.

Gaskell found overwhelmingly negative views about the police (and only the police) amongst the black youths he interviewed. 60 per cent of white youth thought the police were 'good' or 'very good' but just half of the black youth held this view. 41 per cent of black and 16 per cent of white people held the view that the police were 'bad' or 'very bad'. Other studies have also found similar views (Skogan, 1990).

These attitudes were isolated in Gaskell's research and found to be discrete but of course his technique of statistical regression could not capture the pluriform meaning of phenomena or relations between events in context. Riots can be an expression of frustration, rebellion, fear, fun and many other meanings at one and the same time. Meanings flow back and forth as events develop. Nevertheless, whatever the complex mix of meanings of the riots as they took place, young black people involved in them were in significant part motivated by feelings against the police because of the frequency and insensitivity with which they had been stopped in the street. Their experience of the police and the resentment that grew from it were then woven into a more widely shared 'folk history',

> 'of perhaps frightening experiences with the police (which) has worked its way into the shared beliefs of black youngsters. Even without direct personal experience young blacks evoke an unpleasant stereotype of the police, and this, of course, affects any contact they have with them (Gaskell and Smith, 1985, p. 263).

Another limitation of Gaskell's methodology is that it cannot describe and analyse the ways in which this 'folk history' was articulated before and during the Brixton riots, or its relevance to the disturbances in other parts of the country. The idea of a 'folk history' rationalises into a coherent whole a diverse range of snippets of rumour, primary stories and other information that in diverse ways brought a group of people to the streets of Brixton and elsewhere. 'Folk history' does, however, draw the attention of those who sustain it to processes of police policy development and routine police work that construct 'race' as a phenomenon.

Critical of the polarised, sterile debate about black youth's involvement in crime, Jock Young and John Lea have argued that the riots were both a response to police discrimination and the deprivation of social inequality (Lea and Young, 1982). In a characteristically schematic manner they argue that the experience of racial discrimination and social deprivation led to rising street crime in Brixton. As far as recorded crime was concerned, a pattern that directed police attention to Brixton became evident. Between 1976 and 1980 36 per cent of all crime in the larger London Borough of Lambeth occurred in Brixton and 49 per cent of all robberies and other violent thefts occurred there.

The response of senior officers was eventually to place an emphasis on stopping people in the street, which would resonate lower ranks' views of how crime should be tackled. Aggression and insensitivity by the lower ranks led to increased tension and a further separation of Brixton police from the population they policed. Those who in the past might have volunteered information about the identity of criminals became unwilling to trust the police with their information and, as a consequence, the police became increasingly reliant on their own strategies of 'street wise' policing. The whole of the Brixton community gradually came to feel that they were the subject of an oppressive style of policing, rapidly withdrawing their consent from the police until the final response of riot, there being no other effective institutional channel – political representation, for example – through which to express their grievances.

The Collapse of Consensus Policing

Discrimination and Deprivation
↓
Rising level of street crime
↓
Shift towards 'military' policing
↓
Alienation of the community

Mobilisation of bystanders   Reduced flow of information
to police

Collapse of basis for consensus policing

Source: Lea and Young, p. 1982, p. 13

Criticism of this explanation has ranged from an over-reliance on official statistics, which we well know to be imperfect (Blom-Cooper and Drabble, 1982); a lack of appreciation that most calls for police assistance are unrelated to crime, and therefore the idea that a local population became alienated is an exaggeration forced into a preconceived explanatory schema; and that Lea and Young's argument 'The police make the initial connection between race and crime' is flawed historically because – as pointed out in the previous chapter – conflict between the police and black people pre-dates arguments about the extent to which black people are involved in crime (Keith, 1987).

Apart from these specific flaws in Young and Lea's paper its emphasis on the ways in which routine police work in the inner city can reconstruct and sustain racialised divisions is important. Scarman's account of the immediate events that led up to the 1981 riots, when tensions in Brixton were already running high, includes many clues about the reference points of routine policing practices rooted in the occupational culture that heightened conflict and reinforced the racialisation of relations between the police and the local population. Officers' lack of sensitive discretion when dealing with incidents that were escalating towards serious disorder are indicative of the notion of absolute control of the population and territory that are found in the occupational culture.

Scarman, for example, relates an incident in which two officers saw a taxi driver poke something down his sock (Scarman, 1981, p. 24). They made the assumption that drugs were being concealed and insisted on searching the driver and, eventually, his car, despite his protestation and explanation that he kept bank notes in his sock as a security measure. Before long a group of youths gathered and the incident became both threatening and serious.

Knowing how relationships between police and public in Brixton had become difficult; that a taxi driver might well keep bank notes in a sock for security reasons; that withdrawal from a difficult situation by the use of tact and effective discretion is a key aspect of effective police work; that, more speculatively, the conduit between the taxi driver and his possession of drugs was skin colour, we can question the officers' reasoning. One wonders if the same assumptions would have been made about a white taxi driver stopping the same vehicle in precisely the same place?

Basing their action on taken for granted ideas and practices that have been well documented in studies of the occupational culture, the officers sustained racialised relations between police and people in Brixton. I am suggesting that by policing in a different way, or by policing in the same way when stopping white youth they would have avoided the wholesale escalation of pre-existing tensions and there- fore not sustained – constructed and re-constructed – racialised relations of police work.

The point is that although Scarman, albeit briefly and inadequate- ly, documented what he called the 'insecure social conditions' within which the people of Brixton live, by which he meant patterns of social inequalities sustained by differential educational, health, leisure and housing provisions, he also implicitly directed attention to diverse ways in which this structure of inequality is mediated through police action. This is something of what Young and Lea seem to be arguing but they require more evidence about the ways routine police work, not least its reference points in the occupational culture, amplifies or at times reduces the consequences of material inequality and racialised relations that extend beyond the structural and organisational framework of policing itself. Then in relation to the riot, they need to demonstrate how race relations were constructed and changed within the specific context of Brixton.

This is where Michael Keith's recent work adds to our understanding of the riots (Keith, 1987; 1988; 1991; 1993a; 1993b). Keith is critical of the ways in which academics have assumed that, because they identify youth within a particular age range sharing particular socio-economic characteristics to be the 'average rioter', or, in the absence of evidence, that black youth in a racist society are in opposition to all authority, the meaning of a riot or rioting has been captured.

> 'The rioting is considered to be a single generic activity carried out by a holistic unit ('the crowd' or 'the rioters') and is consequently susceptible to a relatively straightforward single explanation. This unit is made up of people each of whom can be characterised by the descriptive term 'average rioter', who is variously either black, young and 'alienated' or either black or white, young and 'alienated'. Reference to the events that constituted any single disorder in Britain in 1980 or 1981 belies such tidy classification (ibid, 1987, p. 280).'

Using official statistics of arrest, and recognising their limitations, he is able to argue that the events in Brixton in 1981 were diverse, occurring in different places, involving a range of people of different ages who belonged to different groups. There were two main classes of participants – 'rioters' and 'looters'. There were what might be called two events in close proximity: 'one was a localised, full-scale confrontation with the police, involving a broad section of people from a very small area of Brixton; the other, which occurred some distance away from this, was an opportunistic reaction to the collapse of social order (ibid, p. 286).'

Keith argues that it is not adequate to derive the meanings of a riot by analysis of the average characteristics of rioters or by an appeal to theory that collates and wrongly attributes dominant motives to people engaged in very different actions on the street. The meanings of what might be interpreted as 'riot' amongst people involved in the Brixton riots were diverse, ranging from a blow against white society, to fun, to a directed protest against some police officers, and so on. The relationship between mental states and physical behaviour is much more complex than sociological analyses of the riots would suppose. These explanations, Keith argues, some of which we have already criticised, rationalise the complexity of the Brixton and other riots into a taken for granted common sense of social science that is stereotypical, simplistic and misleading. Each incidence of disorder should be studied as an entity in its own right before it is compared with what appears to be a similar event.

On the basis of a detailed study of three places in London where riots took place, Brixton, Hackney and Notting Hill, the particular history of police relations with local communities are charted as they become very specific 'symbolic locations' where the past 'lives' as an interpretative tradition that can set alight (literally at times) relations between police and people. Time and space are key organising concepts for Keith's detailed and innovative research and he reminds us that the places where the riots occurred were not just convenient spatial stages for the playing out of frustration but symbolic locations that, through the connotations and denotations they convey, have infused events with rich meanings. The history of relations between the police and people living in the areas of London that are the focus of Keith's analysis is a recounting of events within a particular framework of understanding, leading in time to 'riot'.

This analysis of the riots humbles other sociological accounts in that it demonstrates their tendency to simplify complex events; to conceptualise adequately the relationship between social structure and action; to give attention to ways in which local history provides a material and symbolic context for riots; and to analyse them 'as if' they have an objective status when they are constructed through human action.

My own view is that, though Keith's work is invaluable as a deconstruction of sociological accounts of riots, it also wavers between an extreme form of relativism and a view that, for example, 'race' exists, has causal powers, and epistemological validity, but is not necessarily reified (ibid, p. 241). The extent to which we can regard racialised relations as 'real' is not clear from his work. Nevertheless, the most sophisticated analysis, like Michael Keith's, returns us to basic sociological rather than administrative or methodological questions of the type criminology has favoured.

One of the consequences of the 1981 riots was a gathering up of a history of place to reconstructed 'symbolic locations', creating the framework for policing during the following years. Scarman's report added to this history but we do not know what the residents of Brixton understood by it as it mingled within their own reconstructions of the events of 1981. Neither do we know how police perceptions of the riots and of the local population changed, if at all. There was not to be another riot in Brixton although there were direct conflicts between the police and young people, and some later incidents when the police found themselves on the brink of serious disorder, after Cherry Groce was shot by a police officer, for example.

This change did not occur because the tenor of policing was suddenly transformed, though some important, brave reforms were implemented. Maybe Scarman's report and various police and community initiatives changed the symbolism of time away from one of increasing conflict? We do not know and there is more than enough scope for research that draws on the oral history of the riots to help us understand why there were not further wide scale disorders in Brixton during the following years. Academic criminology has unfortunately tended to be too preoccupied with the immediacy and apparent relevancy of policy and administrative issues to engage in work like this.

1985

Four years after Brixton, a more serious riot took place at Broadwater Farm Estate in Tottenham, north London. The complex circumstances leading to this riot will not be discussed here although the death of Cynthia Jarret during a police search of her home was central to them. The point I want to emphasise is that the Broadwater Farm riot marked a turning point for the policing of public order incidents and for the policing of black people. By 1985 Kenneth Newman had become the Commissioner of the Metropolitan Police and was commanding his force as petrol bombs reigned down on his officers, protected by shields and special clothing. Two further features of Broadwater Farm dramatically changed the scene. These were the introduction of CS gas and other weapons and the brutal killing of an officer by participants in the riot. No longer could the Scarman argument of better community relations as *the* key to the creation of public order be used with such credibility within the police service. Senior officers now had to reckon with the management of a workforce conscious of the murder of a colleague at the hands of rioters and with a public image of a police at times adopting methods of policing more reminiscent of military manoeuvres than community consultation.

Broadwater Farm did not lead to a formal public enquiry, although the local authority, Haringey Council, established an enquiry, chaired by Lord Gifford QC (Broadwater, 1986). I include Broadwater Farm within this final discussion of police responses to the riots because it led to one of three major changes in policing that are not wholly in balance. Two of these, training and community consultation were advocated by Lord Scarman. The third, what has come to be called 'paramilitary policing', was the response of chief constables.[3]

Training

The police are no strangers to training, which has always occupied a position of considerable status within their organisation (Reiner, 1991). The traditional thrust of training has been the provision of information about the law and police procedures rather than the role of police in society, the effective use of discretion when enforcing the law, and related issues. When community relations training was provided it was of the 'visit the mosque to learn about culture' type of event and a very infrequent one at that.

Scarman aimed some of his main recommendations at the reform of police training, concentrating on the ways in which powers are used and duties performed in the course of routine police work. He wanted more emphasis on training officers on the streets during their early period of service rather than in the training school; training throughout a police career; an emphasis on the effective use of discretion; and, most importantly for this discussion, on race and community relations training (Oakley, 1993).[4]

In response to his proposals the Home Office established a working party to review existing training provisions and to propose principles and recommendations for the future (Police Training Council, 1983). As far as existing training was concerned, the working party noted it was restricted to the provision of information and therefore based on a very limited range of methods of delivery that were not assessed for their effectiveness. Recognising that 'race issues' do not present themselves as discrete problems in the course of routine police work, it was recommended that race relations should be integrated into a wider curriculum dealing with community relations. However, it was also acknowledged that some training should be concerned exclusively with race issues.

Placing the subject at the centre of policing, the working party recommended that all officers should receive training in community and race relations. Rural forces without a substantial minority ethnic population could not neglect the subject. A much wider range of methods of training were to be developed, including role play and race awareness training, as well as the traditional provision of information. Both officers' attitudes and behaviour were to be tackled, each related to the teaching of effective policing skills and therefore the requirements of routine police work. To start the ball rolling a pilot project of Race Awareness Training was to be established and evaluated by the Home Office (Southgate, 1984).

Recommendations were also made for the continuation training of each rank and officers holding a specialist function. The policy role of more senior officers was understood and, importantly, there was recognition that they needed to understand not only the ways in which personal attitudes and behaviour could be prejudicial and discriminatory but also that training should 'encourage them (the police) to begin to see their work in a wider context and to impart an understanding of institutional racism (p. 27).' Anticipating the considerable development work required to put their proposals in place, it was suggested that a new national training support and resources centre should be established, to develop materials for the new curriculum, to train trainers and to retain the impetus the working party stimulated.

Virtually all these recommendations were accepted by the Home Office and, in preparation for larger scale innovation, they ran a pilot race awareness programme, which was evaluated by Peter Southgate of the Home Office Research and Planning Unit (Southgate, 1984). Southgate's report identified at a very early stage the basic problems that would dog successive attempts to provide effective training in race and community relations in the police service. There were clear limitations to the small project evaluated, which Southgate acknowledges, but the suspicion of the police, their perception of its irrelevance to routine police work and their lack of understanding of what the training could, should and did provide proved to be uncertain, to say the very least. The fundamental issues of the relevance of training in race relations to routine police work and of what such training can reform remain to this day.

In his recent review of training provisions for race relations, Robin Oakley, a former member of the Brunel University Centre, the initial resources centre suggested by the Home Office working party, and now an associate of the new centre, which is run by an American trainer closely associated with the race awareness programmes of the American armed forces, has identified a number of the remaining problems (Oakley, 1989; 1993). First, there is the police understanding of what training can achieve and, therefore, what it cannot change. In the early days training was perceived as *the* solution to what, I suspect, was an ill-defined or, more likely, undefined problem in the minds of many senior police officers. Training was training, unanalysed in terms of the impact it could have on routine police work. The sufficient and adequate task was to do something called training, without consideration of the extent to which it could effect change in a hierarchical organisation like the police.

Secondly and related, training was not understood as one arm of a wider strategy of policy and practice for organisational change. Few if any forces have undertaken a systematic analysis of race relations training needs, and this work has only just been carried out at national level, a decade after the publication of the Home Office report, by staff of the Police Central Planning and Training Unit (CPTU Community, 1993). This means there has not been a corporate and strategic approach to the integration of training provision within all policies and practices of a constabulary. The role of management in relation to the objectives of race relations training; clarity about the objectives of training and their impact on recruitment and other key organisational strategies; consideration of the relationship between the supervisory work of sergeants and inspectors and race relations training; and other issues have not been adequately addressed.

Thirdly, a potent impediment to change is the tradition of the lower ranks' occupational culture. We know from recent cases of discrimination in employment brought against chief constables by black and Asian police officers that prejudice and discrimination remain woven into the occupational culture.[5] In the absence of a corporate strategy that deals with this 'reality' of policing, not least the ways in which the taken for granted common sense of the occupational culture can militate against the objectives of training programmes, the impact of integrated or separate race relations training is bound to be severely curtailed.

Effective integration of race issues within a training programme is, however, an important and difficult objective for any organisation. The Central Planning Unit for Police Training has only recently been required to develop and implement a curriculum for trainers concerned with the initial training of constables at regional training centres. Their unpublished report of a pilot project suggests that trainers find it extremely difficult to integrate 'race' issues into their existing curriculum and considerably more work is required over a long period before integration can be achieved. Then there is the related issue of when and how specific aspects of race should be introduced. This is part and parcel of the issue of integration of race issues within generic policing but requires a trainer to have an informed and confident approach to the subject. New courses for trainers are just being put into place and we do not yet know about their impact.

In 1989 the Home Office issued a circular to all chief constables advising them to develop equal opportunities policies and practices (Home Office, 1989).[6] Since that time much police and Home Office attention has been given to equal opportunities but one unintended consequence of this has been to distract attention away from the specific issue of racialisation. I will discuss this problem in the next chapter when we deal with racialised relations within the police service. Here I just want to signal the question of how far a rather general approach to equal opportunities and the strictures of law it imposes on the senior staff of an organisation, the police service in this instance, can lead to a perception of 'race' as a rather dangerous subject that one should treat with caution, ensuring it does not lead to allegations and legal proceedings. Equal opportunities can become a negative aspect of organisations. A positive action approach to training and its place within the wider sweep of police policy is therefore not fostered. Race issues remain more a legal matter to avoid than a good and proper feature of policy and practice.

Finally, it is important to point out that the 43 chief constables of England and Wales have freedom to develop their own in-house training provisions and to take as much or as little advice from Home Office race relations documents and training materials as they wish. This has meant that the development of race relations training within constabularies has been patchy, to say the least (Holdaway, 1991). When recently asked about this issue by the Home Affairs Select Committee, Paul Whitehouse, Chief Constable of Sussex, representing the Association of Chief Police Officers, agreed that much more needs to be done to create a coherent, national framework of training (House of Commons, 1994; p. 26). The commitment of individual chief constables to the successful development of race and equal opportunities policy is highly variable and a serious impediment to change. This means that the staff of the Central Planning Unit, who provide material for the more, though far from tightly, co-ordinated work of regional training centres have to contend with this uneven pattern and their work is presently not based on an accepted, national framework of shared principles and commitments.

The training for trainers programmes have similarly suffered from a lack of appreciation of purpose by chief constables. Staff have been sent to the new national Support Unit for Race and Community Relations Training, successfully completed the training programme and therefore been ready to introduce race awareness and other programmes into their constabulary, to find that within a short period of time after their return they have been posted to other duties.

None of these criticisms mean that nothing has changed. Very wide scale changes in the organisation and delivery of police training have taken place since the Scarman Report was published: much more time is spent by probationer constables training with selected colleagues; the curriculum has been thoroughly revised; trainers have been trained in facilitative rather than didactic methods; a structure to create a national training programme has been set in place. However, training has its limitations, some of which have been described. Training is reactive in the sense that it offers police officers skills and knowledge of how to deal with indigenous social conflicts. Policing can quell and prevent the escalation of conflict but not ameliorate it. This does not mean that training is unimportant, it simply reminds us of its broadest limitations.

Community consultation

The accountability of the British police was probably the most vigorously debated issue arising from the Scarman Report. Much of that debate dealt with the powers of police authorities, which Scarman did not discuss in any detail. Less attention was given to measures dealing with what might be called a lower level and rather different form of accountability, consultative groups.

From the evidence of police community relations in Brixton, Scarman chose to direct attention to the local level of liaison and co-operation between police and people. British policing, he argued, is based on two historic principles, 'balance and consent' and 'independence and accountability'. The first principle is of relevance to the necessary levels of intrusion into common life which will permit the police to retain order, while holding and fostering public consent and confidence to continue their work. The second, related principle is that the police should be answerable for their actions — they are publicly accountable through a number of legal and administrative mechanisms — but not be subject to any partial influence derived from political, economic or any other power base.

It was probably the second of Scarman's principles that led him away from recommendations touching on the problems of party political interest associated with police authorities, to the police community liaison or consultative committees he advocated. Once established on a statutory footing consultative committees would bring representative, public opinion to bear on local police policy and, collectively, on the police authority. Police race relations might then be improved, especially by the presence of minority ethnic representation on the committees. Policing by consent would be strengthened and consultative committees could:

> help to provide an agenda for a continuing dialogue between the police
> and the public about the nature of policing in today's society — a dialogue
> which, if it be based on mutual understanding and respect, will serve to

strengthen, without dehumanising, the forces of law and order (ibid, p. 99).

In fact, Section 106 of the Police and Criminal Evidence Act, 1984 did not require all constabularies to establish committees. They were only made a statutory requirement in London, where the Home Secretary is the police authority.[6] Although the flexibility of local arrangements was stressed in two Home Office circulars, it was found in a national survey that most police authority members and senior police officers thought the arrangements were a statutory requirement (Morgan, 1987). Rod Morgan, who undertook this research, argues that in a number of Home Office circulars civil servants and, in their inspection of constabularies, Her Majesty's inspectors assumed that consultative arrangements would be put in place. Chief officers assumed the same and those few who thought otherwise were persuaded to change their mind.

Although the precise form and role of a consultative committee was not regulated one objective for it, relating back to the Brixton riots, was the management of conflict between the police and minority ethnic groups. Consultative committees were to bring to police attention issues of concern to black people, assuming it is indeed possible to find representatives of black groups who truly tap 'community opinion'; that such people are willing to be members of a consultative committee; that their voice will be heard and lead to appropriate change; and that effective change will in time lead to greater co-operation between the police and minority ethnic groups.

Rod Morgan has studied in some detail the working of committees situated in different areas of the country and found very few included members of minority ethnic groups (Morgan, 1989). Consultative committees have had some success in educating their members about policing and thereby strengthened relationships between senior officers and the members of some community groups. Officers have listened to some views about their activities. To this extent consultative committees have been effective but it has not been possible for chief officers of police and the members of local consultative committees to claim a particularly significant measure of consultation and 'community involvement'. Groups boycotting committees can be criticised for not participating in discussion and afforded little sympathy. On the other hand a more general lack of public interest in the work of committees can be interpreted as satisfaction with present levels of police service.

Consultative committees have therefore achieved a measure of success but, as Morgan argues, they have also tended to legitimise present policing arrangements rather than challenge controversial courses of police action.

> Even where police operations are controversial, the police are usually now able to justify their decision with reference to demands from within the community. As a result, the police are less easily typified as oppressors of the community (ibid, p. 237).

This general description of the work of consultative committees may represent the national picture but could also be slightly misleading in that it evens out significant points of tension. In some areas of London, for example, where there is a large black population, they do not appear to have been the rather cosy talking shop Morgan portrays. Michael Keith's study of consultative committees in Brixton describes in graphic detail intense hostility towards senior police officers and more generally points out some of the limitations of their work (Keith, 1988).

Keith takes as his example an open public meeting held by the Brixton Consultative Committee after the police shooting of Cherry Groce in 1985. The chair of the committee, Astell Parkinson, a well known youth worker who had lived in Brixton since 1959 and in the past was personally involved in clashes between the police and the black community, began with 'a moving speech for serious but controlled discussion of the emotive issues that had occurred in the preceding days.' Soon, a small number of people dressed in paramilitary uniforms forced their way into the council chamber where the meeting was held and took control of the microphones. From then on bitter accusations about the police were repeated. Parkinson's contributions were met with a chorus of 'Uncle Tom, Uncle Tom'. Members of the committee could not assuage the anger of the people present, despite the at times outspoken conciliatory comments of Alex Marnoch, the much respected commander of the police division covering Brixton. The vitriol directed at Marnoch and Parkinson was beyond reason and at one point Marnoch was briefly reduced to tears. The meeting broke up in disarray.

This is an extreme example of a consultative committee at work but the extreme example reveals some limitations. Conflicts between the police and black people cannot be adequately resolved within the context of a consultative committee. At extraordinary cost to two people, Astell Parkinson and Alex Marnoch, who took the full brunt of community anger, a holding operation was sustained and tension dissipated but this was far less an achievement than Scarman's expectation that community consultation would reduce sustained conflict. As Keith put it, 'The roots and nature of this conflict were simply not susceptible to being talked away . . . Certainly, antagonism between the police and community had not diminished . . . As individuals Parkinson and Marnoch could not have invested more in the consultative process but they worked within an institutional structure that could offer only occasional palliatives to a social schism (ibid; pp. 68–9).'

Secondly, Keith argues that consultative committees are based on a spurious notion of community and the ways in which it is represented through committee membership. The disruption of the Brixton meeting by a faction of the black community may have represented an expression of widespread dismay and anger but it was also followed by telephone calls of support, from within the same community, to Marnoch and Astell. Which group and which voice was the representative one? To which channels of dialogue should primary attention be given?

Thirdly, within the membership of the committee there was no mandate providing an authority to press for changes in police policy. Local communities, so called, are not homogeneous groups and the assumption that 'there are natural geographic, ethnic and religious groups, hierarchically structured and answerable to the individuals who assume readily identifiable positions of leadership', is inadequate (ibid, p. 65).

Finally, where decisions are reached, the work of a consultative committee is limited by the extent to which it is possible for local police commanders to influence the activity of their lower and more senior ranks in accordance with the wishes of the committee. A tension between policy and practice in police work has already been described, illustrating how the working practices of the rank-and-file can adapt the intentions of senior officers' directives that are perhaps in accord with the views of a consultative committee.

Local police commanders are also dependent on the support of their seniors, who can refuse to co-operate with the wishes of the consultative group, to the detriment of the credibility of local officers. Keith cites an example from the Islington committee where the local chief superintendent was unable to answer any questions about a serious incident because his senior commander was not willing to attend relevant meetings, or brief him with the information required by its members.

These are limitations rather than a negation of consultative committees. They follow the boundaries of Scarman's analysis of the nature of social conflict, not least his view that consensus between police and people can be significantly developed by the introduction of channels of representation to enhance interdependency between police and people. Deeply rooted social divisions of racial inequalities and therefore of conflict can cut through such boundaries of representation, to limit and frustrate them.

Racial conflicts have many dimensions, with a varied impact on consultative group considerations. The under-policing of the ethnic minorities when subjected to racial attack, the over-policing of ethnic minorities during stop and search operations, and racial prejudice within the police and communities policed can be conflated, confused and conveniently played off against each other during discussions about race issues (Pearson and Sampson *et al.*, 1989). In the light of these many difficulties Keith concludes:

> In reality, community consultative groups are neither a panacea for police/black antagonism nor a calculated and fraudulent exercise in cooptation and public relations. Instead, they are a flawed reform: institutions that cannot satisfy one of the main functions for which they were created because of the characteristics of their design (ibid, p. 64).

Public order policing

When Harold Macmillan was asked about the most fraught aspects of being in government he said, 'Events, events.' The reforms Scarman suggested and the Police and Criminal Evidence Act set in place to improve police race relations were not annulled but were certainly questioned by the 'events' of 1985. In that year riots occurred in Handsworth, Birmingham and Broadwater Farm Estate, Tottenham, north London. Two Asians died in a fire during the Handsworth riot and a police constable was brutally murdered during the Broadwater Farm Estate conflict. The extent and ferocity of the riots led Kenneth Newman, the Commissioner of the Metropolitan Police at the time, to bring onto the streets officers in full riot gear and weapons using plastic bullets. It was no longer possible for the commissioner or the chief officer of any other metropolitan force to claim credibility for the strategy former Commissioner Robert Mark described as 'winning by appearing to lose.' Overt force had to be used to win and it became extremely difficult for Newman, in the short term at least, to argue that consultative committees, training in race relations and other social measures could deal with the root problems of police race relations. Officers had to be defended and new strategies were required for their protection. To argue against this was to invite trouble, from within the police and from a government increasingly keen on defining an enemy within.

To deny that the death of a police officer at the hands of rioters was merely a setback to the reforms Scarman suggested, and to which many senior officers were committed, would have eroded Kenneth Newman's credibility amongst his rank-and-file. He and his fellow chief officers reviewed their capacity to control riots and responded by developing new training strategies, purchasing a wide range of riot control equipment and strengthening policy for the control of public disorder.

The events of 1985 normalised public order policing and, although we do not have clear evidence about this, may well have led to an association in the police mind between black youth living in urban areas and the potential for wide scale public disorder. One can only speculate if or how this perception altered the routine policing of black people. At the national level the Association of Chief Officers of Police developed a manual for public order policing, circulated to all their members.[8] The Home Office advised all chief constables to identify 'symbolic locations', where widescale disorder might occur, to monitor activity in and around them and to rate the level of disorder on a scale of social tension. When tensions move towards the higher end of the scale officers would be placed on alert and preparations for a policing response put in place. Immediate response units staffed by specially trained officers skilled in techniques of riot control would be deployed if events escalated. Their training took place at a newly established public order training centre. CS gas was purchased by virtually every constabulary, even when a police authority expressed a strong wish that its chief constable should not use the budget for such resources, South Yorkshire being a case in point. Riot shields, transit carriers with protective armour, flame-proof suits and special protective helmets became the standard equipment for the officer deployed on riot control. CS gas and other weaponry were held in the background. The decision to prepare for the policing of wide scale public disorder was clearly placed within the operational realm and therefore the autonomous province of the chief constable. Senior officers were trained and became proficient in the command and control of the policing of large scale social disorder.

These changes, which have been very significant in the development of policing during the last two decades or so do not immediately translate into routine patrol work in the policing of minority ethnic groups. We are talking about large scale situations of potential or actual disorder, which range from demonstrations to carnivals, small gatherings after an incident involving the police, to intentional confrontations with the police. The ways in which large scale disorders remain in the collective police memory, translated across time through the occupational culture and related to action on the streets, is of course extremely difficult to research and we can at present only speculate about them. Established features of the occupational culture like action, challenge to disorder and excitement could feed from the expectation of wide scale disorder officers glean from mundane incidents.

Officers would on the one hand be wary of dealing with black youths, expectant that trouble was round the corner and therefore ready to use force prematurely. They may well be more apprehensive and fearful of injury, even though they overestimate the risks of being hurt. This could provoke a willingness to avoid confrontation and it may be that the emphasis on dealing with incidents with discretion found in basic police training has tempered the approach of many officers, we do not know. On the other hand, when the occupational culture is taken into account, a quest for a measure of action and challenge to black youth seems likely.

As far as academic debate has been concerned, interest has focused on the consequences of new strategies to police disorder. This has mainly been articulated in the pages of academic journals and in particular the different interpretations of paramilitary policing by Tony Jefferson and Peter Waddington (Jefferson, 1987; 1990; 1993; Waddington, 1987; 1991; 1993).

The bones of this dispute are that Jefferson argues that paramilitary policing is 'the application of (quasi) military training, equipment, philosophy and organisation to questions of policing (whether under centralised control or not)' and Waddington prefers the core of his definition to be the less pejorative 'co-ordination through superior command and control' (Jefferson, 1993, p. 374).

For Jefferson, the developmental seeds of paramilitary policing were sown when police authority required renewed legitimation. There has since been an inevitable ratcheting of paramilitary policing at major public disorders and, 'military discipline cannot simply be transferred to policing without altering the nature of policing.' This is a historical change from the efforts of police and government to stress that officers are civilians in uniform, not quasi-military personnel. Further, the stance of paramilitary policing is essentially confrontational; it escalates rather than quells conflict. To illustrate his point, Jefferson argues that the night before the Broadwater Farm Estate riot erupted a protest took place near Tottenham police station. This was controlled by beat officers, while the specially trained 'paramilitary' units remained out of sight. The demonstration, though threatening and vigorous, was policed in a controlled and minimal manner. There was no escalation of violence. This for Jefferson, drawing on Lord Gifford's report of his inquiry into Broadwater Farm, was a 'traditional response'. The paramilitary reserves waiting in the wings took a different view, 'the atmosphere must have been charged with anticipation of trouble' (Jefferson, 1990, p. 87).

Waddington's view of paramilitary policing is different, very different. Unlike Jefferson, he does not begin his analysis from a macro-analysis of the historical juncture at which particular changes in police work coincide with wider structural change. There is, however, more than a hint of inevitability about his understanding of paramilitarism. Although Waddington recognises the social context within which the riots occurred, he argues that the police are primarily responding to the disorder that faces them rather than any wider precipitating factor.

There is a strong managerial logic to much of Waddington's work as he writes of the controlled and disciplined way in which the policing of public order has not escalated, as Jefferson argues, but has been retained within bounds. His methodology is far more positively empirical that Jefferson's and he is able to point out, for example, that the so-called routine policing of the demonstration outside Tottenham police station on the night before the Broadwater Farm Estate riot was in fact policed by officers from the support group Jefferson is so keen to criticise. Jefferson has simply got his facts wrong. A clear line cannot be drawn between 'routine' and paramilitary styles of policing.

In more recent work, based on the close observation of the policing of many public order events, Waddington argues that it is not the iron fist of law, in the guise of the Public Order Act, that frames police perceptions of their planning for and action at such events (Waddington, 1994). The law and the police are the means through which structure is mediated in practice. The police are as keen to avoid what Michael Chatterton has described as internal and external 'trouble' by bringing public and senior officers' attention to their mistakes (Chatterton, 1979). This strategy can minimise their reliance on the enforcement of the law. Through a variety of tactics and strategies officers in command of public order events both accommodate and exclude the wishes of the organisers of marches, demonstrations and the like. Officers remain in command and try to minimise conflict.

Jefferson's work certainly reminds us of the changes in policing that have introduced paramilitary organisation and equipment into the police repertoire. Black people may well no longer afford the police as much legitimacy as they might have done without the changes of paramilitarism we have described. He also reminds us of the conflict between different policing functions and styles that need constant management. On the other hand it is perfectly fair to ask of Jefferson, as others have, how he would have responded to the riots facing the police? One is tempted to say that his only available reply is to point to the wider structures determining (not his term) police action. Police reform basically awaits wider social structural change – but in the interim, what?

Waddington is reasonable to point to the limited options facing the police but he leaves us with the problem of deciding the boundaries and desirability of a continual, increasingly militaristic (not his term) and aggressive police response to public disorder. He could lead us to the routine arming of the police and, eventually, to the use of firearms simply because others possess them. The consequences of this for black peoples' perceptions of the police and, indeed, police perceptions of black people do not bear thinking about.

The development of paramilitary policing has therefore had definite effects on the policing of large scale events involving minority ethnic people. Much more empirical research of the type Waddington has recently completed is required, however, before we can understand how various pressures on police officers controlling demonstrations are articulated in action through strategies of accommodation and active control.

Large scale disorder involving black people has led to new police strategies that may make an impact on their understanding of routine policing. We have certainly moved well beyond the view that problems of police, community and race relations are primarily those of cultural misunderstandings, to be assisted by a process of assimilation. Consultation and training initiatives continue in a rather halting manner, having a limited effect on the quality of policing and relationships between some black and Asian people and the police.

Many serious incidents involving the police and black and Asian youths have occurred since 1985 but have not received the headlines they attracted in the past. We do not know why these have not developed into much larger incidents. Public order policing has been naturalised, becoming an expected and in large measure accepted strategy. But we cannot straightforwardly point to an increasingly authoritarian police using increasingly oppressive measures. Crises of police legitimation forged by wider structural pressures have no inevitable outcomes. Structure and action have to be considered in their complex relationship but the evidence so far suggests that 'action will out'.

Chapter Six

An enemy within – racialised relations within the British police

The organisational boundaries of constabularies cannot withstand questions about 'race'. Although most research attention has been given to the policing of minority ethnic groups, the racialisation of relations *within* the police service is an important, fruitful area of study. In this chapter various aspects of race relations within the police service will be considered, especially the recruitment of black and Asian people into the ranks; their experience of employment within the service; and police initiatives to create a multi-racial police service within England and Wales.[1]

A multi-racial police

As long ago as 1976 the Home Office supported a national advertising recruitment campaign in the black and Asian press. Thirty-two applications to join the police materialised but none led to an appointment. When questioned in the House of Commons about the impact of the campaign, the Home Office minister with responsibility for police recruitment at the time described the perspective that underpinned this and similar recruiting initiatives throughout the 70s: if special campaigns fail to recruit in the short term, the number of coloured recruits, as they were then called, would nevertheless increase adequately in the long term (Runnymede Trust, 1976). An assimilation of immigrants into British society would encompass police recruitment. In time the number of black and Asian serving officers would grow and England and Wales would have a multi-racial police. Nothing approximating a positive action stance, requiring constabularies to accept the primary responsibility for increasing recruitment from minority ethnic groups, was at this time written into the police or Home Office agenda. 'Assimilation' would provide.

The 1981 riots and Lord Scarman's report (once again) brought a significant change to this subject. Scarman commented on recruitment from minority ethnic groups, basing his analysis on the assumption that 'the composition of our police forces must reflect the make-up of the society they serve. In one important respect at least, it does not do so: in the police, as in other important areas of society, the ethnic minorities are very significantly under-represented' (Scarman, 1981, p. 76). He then argued that his perspective did not imply the setting of employment quotas or the lowering of entry standards. Scarman's requirements were prominent, committed police policy involving special initiatives to recruit from ethnic minorities and demonstrable support from the leaders of black and Asian communities. The police were to take the lead. There was no time to wait for a process of assimilation to run its course.

The Home Office response to Scarman's report was the appointment of a working party, which reported in 1982 (Home Office, 1982). They related black and Asian peoples' perceptions of the police to the manner in which individual officers conduct themselves when patrolling the streets. A single officer's insensitivity or rudeness towards a black or Asian person can seriously harm recruiting policy. Recruitment from minority ethnic groups is not a specialist activity for the staff of a specialist police recruiting department; it is an aspect of all officers' work. Within the police ranks black and Asian officers are to be held in the same regard as their white colleagues.

In a more specialist vein, all forces were advised to develop methods of identifying black and Asian applicants and to introduce a range of special recruiting initiatives. Training for selection interviewing was suggested, as was a review of recruitment procedures, to identify and remove any features that might disadvantage minority ethnic applicants. Importantly, it was recognised that a responsibility to initiate special recruiting measures lay with the police. Their approach was now to be a positive one, giving impetus to increased recruitment from minority ethnic groups.

During the years following publication of the 1982 Home Office report a small number of forces began developing special recruiting initiatives. The West Midlands Police, for example, whose officers serve a large black and Asian population, planned an educational access course for intending applicants, street-to-street leafleting campaigns, public meetings at community centres used by black and Asian people, and a range of other initiatives. Leicestershire Constabulary planned a year-long recruiting campaign which included many different types of initiatives, public meetings, leafleting, radio and television broadcasts, and so on. Both these forces have enjoyed significant increases in their number of black and Asian recruits. The Thames Valley Police produced a promotional video and organised weekend courses for enquiries from ethnic minorities who might later apply for appointment to the force. All these activities and many more in other forces were initiated by the police, who have probably carried out more specialist recruitment work than any other organisation.

Despite these efforts, general progress in police recruitment from minority ethnic groups remained slow. In 1986, following the 'second round' of urban riots in 1985, Douglas Hogg, then Minister of State at the Home Office, organised a conference of recruiting officers to launch a further raft of proposals designed to increase minority ethnic recruitment (Home Office, 1986). The minister accepted that there was no short term solution to the problem. Standards applied to applicants could not be lowered. These points, however, should not divert attention away from key issues the police must face. The image of the police among black and Asian people was acknowledged to be a serious stumbling-block to recruitment. A determination to eliminate any racial prejudice or discrimination found among police officers must be conveyed to the public. Officers of all ranks should realise that insensitive behaviour when dealing with a person from a minority ethnic group can ruin months of recruitment work. The Home Office would provide background support to the recruitment initiatives forces must spearhead. Among other tasks, they would take responsibility for the revision of the initial police recruitment educational test, which was potentially open to challenge on the grounds of cultural bias. A staff officer from Her Majesty's Chief Inspector of Constabulary office would be appointed to take responsibility for advice about ethnic minority recruitment and dissemination of examples of good recruitment practices.

Douglas Hogg's emphasis, both at the conference and later in a letter to all chief constables, was that he regarded the event as a 'springboard to positive action and I hope, therefore, that you personally will consider what else can be done in your force to follow up the main points which were made at the conference (Home Office, 1986).' Chief constables were advised to prepare a race relations policy statement which should be effectively communicated to all staff. Attention was to be given to monitoring recruitment procedures; black and Asian officers in post were to be supported; special recruiting initiatives were to be undertaken.

The nature of the advice offered to forces about the recruitment of black and Asian people was now shifting somewhat. While the Home Office would play a supporting role, the major impetus for the development of policy was to come from chief constables. Furthermore, the advice offered ranged across a wide area of police work. The police were to analyse their internal recruiting procedures as much as their special, outgoing recruitment initiatives.

In 1982 the Home Office working party argued that 'sustained effort' over a long period of time was required if minority ethnic recruitment was to increase. In 1986 the Home Office minister re-emphasised this long term perspective but also strongly advocated a programme of what he called 'positive action', to realise some recruiting gains in the short and medium term, with the police taking the main responsibility for a vigorous recruiting policy and programme of initiatives.

Despite that advice, the number of police recruits from minority ethnic groups has remained low and there are few signs that the general trend is likely to change dramatically. In 1993 just 1.45 per cent of serving officers were from minority ethnic groups (Her Majesty's Chief Inspector of Constabulary, 1994). Further encouragement and advice has been given by the Home Office through their circulars on equal opportunities and on ethnic minority recruiting, reiterating many of the points made in various reports and other documents (Home Office, 1989; 1990). In his 1993 annual report, however, Her Majesty's Chief Inspector of Constabulary described a police work-force far short of the percentage of minority ethnic groups in the population at large and he criticised the racist banter and other insensitive practices that turn potential recruits away from a police career (Her Majesty's Chief Inspector of Constabulary, 1993).

The context of recruitment

We know from research studies that the attractions of a police career are broadly similar for the majority and minority ethnic communities in Britain. When representative samples of black, Asian and white youths have been asked about the potential attractions of a police career, they have cited similar features. 'Job security', 'variety of work', 'pay', and 'prospects' have been ranked in the same order by members of all groups (MIL, 1979; Harris, 1982). There is also evidence of a continuing reluctance among black and Asian people to apply for appointment to a force. And we know from other research that serving black and Asian officers frequently face racialist banter from their colleagues and, to a lesser extent, from the public. A study in which a national sample of black and Asian officers serving in seven constabularies were interviewed indicated that the most frequently mentioned factor that may prevent recruitment from minority ethnic groups into the police was prejudice from future colleagues. Over half the officers interviewed said they had been the subject of name-calling, which they accepted as part of the general banter of canteen conversation (Wilson, Holdaway *et al.*, 1984).

In their study of the Metropolitan Police, David Smith and Jeremy Gray observed over a period of time how six constables of Afro-Caribbean or Asian origin were treated by colleagues: 'Overall, it is clear that for most black and brown people, being a police officer puts them under considerable strain. They have to take abuse from the public and put up with racialist language and jokes from their colleagues, and they are subject to a conflict of loyalties' (Smith *et al.*, 1986; p. 145). Studies of the occupational culture of the lower police ranks have emphasised the frequent use of racialist language by officers (Holdaway, 1983; Keith, 1993).

Research shows that black youths have less confidence in the police than their white peers, but the evidence does not indicate a general rejection. In a recent 'customer survey' conducted within the Metropolitan Police District it was found that black people were markedly less satisfied than white people when asked about the service offered to them by the police. Levels of satisfaction, however, tended to be high for both groups. Black and Asian people's views of the police are therefore somewhat varied, but the general conclusion to be drawn from the available evidence is an attitude characterised by reservation rather than either clear support or contempt (Research Services, 1990).

These findings have to be placed within the wider context of inequalities outlined in earlier parts of this book. The attractiveness of a police career to a black or Asian person is not immediate. Highly publicised individual cases where a black person has received poor treatment at the hands of the police; question marks against police handling of riots; concern about how one will be treated by future police colleagues; and other, related issues will be weighed in the balance when a police career is considered. As the Home Office minister pointed out in his address to the 1986 recruiting officers' conference, years of work building up confidence between the public and the ethnic minorities can be undone by one act of insensitivity.

The legal context

There are also particular legal constraints that frame the recruitment of people from minority ethnic groups. In his study of the recruitment of black Americans into the police, John Leinen argues that the United States legal framework of positive discrimination was crucial for the significant advances made by black police officers (Leinen, 1984). Civil disturbance acted as a catalyst to a public consciousness of civil rights and a protest movement among black Americans. Legal change followed, first within a framework of equal opportunities. Affirmative action then developed as a prelude to the acceptance of positive discrimination and the setting of formal hiring quotas. Other American research on this subject has suggested that changes in patterns of recruitment experienced by the police have been primarily achieved by the existence of employment quotas (Conley, 1982; Hochstedler, 1984).

A particularly important role in reform has been played by American black police officers and their representative associations, who have sought legal redress for discriminatory employment practices within the police (Alex, 1969; Sherman, 1983). The notion of legal rights, which forms the foundation of the United States constitution, has provided a justification for and impetus to this type of action. Furthermore, the gradual political representation of black people through their election to state and federal legislatures has also been an important means of exerting pressure and gaining influence.

In Britain, positive discrimination, and therefore the setting of employment quotas governed by the criterion of ethnicity, is illegal. Some special measures can be taken in the area of training for people from ethnic minorities and their access to employment provisions. These do not extend to positive discrimination in the sense of preserving a quota of jobs for people from particular ethnic minorities and therefore excluding white people from applying for them. It is possible, for example, under Section 37 of the Race Relations Act 1976, to offer special training to people from identified ethnic groups who are under-represented in the work-force of an institution. The police could use this provision to fund access courses for the educational selection test. Access courses have been mounted by some forces from their own resources or in partnership with a local educational establishment but they have not so far been funded under this provision.

During research interviews about their experience of police employment and recruitment policies I conducted with black and Asian constables it was clear that they disliked and in most cases rejected recruiting strategies that appeared to include special procedures for people from minority ethnic groups (Holdaway, 1991). Assistant chief constables and recruiting officers, who were also interviewed during the research, were similarly cautious when asked to comment about a programme of positive action. Some positive action measures to recruit from the ethnic minorities, however, were seen as desirable and necessary but they were viewed as perilously close to positive discrimination. All officers rejected positive discrimination measures and in particular the use of ethnicity as a criterion for setting formal employment quotas. They argued that any element of positive discrimination would stigmatise black and Asian recruits as second-class police officers.

The assistant chief constables understood 'positive action' in a number of different ways. This is not surprising when the unfamiliarity of the notion within Britain is taken into account (Young, 1983; Edwards, 1987; Burney, 1988). In some forces positive action meant the careful review of individual applications for employment from members of minority ethnic groups. A double check was made on decisions about the relevance of and weight given to educational qualifications, previous work experience, and so on. In another force it was taken to mean a wide range of special initiatives, introduced to take account of the substantial problems experienced by black and Asian people when seeking employment, including their perception of the police force as a difficult working environment. Positive action was altogether more muted in the third force where research was undertaken. Here it meant a measure of flexibility with recruiting standards, the height and eyesight standards of applicants, for example.

Without doubt, positive action is a difficult notion to define, merging with positive discrimination on a continuum. As John Edwards has put it in his discussion of the notion within social policy, 'Positive discrimination and positive action lie on a continuum where anodyne positive action merges into "soft" positive discrimination and the latter into "hard" positive discrimination (Edwards, 1987, p. 209). The diversity of views about positive action found within and between forces during the research, however, indicated that the notion had not been defined by chief police officers, incorporated into a coherent strategy, and adequately communicated to staff working at any level of their organisation.

To the recruiting officers, positive action was always associated with and dangerously close to 'hard' positive discrimination, with the connotation of rigid quotas and so on. This did not mean that they considered police forces could not take a vigorous stance towards ethnic minority recruitment. It did mean they had not defined for themselves or communicated to their staff the distinction they drew between positive action and positive discrimination. The legal framework they perceived led to caution rather than positive innovations of policy and practice.

The policy context

Within this social structural and legal context, the police have developed their response to the recruitment of black and Asian people. Their perception and response, however, has not led to an inclusive approach, taking race relations within and without the police as integral aspects of a recruitment policy. During my research it became clear that senior officers in many forces did not relate recruitment to wider concerns of police race relations. For them, ethnic minority recruitment was primarily a recruiting issue of long or short term importance, with more or less emphasis on black and Asian people as target recruitment populations. 'Race' was not perceived to be a key issue of relevance to recruitment policy and practice.

Very few constabularies, for example, have published a race relations policy statement and codes of practice covering an interrelated sweep of police work.[2] All forces have an equal opportunities policy statement but, despite the very clear and firm advice of the

Under-Secretary of State in 1986 that they should do otherwise, very few chief constables have developed an accessible race relations policy.

Race relations policy statements bring clear benefits to a constabulary. They include clarity of information for staff and the public about a force's commitment and approach to race relations, and the enhancement of public accountability. Further, staff who want to question any policy or practice they think is discriminatory can point to a race relations policy statement to justify their stance. A race relations policy statement is therefore the starting point for the development of specific work in any area of policing, including recruitment from ethnic minorities. Few chief constables, however, have perceived their approach to race relations in this way. Ethnic minority recruitment has not been clearly defined as an area of police work centrally related to race relations within the police service and between a force and the public it serves.

Another indication of the separation of race relations from recruitment is its specialisation within constabularies. 95 per cent of constabularies in England and Wales (41) have a specialist department for community\race relations work but just four of these are routinely involved in recruitment planning.[3] Clearly, this is a needless and wasteful marginalisation of knowledge and skill. Race relations has been relegated to a specialism and neglected when policy and practice for police recruitment from minority ethnic groups has been considered.

A further dimension of this separation of race relations from other aspects of policing was apparent in evidence from recruiting officers who had worked on special initiatives to attract recruits from minority ethnic groups, and from serving officers' accounts of routine police work. The basic point here is that the tenor of the routine policing of black and Asian people on the streets is clearly related to racialised relations within the police, and to the effectiveness of recruitment strategies. A black officer might be patrolling with a white colleague and a black youth is arrested. The white officer is racially abusive to the youth but the effect of his remarks on his black colleague is not taken into account. A black youth is in the charge room of a police station, in custody for an alleged offence. A black police officer walks through the charge room and hears racialist remarks directed at the youth. White officers will say that no harm is meant to their black colleague, as if 'race' can be separated into discrete channels of communication.[4]

Similarly, if relationships between a local police and black or Asian people become tense, as was the case when a black youth was allegedly wrongfully arrested in one of the areas where intensive research was undertaken, the impact is felt by officers concerned with recruitment initiatives in those areas. On one occasion a recruitment officer told me that enquiries at a special recruiting caravan had come to a standstill after an incident involving the arrest of a black youth and the caravan became a place for youths to lodge their complaints about the police. An Asian officer employed at the caravan then spent a good deal of time fire-fighting the suspicions and dissatisfaction of local people. Relations between the police and black and Asian people cannot be separated from racialised relations within the police. They are interrelated, structuring and sustaining racialised relations within and without the police.

Officers' views

Assistant chief constables (ACC) with responsibility for recruitment and a sample of serving black and Asian officers were interviewed about recruitment issues and the experience of police employment during this research (Holdaway, 1993, pp. 128–34). Although I think the situation is now changing somewhat, it was striking that the ACCs' views were markedly different from those of the black and Asian constables.[5] The ACCs minimised problems of prejudice and discrimination their black and Asian officers might face; these same issues were of primary importance to the constables.

When asked if he thought racial prejudice or discrimination within the work-force was an issue for his constabulary, one ACC responded that his perception 'is that racial prejudice is less now within the police service than it is in the general community. Probably I've said something that would fly in the face of a lot of opinion but I do believe that.' Another ACC said that he did not have any evidence of a measurable prejudicial attitude among police officers in his force. If prejudice existed it was unlikely to be detected. Racist officers were too canny to use racialist language openly and be identified. This view, however, did not mean that the problem of racial prejudice and discrimination was unimportant. He explained,

'Now, if you are saying to me what evidence have I got in this force that there is a definite and measurable discriminatory attitude by police officers, I have got to say to you, the evidence is that I haven't got any evidence. If you say to me does that mean there isn't a problem, the answer is 'No.' I haven't any evidence of a problem or not a problem . . . Frankly, I am more concerned about our general levels of service than I am about . . . I think discrimination is just one of those other elements. I mean, you know, we could phone a police station now at random and get a very good reception or we could get a fairly mediocre reception. Now I think that happens to white people and to black people.'

The ACC in the third force drew attention to 'weeding out those officers who are racist' and he recognised that many black and Asian parents did not encourage their children to pursue a police career because they considered the police 'violent, racist, bigoted, anti-Asian, and so on.' However, when it came to views about his work-force he adopted a rather more relaxed stance:

'I'm not that naive to say to you that there are not problems. There are problems and there's a lot of healthy banter goes on. I've heard some of it myself when they don't know I'm there, between black and white officers, two-way. I think the problems can start to occur when there is no banter at all, when people are shunned and people are talked about behind their back. If there is healthy banter, some of which may be mildly racist but is in jest, then you are on the right track, I think.'

These interviews revealed a consistent misunderstanding of the extent and impact of racialised language among the police rank-and-file. Constables of Afro-Caribbean or Asian origin interviewed presented a very different picture of life in the police. Thirty constables were interviewed and just four did not mention racialist comments and jokes as a regular feature of colleagues' conversation (Holdaway, 1993, pp. 135–56). One of the four had recently joined the force, two identified a specific incident but did not find it to be of major significance, and the other had no comment to make.

The other officers accommodated to their employment in four basic ways. Some made a distinction between jokes that were malicious and those that were benign. Although their colleagues frequently engaged in racialist banter they reckoned to know whether or not it was derisory.

> 'Oh yes, I mean you are going to get jokes. You are going to make jokes. Then again, I make jokes back, you know, at their expense, so it's a bit of give and take really. I think you do know if someone means something, I think everyone does. If you are a coloured officer, well, if you are a coloured person, forget about officer, if you are a coloured person, you know if someone makes a racist remark. You do if it's purely and simply by the way they say it, the accent they put on, so you know if they mean it or not. I've not come across any officer that's said anything that's racist that has not been in fun.'

Another officer put it this way: 'After five or six years of jokes you learn, you learn who are the idiots.'

For other officers, police employment was a continuation of a lifelong experience.

> 'I grew up with it so I don't know any different. If I went to an Asian school and I went into the police force and people started calling me names and that, I probably would be very hurt. I don't know, I really don't know.'

A colleague who also expressed this view linked his experience of what he called 'police racism' to an apprehension about recruitment amongst black and Asian people: 'I think it is because they are frightened. They have heard so many stories of racism in the police that they won't join to find out because they are frightened of what people will say or their friends are going to turn round and say "Traitor".'

Seven officers said they accepted a situation they disliked because they were committed to a police career. They wanted to get on with the job of policing, 'Other policemen. I find more racism in the actual force and amongst colleagues than I've ever had in my whole life . . . that's the only thing that annoys me. I accept it because if I don't then I can't do the job.' However, there were costs associated with this coping strategy. This officer said he tolerated racist comments but when asked 'Do you think they sometimes go too far?', said: 'There are times, yeah, where they overstep the mark. Because I've given, well, if you like, because I've given (them) free licence to say what they want. I mean I wouldn't try and suppress a person's views anyway. But because I've given them free licence to say or think whatever they want, then they do tend to just come out with it, irrespective of whatever the situation is.'

Fewer officers, six, resisted colleagues' remarks in various ways. Sometimes they let them know that, 'I'll give them some back and that's the way it goes, you know.' Others took a less prominent but nevertheless active stance: 'If it annoys me I'll say something and they are well aware of the fact that I thought what they said wasn't quite right.'

The black and Asian officers serving in the research forces were therefore resilient, coping with their work situation by the use of one or more of the strategies identified. Their description of police service is hardly encouraging for people from minority ethnic groups thinking about a police career. Yet this is the work context the assistant chief constables described in mundane terms and failed to tackle by managerial intervention. For them, 'race' was not a key feature of recruitment policy. Recruitment policy was not clearly related to the task of managing a multi-racial police force.

Recent changes

The research I have been discussing was completed about four years ago and since then some important changes have occurred in this area of police work. Some of the movement, the most significant, has been driven by the initiative of black and Asian officers, and some by chief constables. In the round they indicate a changing but less than clear understanding of the ways in which relationships within the work-force are racialised.

The initial factor to note is a number of important industrial tribunal cases in which police officers from minority ethnic groups have successfully brought an allegation of racial discrimination in employment against their chief constable. The first of these was brought against the Metropolitan Police in 1990 by PC William Halliday. He alleged extreme racial abuse by colleagues and that this was part of an atmosphere orchestrated by the inspector in charge of his shift. In 1991 PC Surinder Singh, Sergeant Anil Patani and Sergeant Satinda Sharma sued the Chief Constable of Nottingham-shire for racial discrimination and victimisation. They received compensation of £35,000. Two years later another Asian officer, PC

Joginder Singh Prem, agreed a settlement of £25,000 with the same chief constable for racial discrimination, citing evidence of jokes – senior officers were alleged to have called him 'towel head' – victimisation by fellow officers and discrimination when he applied to join the CID. This second case was brought despite Nottingham-shire Police's introduction of an equal opportunities policy and the appointment of its chief constable, Dan Crompton, as chair of the Association of Chief Police Officers Race and Community Relations Committee.

Other cases have followed. Detective Constable Barry Thompson settled with Kent Police after he was the subject of racial abuse when the member of a vocational course for trainee detectives. He alleged he was the butt of racist jokes about the size of black male genitalia, that his BMW car was a 'pimpmobile' and that as he was black he must be a money-launderer and a drug-dealer. Finally, it is worth mentioning the case of PC Sarah Locker who successfully settled a case of racial and sexual discrimination against the Metropolitan Police. Locker alleged that as part of a continuing experience of jokes about her Turkish origins she was given a letter containing racist abuse by a detective chief superintendent. The letter was written on an official police form! A second allegation was that she had not been selected for service in the CID when less qualified officers had been appointed to the branch. Locker agreed a settlement of £32,500, a post in the CID and a period of re-induction into her force.

These and other cases, the Nottinghamshire Singh case in particu-lar, have brought the ways in which officers from minority ethnic groups are continually subjected to racialist jokes, banter and other forms of prejudice and discrimination to the attention of chief constables and the Home Office. Other cases are in the pipeline and, as happened in America, they give confidence to minority ethnic officers who see a very public means of changing their conditions and experience of employment.

The most recent development, partly a response to the cases mentioned, is the launch of the Metropolitan Police Black Police Association. The Association encompasses both police and civilian personnel working in the force and one of its objectives is to secure equal opportunities for its members. At its launch the Commissioner of the Force, Paul Condon, gave his unreserved support and recog-nised the need for the Association when the history of the employ-ment of black officers is considered. The Police Federation, the police union, were unable to agree to send a representative to the launch and there is uncertainty about their stance on what for them appears a potentially divisive development.

My judgement is that the formation of the Association will prove to be one of if not the most effective reforms within the police. Although recently confined to the Metropolitan Service, the many other black and Asian officers present at the launch will either establish their own regional organisations or become associate members of the London based group. Chief officers and the Home Office will then be faced with black and Asian officers arguing from a stronger power base than has been available to them in the past. The modes of accommodation to racial abuse found among the serving officers interviewed during my research could gradually move towards resistance and in the longer term much will change.

This does not necessarily mean that officers will heighten their consciousness of being 'black' or 'Asian', or develop what might be defined as a political stance. They might but it is not inevitable. The strong view of black and Asian officers is that they are police officers who happen to be black or Asian, not that they are black people who have joined the police as part of a personal strategy to change race relations (Wilson, Holdaway *et al.*, 1984). This is not wholly true of all black and Asian officers, but it is so of the vast majority.

The Bristol seminars

In response to concern about the work experience of their black and Asian officers, in July 1990 the Metropolitan Police Service organised a number of seminars – the 'Bristol Seminars' – to discuss 'the causes of and possible solutions to its current high wastage rates, especially amongst black and Asian officers (Metropolitan Police, 1990)'. The seminars were organised in five groups, each with a membership of about 70 officers. Each group was further divided into a smaller membership of about 14 officers, who discussed questions about a wide range of subjects: racial issues, recruitment, training, grievance and discipline, support mechanisms, force policy, career development, public relations and constraints. In all, four of the groups had a sole membership of black and Asian officers and the fifth had a membership of white officers, allowing a comparative element in the analysis of points raised. Groups were also matched as far as possible by gender, length of service and age.

These seminars mark an important innovation in the history of race issues in the British police. No other constabulary – and probably no other work organisation of any type – has so directly faced prejudice and discrimination within the work-force or engaged black and Asian officers in open discussion. Following the seminars a small team of black and Asian officers wrote a report of the findings with recommendations for reform. Working parties were then formed with a remit to bring forward suggestions for change in all areas identified during the seminars.

The general message of the report was that race issues were of much more importance to the black and Asian officers who attended the seminars than to white officers (Metropolitan Police: Analysis Team, 1990). It was clearly demonstrated that black and Asian officers have a different perspective than white officers on the organisation that employs them and that many of their particular needs are not met by their colleagues. One of the more specific, key findings of the seminars was the crucial part the occupational culture plays in sustaining the racialised divisions identified by the black and Asian officers. Racial jokes and banter were said to be rife; supervisory staff rarely intervened to challenge prejudice or discrimination; there was a lack of confidence in more senior officers' commitment to change the culture.

Few white officers identified these features of their work environment. They did not recognise that their black and Asian colleagues had any specific problems and were therefore unable to address themselves to them. They made a wealth of unintentionally revealing observations on the subject of racial integration within the service but the greater part of their presentations centred around general service conditions and individual grievances. This perspective reflected a wider feeling within the Metropolitan Police rank-and-file that there was not a problem for discussion. In their report of the seminars the reporting team mention vociferous criticism by their white peers of expenditure on the 'Wogs Seminar' and of their 'Black Report', as some officers have called it (Metropolitan Police: Analysis Team, 1990).

The idea of a black police association was given a final fillip during the seminars. Although extremely difficult and uncomfortable for both complainants and plaintiffs, the cases of racial discrimination in employment have made chief constables think hard about the management of their staff from minority ethnic groups. Black and Asian officers in the Metropolitan Police, and in the longer term in other constabularies, are not as isolated as they once were. Racial prejudice and discrimination has become an organisational rather than a personal problem for individual officers. Networks of minority ethnic officers have been established and they will be strengthened. It is certainly early days and change is not fast but the first signs of reform, largely driven by the activity of black and Asian officers, are becoming clearer. In America black officers and their representative associations pushed forward the pace of change and sought legal redress to do so. A similar path of change may be developing here.

Quality of service – management and race relations

Chief constables now recognise the existence of an occupational culture within their constabularies. The term they have often used is 'canteen culture', which tends to sanitise and restrict its scope to talk rather than talk and action, but the recognition is there. They also now accept that there is an association between the internal and external dimensions of police, race relations.

A corporate management strategy encompassing both of these aspects is now advocated by the Home Office and the Association of Chief Police Officers. In October, 1990, for example, the Association of Chief Police Officers launched its strategic policy document, *Setting the Standards for Policing: Meeting Community Expectation*, in which equal opportunities policy is afforded a central place: 'Forces should strive to improve equal opportunities within the organisation . . . there is a direct correlation between attitudes within the organisation in these areas and officers' attitudes towards members of the public (ACPO, 1990, para. 3.7).' A similar view is also evident in the Association's 'Quality of Service Initiative', where clear recognition is given to the relationship between and interdependency of all aspects of police policy and practice (ACPO Quality of Service Committee, 1993). What is not clear, however, is the extent to which these and other contemporary police developments concerned with the central but rather general motif of 'quality of service' are adequate to incorporate the particular issue of police race relations?

This question is raised because it is debatable whether or not race relations is a generic 'quality of service issue'. A substantial body of systematic research has identified the particular lack of confidence black and Asian people have in the police service (Skogan, 1990; Home Office, 1992; Southgate and Crisp, 1992). A further, substantial body of research evidence demonstrates the particular work experience of black and Asian officers (Wilson, Holdaway *et al.*, 1984; Smith *et al.*, 1986). Their experience of police employment is certainly related to that of white officers but it is distinct nevertheless. Race relations within the police and between the police service and members of minority ethnic groups raise particular problems begging particular solutions.

Throughout the discussion of sites of racialisation the need to place 'race' within the social context of the police as an organisation, with its distinctive occupational culture, has been stressed. This perspective allows us to analyse common, shared *and* particular features of the occupational culture that construct racialised relations and the processes through which they are sustained.

The following person interviewed during a study of black and Asian officers' reasons for resigning from the police service makes the general point (Holdaway, 1993).[6] Being treated differently is not just the fate of members of minority groups. Most minorities are regarded differently by the rank-and-file.

> No, they didn't treat me differently, not necessarily because I was black, the thing is it's down to attitudes really . . . It wasn't just about blacks, it was about women who were beaten up, it was about women who were raped dressed up in loud clothing shall we say, it was about Irish people, it was just about everybody – and I just didn't, I didn't really share the ideas, I didn't really.

White resigners made similar comments but a difference between white and minority ethnic officers' views became clearer when they talked about the power of the occupational culture and its particular relevance to black people, and to women. The following quote is from a white male officer whose view was challenged by the majority of black, Asian and white female officers interviewed. If you are not on the butt end of prejudice you can afford to say that you 'never felt it was racist and it was never sexist.' When you stand as a target, your perception is rather different.

> But I always felt that it was never racist, and it was never sexist, it was simply part of − I mean they'd take the mickey out of a man who's fat, and they'd take the mickey out of a man who's bald. It's part of just seeing how far they could push you and, you know, making sure you understand. And the lads who work out on the unit, they want you to understand them. They want to know that they can trust you, that you're there and that you're not going to blow up every time you talk.

The occupational culture is an oppositional culture that engenders negative views among the rank-and-file. Rather than placing a primary emphasis on positive and hopeful aspects of police work in which social order is preserved, people helped, crime prevented and community bonds affirmed, its heart is a triumphant defeat of what, by rank-and-file definitions, is not normal and taken for granted. Officers, not least those thinking about resignation, therefore have to weigh the value of the negative views that surround them.

> Yes, unfortunately. There are some aspects of it that aren't very savoury but by and large it tends to indoctrinate you, well brainwash. Because the police culture, it applied even to me. I found myself regurgitating and spewing it up at home. It was like I was a third person. I could actually see myself making all these comments, thinking, 'Well, that's not quite right.' I found myself doing it. I mean, specifically, I started picking people, putting them into little compartments. I found myself thinking 'Well, that's not quite right, perhaps coming from an ethnic minority myself and having experiences at first hand, I should know better but I found myself doing it.

Time and again the resigners interviewed talked about the all-embracing way in which the occupational culture had formed a framework for their experience of work, whatever ethnic group they come from. 'Race', however, is manifested in particular ways.

Stereotypes

The essence of a stereotype is a rigid and one-dimensional presentation of a more diverse and multi-faceted phenomenon. Stereotypical thinking has been identified as a characteristic of rank-and-file police thinking *per se* (Manning, 1977; Chatterton, 1992; Keith, 1993).

Stereotypes are different from what sociologists call 'typifications'; they are rounded and therefore somewhat inaccurate résumés of information about people, situations, places and so on of relevance to a social position, the position of police officer being the case in point (Schutz, 1967). The complexity of the social world requires us to simplify information to some extent, to disregard in some measure evidence that is contrary to our own beliefs, to justify the relationship between our ideas and actions with a retrospective gloss of constancy rather than inconsistency. Conversation would be endlessly laced with qualifications if we did not routinely use typifications. Typifications, however, are not stereotypes, which are less complex, more rigid and virtually irrefutable, except in extreme situations.

Being particularly rigid, stereotypical ideas are difficult to challenge and they become increasingly entrenched within organisational thinking. The task of the policy maker and manager in this situation is to present alternative images of people to whom stereotypes are applied, and to ensure that they are consistently reinforced when officers articulate contrary ideas. There is nothing patronising or exceptional about this matter of good policy and practice; it is a key aspect of positive action. Where stereotypes are left unchallenged, when there is no organisational strategy to change them through the implementation of a consistent and concerted policy, life within the police work-force remains difficult for black and Asian officers.

When researchers have asked serving black and Asian officers about their occupational identity they have stressed that they regard themselves as police officers who happen to be black or Asian (Wilson, Holdaway *et al.*, 1984; Holdaway, 1991). Their colleagues regard them rather differently, as black and Asian people who happen to be police officers and therefore as different from the mainstream.

From the perspective of many white rank-and-file officers, to be a police officer is to be white (Her Majesty's Inspectorate of Constabulary, 1992). In the most routine of situations, 'race' as a social category that summarises differences seems to be of immediate relevance to white officers. This is a black officer describing his colleagues who regularly talked about black and Asian people in derogatory terms.

I would say, 'I don't think you should be saying that' and those people that said, 'Sorry, I didn't know you were there' would say, 'Well you know what it's like, you get used to it.' 'Well get un-used to it then,' I would say, you wouldn't like it if I said, 'You so-and-so, I mean how would you feel if I said that to you?' . . . They like to put people in boxes. If someone was black they could call them some derogatory name but instead they put us in boxes. They were just trying to identify us with the sort of person that was socially deprived or any person that's black. But I should say they should just give it a bit of thought before they open their mouth and that's what I told them. I don't know, I sort of give up. I never got any sort of commendation because I'd said that. Nobody takes any notice.

The prevalence of stereotypical thinking within the rank-and-file therefore amplifies racial prejudice and, possibly, discrimination. It is a stable feature of the occupational culture but one that nevertheless has particular implications for the tenor of race relations within the police work-force.

Team membership

Rank-and-file officers define police work as team work. There are without doubt occasions when groups of officers work together to a common end; when an individual needs to call urgently on the assistance of colleagues and be sure it will be forthcoming. The bulk of police work, however, is not of this type; officers mostly work on their own.

Their notion of being the member of a team has a further implication. Team membership implies acceptance of the rank-and-file definition of police work, the ways in which it is practised and the values that underpin it, including stereotypes of members of minority groups. This does not mean that an officer joining a shift from training school who places primary emphasis on community based crime prevention, for example, will be completely shunned by colleagues. The point is that most colleagues' assessment of such an officer will be compared to their stereotypical view of what constitutes a police officer and police work, including attitudes and beliefs about minority ethnic groups.

Membership of the work group implies a significant measure of acceptance of the rank-and-file culture, including its racialised elements, which makes it difficult for a black or Asian officer to find an agreeable reception from colleagues. Stereotypical thinking and team membership go hand in hand.

Various routes lead officers into team membership. One is by demonstrating the acceptance of an occupational trait with a higher status than one relevant to 'race'. An ability to use physical force to protect a colleague is such a value and the following illustration is concerned with a black officer who found a greater measure of acceptance amongst colleagues precisely because he demonstrated physical prowess when dealing with an offender. I am not arguing that all colleagues at this officer's station placed the same degree of credibility on defensive skills or that the officer's skills are entirely unrelated to police work. If I argued thus the occupational culture would be presented as a stereotype. The officer quoted here has nevertheless found himself integrated into his team of colleagues since he demonstrated he could 'handle himself'. The irony of his remarks is that in his colleagues' minds he has moved from one stereotype to another. At first he was straightforwardly perceived as a black person. Once integrated he is *the* officer who can deal with difficult situations requiring physical force. Also notice that being the member of the police team is, in the officer's words, 'being one of the lads'.

At first he talks about the way in which colleagues assume he and his parents were born in Jamaica, that all black people are unintelligent, and that derogatory language about black and Asian people is commonplace. The situation then changed.

> But then finally another one of these breaks. One night there was quite a bad disturbance in the town centre and we actually had to wade in. One of the officers was overpowered so to speak and he was getting a damn good pasting. Now because I had done quite a lot of self-defence and I'd done quite a bit of martial arts I didn't find any problems. I was able to dig him out and get him back to the van. And from that point onwards I was one of the lads . . . That was it. I was one the lads because I'd actually gone out and proved myself in a situation and they thought well that's it for us, he's one of the lads. And from that point onwards I was always being dragged off, 'Oh we need someone to come with us. Call Bob, go and find Bob, wherever is he, go and find Bob.' You know, if I was sat at the station desk doing something else, 'Can I have Bob to come with me please?'

Another sign of acceptance by the team draws us beyond the working day to socialising after work and the implicit expectation lodged in the occupational culture that officers will congregate for a drink.[7]

Probationer constables joining the shift in a pub after work are eased into membership of the team of colleagues; an invitation to socialise is a sign that closer team membership is being offered. The problem for many Asian officers, however, is that for religious reasons they do not consume alcohol and although the same is true of some white people, it is more likely to be the case amongst Asians. This makes the 'drinking route' into team membership difficult because although it is perfectly feasible to drink non-alcoholic beverages in a public house it seems hardly commonplace for police officers. This Asian officer describes how be believes abstinence has contributed to his experience of policing.

> Even those I had a good rapport with probably wanted to draw a line and after tour of duty, that was it. I mean after a while I talked of going to pubs and things. Some people would obviously have social occasions in their homes and things and I wasn't invited to some of these things – because 'What's S* going to do, he doesn't drink, he's not going to have a piss-up'. I felt a little bit isolated at that time.

> I tried a hell of a lot to, or I feel I tried a hell of a lot to integrate myself. The first Christmas that we were there, for example, we were on duty. 'OK, what are we going to do this Christmas?' People were starting to talk. I can prepare quite nice stuff so I prepared an Indian meal for everybody. I got my parents to do this, bought it out of my own pocket. I didn't get them to pay. We had a really fantastic meal and it was a good time. Everybody enjoyed it. So I wanted to say 'Look, I want to join in with you.' I tried as far as possible but as time went on . . .

Team membership, another stock feature of the occupational culture, places particular obstacles in the path of black and Asian officers. Interwoven with stereotypes that structure so much of police thinking, team membership is fully afforded to probationers on the basis of criteria that are unrelated to the quality of their formal work performance, equal opportunities, justice, fairness or any other stated grounds. Rank-and-file definitions and perceptions of black and Asian officers compared to those of white officers structure membership of and relationships within the rank-and-file team.

Trust

Secure human relationships are based on trust (Gambetta, 1988). This means that, ideally, others accept us and we can be reasonably sure that their regard for us is constant, whether or not they are in our physical presence. Trust in relationships also has other, more instrumental meanings. In the police service, for example, it means that an officer dealing with a violent situation who needs assistance from colleagues can be sure that support will be forthcoming.

Black and Asian officers can be trusted by and assume colleagues' trust in this sense of being afforded physical security. However, they cannot be similarly assured about the sincerity and human regard afforded to them by the same colleagues. Exacerbated by the rank-and-file premium on team membership, insecurity and dis-ease can enter working relationships between ethnic majority and minority officers.

When we know that people are 'speaking behind our back' in derogatory tones it is difficult to be completely relaxed in their presence. This breach of trust may be manageable at the individual level but when it involves a number of work colleagues it is more difficult to cope with. We know that many white officers speak in derogatory terms about their black and Asian colleagues and minority ethnic groups in general. Black and Asian resigners told us about the difficulty of becoming fully accepted as members of their work team. Their work environment is often an uncomfortable one and they cannot assume the common level of trust among colleagues afforded most of their white colleagues. Again, the emphasis the rank-and-file place on the occupational value of team membership, their attitudes to and beliefs about minority ethnic groups and stereotypical ways of thinking combine to present black and Asian officers with the distinct experience of employment they have to manage.

This officer could not trust his colleagues and, as a consequence, his relationships at work were laced with cynicism. Faced with the prejudice and discrimination he found in the police service and its constancy beyond the world of work he concludes, 'you can't change people's minds.'

I found I got on well with my colleagues but I couldn't trust them, well, to my face. I knew what they were thinking behind my back. It wasn't a general feeling. I knew what their feelings were towards racism anyway, on Asians, on racism, I knew what their views were. I knew what exactly they thought of coloured people living in this country. And I thought 'Well why should it be different for me? I'm doing the same job as them but I'm still one of these people whom they are on about.'

Interviewer: How did you know their views of black and Asian people in general? How did you feel about those views?

A lot of it was while they were talking and some of it was said to my face. People would say 'Well I'm not racist, but . . .' 'I'm not racist but . . . this, this and this.' Let's just say you know, 'This is what I think. I'm racist, but I don't want to think about it.' I suppose, at the end of the day, they are sort of entitled to their own opinion. You can't change people's views. If that's the way they've felt all their life then there's not much you can do about it. It just made me feel very insecure.

The idea that 'you can't change people's views' may be right but it is nevertheless possible within an organisation to encourage an alignment of what he calls 'views' with actions, to ensure prejudice and discrimination are not sustained. An organisation that places an emphasis on equal opportunities policy and practice aims to provide a work environment within which black and Asian people, and the members of other groups too, are assured a requisite level of trust between colleagues that does not foster the fatalism this and other resigners expressed.

In one sense the constancy and pervasive nature of racialism within the police is not surprising because an occupational culture is a framework that embraces all the work of the rank-and-file. This is an organisational problem rather than one created for the organisation by a few individuals. 'Race' seems an obsession amongst some groups of officers.

I think well, through the 365 days of the years barring holidays, I think I had some comment made about me being black and normally it was in the form of a leg-pull. Or they would say things about black people in general to try and wind me up. But I would make a suitable reply and that was the end of it. They would all fall about laughing and that was it.

That's mainly what it's all about you see – they're always . . . You've got to realise that it's not a little bit, it's continual, day and night, they make you realise that you are not the same as them. You're not an officer first – to them you're an Asian officer . . . but you see they make you feel like, that you're just an Asian officer. You're an Asian person and then an officer.

And continually day and night when you're on the shift, it's always reinforced this thing that you're an Asian. The name they give you, 'Gupta' that type of name or 'Gandhi' or whatever. Whatever your name in canteen culture was – it's always to do with race issues. If you've made a blunder outside as a police officer that would be brought round to a race issue, 'Oh Asians can't do that.' That was what used to annoy me. If somebody just says, 'You clumsy old fool,' because you've done this that or the other, that's fine. But when they bring race into it 'because you're an Asian' and keep reinforcing it day and night, that's the wrong thing.

One strategy to overcome problems like these might be to socialise with colleagues and to hope they understand that joking, name calling and so on are not welcome, but this seems unlikely and unreasonable. Although this resigner, who did socialise with colleagues, was afforded the courtesy of being warned that a racist joke was about to be told, little or no consideration was given to its effects.

If we'd been out at the pub or something and there's jokes going round, inevitably the joke about a coloured person comes up. They always said 'No offence, it was a joke about . . . and they tell the joke. A joke's a joke, and I'm not bothered like. When it came to that point something flashed into their minds, 'John's coloured,' and made sure I'm not going to take offence to it rather than just coming out with it and then thinking 'Oh no, John's here.'

Interviewer: How did you feel about them saying that?

I wasn't really bothered. I suppose I'm glad they did in some ways because if they'd just come out with the joke and if it's a shock and you didn't know the joke was coming up then you think 'Right, I'm glad they told me there was going to be a joke about a coloured person coming up.' Even though they tell jokes about Scottish and Irish and whatever, they can tell them jokes and I suppose that's just about their accent. When it comes to a coloured person you're actually talking about his

features and his colour of his skin. I suppose I was glad they did say
something before they said it.

Other, more serious situations can arise from this basic disregard for
black and Asian colleagues. Officers who express a particular dislike
of people from minority ethnic groups – out and out racists – think
their behaviour is supported; colleagues' lack of dissent to their
behaviour implies as much. Although this is a particularly stark and
nasty example that stood out from the vast bulk of the research
evidence, other incidents also indicate how the occupational culture
places in the ascendancy assumptions about behaviour that are
utterly contrary to equal opportunities.

Two youths, one white, one black, had been arrested for burglary.
They were in the police station and the black youth was cheeky
towards officers. This led to a number of officers abusing him, one
of them being particularly influential. The officer went on to describe
what happened in the station:

> So basically he wasn't fighting back at all, in effect he was defenceless
> and I said to D, 'Is that really bloody necessary,' to which he replied
> 'That's a stupid tone of language.' So I stepped out the cell block. That
> particular night there was nobody to turn to in terms of what do I do.
> As far as I could tell this had been sanctioned at high level. Do I make
> a fuss or keep still and keep my head down? So I thought, keep my head
> down, I was still on my probation – which I thought was the right thing.
> Looking back it wasn't. And I said 'How would you like it if you were in
> a restricted place and you had seven or eight people queuing up to abuse
> you, how would you feel?' 'Totally irrelevant, I'm not black am I.' 'Fine,
> I said, let's go in the locker room and sort this out.'
>
> That was the only time I can honestly say I lost my rag. D and I were
> in the locker-room and he said to me 'Well come on then, you black
> twat.' I won't forget the words. I hit him and he didn't get back up –
> 'Come on make your first move,' I said, 'D I'm not going to hit you, I
> want to talk. Me and you, one to one and get this sorted. If you don't
> like me, fine, don't take it out on anybody else, they can't fight back. I
> can, whether it be here or out the street. I'm clear, I can fight back but
> they can't. By the same token you got no place to give that guy grief. D,
> he's also a human being for Christ's sake, he's out of luck on that.' He
> swung – I hit him once and he stayed down.
>
> I didn't realise that people were gathering behind me, that's why he

swung, others were gathered in. He swung and I just moved out the way. I pushed him once, a body blow, enough to put him on the floor, at which time he must have thought 'My god, he must have lost his rag.'

An extreme situation like this reveals in a particularly stark way what is taken for granted about routine police work and assumed below the surface of daily life in the police station. Many facets of the occupational culture are illustrated by it. We see, for example, that team membership is essential and it is implied that full team membership is reserved for officers who have passed their probationary period. We see that supervisory officers are drawn into the team and affirm rather than challenge the values of their subordinates. We see that the use of physical force can get out of hand and it cannot be assumed that supervisors will intervene. 'Race' is moulded by and finds expression in this context. This is the setting in which a black or Asian officer has to build trusting relationships with colleagues.

At a minimum the officer could have expected a supervisory officer to intervene to restore a situation that was clearly getting out of hand but he is not the only resigner who spoke about the connivance of senior officers (also see Metropolitan Police: Analysis Team, 1990). This next officer was name-called by colleagues during a parade before duty. His inspector was present at the time but when the officer protested he did nothing.

> That's when I became uncertain with the shifts, and uncertain with my supervising officers. I didn't feel comfortable. Because I felt that today it was this, tomorrow it could be something else and nothing would be done about it.

Confidence was eroded by this and other situations. The officer became increasingly uncertain about the extent to which he could trust his colleagues.

There seems to be one exception to this situation. A different tack is taken when a black or Asian officer is in the presence of a white officer and name-called by a member of the public, or supervisory intervention is required in a situation where a member of the public has abused a black or Asian officer.

> You see if I went out on the street, people out there, I mean specially the youngsters, I mean you hear them say 'nigger'. So of course the first

thing the officer would do, the one with me (I mean I would take no notice, I've got broad shoulders), but the first thing he'd turn on his heels, he'd sort of start striding towards them, he'd get hold of them and he'd say something.

I remember being sent to a job, domestic dispute, different part of the patch, and of course the door opened and this guy says 'What do you want nigger?' And I said 'Domestic dispute, come to sort it out for you, what's your problem?' He said 'I don't want a nigger policeman dealing with my family, send me a real policeman.' So I said 'OK,' turned on my heels, just radioed through to the control room, said, 'Here sarge, got a guy here doesn't want to see a black policeman, I'm clearing, over.' He said, 'Yes, fine, log off, not requesting police attendance' – nobody went. He rang back and nobody went.

My interpretation of this and similar incidents is that when a member of the public makes a racial remark, white colleagues will intervene to defend their colleague. When police colleagues make similar comments their actions seem to pass unchallenged.

This situation offers little comfort to black and Asian officers who are often confronted by racial jokes, banter, comments and, at times, discriminatory behaviour. Little wonder that many of the resigners interviewed spoke about their isolation within the police service.

No, I always stayed out of that because I was being drained, drained. It's like being drained daily because of all these incidents. They did take their toll. I tended to keep most to myself because of these incidents and reports kept coming in, 'He's not socialising.' They expected me to socialise. With these reports coming in, these remarks being made, how can you socialise? No matter how hard or strong you are it does affect you, especially when you have to come there every day, and work with your colleagues, with other people.

Interviewer: You kept apart from it?

I slowly started keeping, you know, not at the start, I slowly started keeping apart and thinking – you start thinking what's all this about, you came into the police force, you took a big step, you're going to settle. Then you do something and you think about it, you're right, because all these attitudes, which you thought might not exist, do exist. You start being apart from everything else, you start staying away from people who are on your shift, you don't play snooker with them. I'm no good at snooker, but – it just slowly starts draining you.

Given the exclusive character of the work group, a probationary constable who already feels marginalised by colleagues has to be extremely determined to protest to colleagues about their behaviour. Probationers – all probationers – are not just regarded as inexperienced officers but also seem to be given a very subordinate status in the hierarchy of the rank-and-file. When this status is coupled to being black or Asian, and the language used by colleagues to describe people from one's ethnic group is demeaning, it is not surprising that many of the resigners interviewed chose to 'keep their head down' rather than protest.

Language

Resigners were also asked if they had heard colleagues discuss or refer to black or Asian people in derogatory terms during their period of police service? Just four of the 28 black and Asian resigners said that they had not heard colleagues speak in this way. Some of the four who said they had not heard derogatory language were in fact demonstrating high levels of tolerance and accepted that police officers tend to think and speak in stereotypical terms. They therefore, as one put it, 'pigeon-hole' everyone, not just black and Asian people. However, over 75 per cent of the black and Asian resigners interviewed said that derogatory terms were used to describe people from their own ethnic group. This was not a reference to one or two officers at each station speaking in this way but a general, commonplace language that none of them welcomed.

Similar proportions of the sample of white resigners said they had heard racialist banter and jokes as commonplace but the meaning they attributed to it was different to that of black and Asian resigners. The white resigners drastically underestimated the acceptability and effects of derogatory language on their black and Asian colleagues. Although just two of the white sample said they found the banter offensive and tiresome, their colleagues in the sample did not consider that white people might also take exception to their behaviour. For most of the white resigners racialist banter was 'part of the job'.

The following quote is from a white resigner who perhaps represents a rather extreme version of the 'it's all part of the job' scenario. His views, however, make clear the demeaning situations black and Asian officers have to face and, again, in the extreme situation we find assumptions that are below the surface appearance of routine policing. Asian and black officers are 'white really'; they have probably faced racial prejudice and discrimination throughout their life. The same situation in the police service will be no surprise to them.

> *Interviewer:* Were you aware of any language that might have caused offence to them?
>
> Yes, all the time.
>
> *Interviewer:* Did you discuss this with them?
>
> No, no, it was working in such a multi-cultural environment. Basically it was just them and us. People used to talk in, bobbies used to talk in West Indian patois or refer to 'niggers and pakis' really.
>
> *Interviewer:* They would do this in front of the other black or Asian officers?
>
> Yes but it was all right because although he was Asian, he was white really. He was a good lad because, I mean, I know he's got a brown skin but he's just like the rest of us really, that was the attitude.
>
> *Interviewer:* And how did the ethnic minority officers react to this?
>
> Put up with it basically. They knew they were going to get it. When they joined the job they knew what the situation was. They'd probably had it all their lives, through school and everything else. So it was no big deal for them when they got there you know. But that never came across really from bobbies, ethnic officers that I served with. The racial abuse or whatever was never really a point for them.

White officers from different forces also described in similar terms the situations black and Asian colleagues faced. Here is one further illustration of the working environment of a black officer who resigned. His erstwhile white colleagues described his reception at the police station and a difference between the working environment of white and minority ethnic officers.

> Yes. He didn't last very long. Because he was made very unwelcome by the whole station.
>
> *Interviewer*: In what way?
>
> 'They don't like black heads or sooties', was the statement that used to go about with it.
>
> *Interviewer*: So do you think the officer picked up that sentiment? Oh yes. Because without being disrespectful or sounding racial I am white and I don't notice any bias. But when I notice it, obviously, he must have felt it as well.

We can now more fully understand how stock features of the occupational culture construct and sustain racialised relations within the police. For example, a stress placed on officers' team member-ship often excludes black and Asian officers from full participation. Team membership depends in some measure on drinking alcohol after a shift ends, which is not possible for many Asian officers, and requires a loyalty that prevents a questioning of the acceptability of racial jokes and banter. This is a clear, well-documented feature of the occupational culture (Holdaway, 1993). The notion of being a member of a police team is central to the occupational culture and its exclusionary character sustains racialised relations between offi-cers.

Despite these well documented features of the police work force, the recent ACPO Quality of Service Committee report *Getting Things Right* (ACPO Quality of Service Committee, 1993) regards team-work in policing as a positive asset (ibid, p. 14). The committee, however, does not take any account of the ways in which teamwork can and in the past has led to black and Asian officers' exclusion from full participation in the work-force, and a consequential inten-sification of racialised prejudice and discrimination. No black or Asian officers were consulted by the committee that drafted the report. 'Race' was not a conscious part of their agenda and evidence of a failure of chief officers to incorporate into a major document a notion of equal opportunities and 'race' issues grounded in the routines of their organisation.

Unless the general and particular subjects of the occupational culture *and* the racialisation of police work are tackled, problems routinely faced by black and Asian officers will not be fully addressed. Put another way, if the occupational culture in general is addressed, white officers will benefit. If the occupational culture in general *and* its particular features that exacerbate good relationships between the majority and minority ethnic groups within the workforce are also tackled, all officers will benefit.

The shortcomings of the quality of service approach are also evident in another document recently published by ACPO, in association with the Commission For Racial Equality. *Policing and Racial Equality* places race issues within the framework of quality of service (ACPO and Commission for Racial Equality, 1993). This framework is part and parcel of an initiative introduced by the Home Office and ACPO that places the idea of the citizen as the customer of the police service at the centre of management; that customer satisfaction is of paramount importance and, therefore, the product or service the police offer the public should be tailored to public demand, so far as it is possible.

The foreword to the pamphlet recognises that mutual mistrust has too often characterised relationships between the police and ethnic minority communities. However, helped by the routine collection of relevant monitoring data and other information, it is suggested that, 'The recommendations in this guide will enable the police to rectify this difficulty, but they will also assist the police to develop a full, non-discriminatory service delivery programme in their relations with the public (ibid, p. 5).'

A startling omission from the document is a discussion of race relations! At no point åre recommendations about quality of service principles related to the specific challenges race issues pose to the police. Recommendations rightly cover ethnic classification for data collection and analysis; functional responsibilities for equal opportunities within constabularies; and so on. The particulars of racialised prejudice and discrimination, however, are not addressed in *Policing and Racial Equality* and the question of how far the advice offered will in fact sustain lasting organisational and cultural change is left unanswered.

The basic problem is that ACPO seems to have accepted uncritically the doctrines of total quality management. All organisational conflicts and dilemmas are reduced to a generic minimum and the distinct ways in which racialised relations are sustained within the police are not considered. Absolutely no critical attention is given to the features of the occupational culture that redefine what, on quality of service criteria, are 'good' and desirable features of a work environment – membership of a work team of colleagues, for example – but exclude minority ethnic officers from full and active membership.

The Quality of Service Initiative is important and has its good points. Race issues are not wholly separate from what might be called generic organisational structures that have an impact on all ethnic groups. Teamwork is a feature of policing for all officers and at times desirable, when dealing with large demonstrations for example. However, as we have seen, there is a distinctive aspect to teamwork that affects relationships between white and minority ethnic officers.

Similarly, jokes and banter are a stock in trade of rank-and-file officers. The occupational culture 'lives' through jokes and story telling. Officers who are overweight, religious, short in height, and others defined as deviating from what is regarded as the norm will be the subject of jokes. In this sense jokes and banter are generic. They are also distinctive when racialised because they sustain inequalities that exclude minority ethnic officers from full and equal participation in the work-force.

ACPO and the Home Office must find an appropriate balance between the generic and particular reference points of racialised relations within constabularies. In particular it is essential for them to understand the ways in which generic relationships are racialised within the occupational culture. If this issue is not considered, organisational change will be severely limited and disappointing. In many ways the effectiveness of the quality of service initiative, which is clearly intended to create a framework of strategic planning within the police service, will be most adequately tested by its impact on the aspects of policing that are clearly racialised, including relations within the work force.

Management and discipline

Senior police officers now perceive themselves to be managers and there is a history of the twists and turns of police management ideology which is yet to be fully written. The latest turn of this history has directed chief officers' attention to 'Total Quality Management' and we have seen how it tends to reduce conflicts, including racialised conflicts, within the organisation of policing to a generic minimum. Constabularies are large, complex organisations; management techniques are essential to the development of an effective police service. There is a remaining question, however, about the extent to which management techniques alone can deal adequately with racial conflicts within the police.

The point is made clearly by the questioning of Chief Constable Paul Whitehouse of Sussex Police (previously Deputy Chief Constable of West Yorkshire), who presented the ACPO evidence to the last Home Affairs Select Committee enquiry about police race relations. Whitehouse was asked about the extent of racial prejudice within the police and he answered that he was 'convinced that there was some degree of racism in the force amongst some officers (House of Commons, 1994, p. 24).' Donald Anderson, vice chair of the committee then asked a perceptive question,

Anderson: I am puzzled because I put alongside two of the answers which you gave to earlier questions. One said you were satisfied, or perhaps as Dame Jill Knight said, 'convinced that there was some degree of racism in the force amongst some officers.' You also said that during your six years in West Yorkshire you had not had cause to discipline any officer either, presumably for racist attitudes towards a fellow officer, or to the public as a whole. You have some racist officers, yet over your long experience, no one came to you. Are there obstructions in the pipeline which prevented their getting to senior officers? What are the problems? (ibid, p. 24).

Whitehouse: No, I do not see that as being the case at all, chairman. If the matter which came to notice was minor, then I would expect it to be handled at divisional level, quite properly. If it was recurring or was not minor, I would expect it to be brought to my level, but the fact of the matter was that the question was, 'Had I had cause to discipline anybody?' The rules, as set out for disciplining police officers are quite clear, and I can only discipline in certain circumstances. That opportunity did not rise in West Yorkshire.

Edward Garnier: Were you aware of any police officers within West Yorkshire having been disciplined by senior or more junior officers than yourself?

Whitehouse: I was aware of two or three occasions of that nature and I agreed that in the circumstances advice should be properly recorded so that if there was any recurrence it would serve later to correct it. I believe, in any case, it is always proper to tell people because often the sort of behaviour we are talking about is improper, only because the person who is exercising it does not realise it is improper . . .

The questioning then went on to why so few cases had come forward? Whitehouse pointed to the difficulties of gathering adequate evidence of racial prejudice or discrimination, partly because black and Asian officers might fear recriminations if they complained to their supervisors. One answer to his problem was that in his force an assurance of his personal protection would be given.

The point I want to pick up from this evidence is the tension between managerial and disciplinary means of dealing with racial prejudice and discrimination within the police service. Management has its place but one of the difficulties faced by black and Asian officers is the lack of attention supervisors, sergeants and inspectors have given to the problems they face. We also know that in spite of his own assurance of protection to officers bringing a complaint, many other chief officers have not clearly demonstrated to their constabulary that racial prejudice and discrimination are intolerable. Very few forces have published a race issues policy statement to which those officers objecting to prejudice and discrimination can appeal. Positive action is not clearly defined or understood by the same officers. The ACPO statement on 'race' does not address 'race'.

A balance has to be struck, of course, and the wishes of the victim taken into account but racial prejudice and discrimination are intolerable and a disciplinary matter. This does not mean the creation of a climate of fear within constabularies where one is called a racist and disciplined for the smallest error. It does, however, point to the need for a more concerted, vigorous police approach to racialised prejudice and discrimination that includes disciplinary intervention by supervisory officers. The important disciplinary interventions have so far been driven by black and Asian officers bringing complaints to industrial tribunals. The onus is now on chief officers to place 'race' and discipline within their framework of 'Total Quality Management'.

Equal opportunities

In addition to the Quality of Service Initiative, the Home Office has consistently supported the development of an equal opportunities framework within all constabularies. Update reports about equal opportunities have been issued periodically to all chief constables (Home Office, 1990; 1991). These have described current policy developments and offered a great deal of advice about ways in which central resources can be used to improve the quality and pace of equal opportunities within the police service. Reference to lessons learned from tribunal cases brought by black and Asian officers is made in them. A keynote of each report is that the pursuit of equal opportunities benefits both staff relations and the public perception of the police service. In the 1991 report, for example, it was stressed that,

> There is more work to do to translate the principles of equal oppor-
> tunities into all aspects of police organisation, and in linking those
> developments to the external objectives of delivering a fair, non-discrimi-
> natory and quality service to all members of the public.

It is clearly important for the various departments of the Home Office to disseminate as much information about good equal opportunities practice as is feasible. Their reports contain valuable information for all chief constables to consider and act upon, if needs be. A further, vital function of such reports is the establishment of a network of personal contacts within and between forces, to facilitate the exchange of practical information about problems of policy development, implementation, and so on.

Again, it has to be acknowledged that the police service has done a great deal to develop an effective policy of equal opportunities, far more than universities, for example. However, in 1992 an important thematic inspection of equal opportunities found inconsistency of equal opportunities policy and practice within and between forces; a lack of adequate monitoring of policy; and the crucial context of the occupational culture that sustains inequalities of gender and race within the police service (Her Majesty's Inspectorate of Constabulary, 1992).

The notion of equal opportunities, however, encompasses different patterns of prejudice and discrimination, racial prejudice and discrimination being but one. At this relatively early point of development it is perhaps understandable, but not inevitable, that the focus of Home Office attention has been on the general theme of equal opportunities rather than its specific manifestations. The danger, however, is that the general emphasis on equal opportunities within the police service does not direct adequate attention to the specifics of racialised prejudice and discrimination; that, just as in the Quality of Service Initiative, processes of racialisation are dissolved into a more general concern for equal opportunities.

An additional problem with equal opportunities within the police service is that it may encourage a legalistic approach, so familiar to police officers in their routine work. One unintended consequence of the settlements for racial and sexual discrimination brought against chief officers may be that equal opportunities law is perceived as prohibitive, negative law, rather than a positive one allowing risks and innovation in policy and practice. Equal opportunities then becomes something a chief officer is wary of, a wire one does not trip over. Any notion of positive action, with a chief officer accepting responsibility for the development of innovative policies and initiatives may be brought into question by an over-emphasis on equal opportunities as primarily a legal issue.

Conclusion

It is clear that virtually no constabularies have taken a positive action stance towards policies to deal with processes of racialisation within constabularies. By a positive action stance I mean chief constables taking primary responsibility for the development of policy and practice to deal with race issues, both within and without their force. Positive action means the establishment of a range of provisions that border positive action and the 'soft' positive discrimination on John Edward's (1937) continuum spanning positive action and 'hard' positive discrimination. The rationale for giving a high priority to the development of policy and related practices to recruit from minority ethnic groups would be that, on the basis of the accumulated evidence of the small number of black and Asian applicants to the constabularies of England and Wales, and the even smaller number appointed to serve as constables, ethnicity becomes a criterion for the allocation of resources.

Chief constables should accept responsibility for a programme of action for recruitment from minority ethnic groups on the basis of the need to develop the potential of new recruits and serving officers, which past discrimination and disadvantage have frustrated. The central feature of this policy would be, as John Edwards points out when defining positive discrimination – and, in this case, 'soft' positive discrimination – that:

> beneficiaries and potential beneficiaries are different from those for which the benefit is given. If the reasons for giving a benefit or social good are need or merit or restitution or rights, that is not positive discrimination. If, in fulfilment of the same objectives, recipients are chosen according to other criteria, such as ethnicity, sex, race and – more arguably – age and residential location, that is positive discrimination (Edwards, p. 18).

One implication here is that chief constables would assume the primary responsibility for reform rather than taking the view in the area of recruitment, for example, that suitable candidates will apply and be appointed to a force as part of general recruitment efforts. To help them the Home Office and other organisations have distributed a considerable amount of advice that will not completely solve but will certainly to some extent alleviate the problems chief officers face. This advice has not been implemented in action in most constabularies. Knowing what could be done most chief officers have chosen to do little or nothing. A passive avoidance of processes of racialisation within police forces by most chief constables has led to the sustained relations of conflict that research has documented within constabularies.

There is a further need for chief officers to address 'race' as a clear dimension of their organisation. The reasons for the adoption of quality management within the police are not altogether clear. It may be that, with half an eye on the racialised conflicts within their work-force, chief constables are trying to deal with the issues in as oblique a manner as possible. The language of total quality management is one of equal service to all consumers of police services. But not all customers of police service are equal and measures to deal with racialised prejudice and discrimination that sustain inequalities do not appear within it. There is every indication that if this is the strategy chief officers pursue it is inadequate to tackle the conflicts that exist within constabularies.

Despite a great deal of Home Office advice about how race issues policies and related practices should be developed within all constabularies, chief constables have taken a piecemeal approach and given inadequate attention to what was required to ensure they are developing as equal opportunities employers. Race issues policies have not been developed and implemented, selection processes have not been reviewed for bias, race training programmes have not been undertaken, special recruitment programmes have not been implemented and evaluated, and so on. It is more the absence of action than what chief officers have actively pursued to deal with race issues that has sustained racialised relationships within the police. At the moment the Quality of Service Initiative is what has been called 'colour blind', an understanding of race plays no part in it. Racialised relations are sustained within and beyond the organisational boundaries of the police.

When we turn to the occupational culture we find an active rather than passive stance of the rank-and-file has sustained the racialisation of relationships within the work group. Mediated through the particular structures of the occupational culture, through jokes and banter, an emphasis on team membership, through stereotypical thinking, and so on, 'race' has been reconstructed to pervade relationships between white, black and Asian officers.

The major points of change to create a multi-racial police within England and Wales occurred in 1981 and 1985, when the issue of 'race' was writ large onto the political agenda by riots on the streets. It would be foolish to argue that only such events can move this process on. The most significant recent changes, however, have been mostly prompted by black and Asian officers taking action to remedy the inequalities they face and there are clear signs that they are now developing as a defined group. My judgement is that an increased number of industrial tribunal cases and the collective power of black and Asian officers within forces will remain the most potent impetus for change.

Chapter Seven

Emerging themes

The subject of each chapter in this book has taken an aspect of policing – victimisation, crime, riot, recruitment and so on – and tried to understand how notions of 'race' are constructed and sustained within each one. Processes of racialisation have been central. This does not mean that 'race' is always of overriding importance for policing. Importantly, it is contextualised within routine policies and practices, ideas, beliefs and actions as officers go about their everyday work. It has not been possible to isolate a subject called 'police race relations' and separate it from other areas of police work. The social world is not so neatly packaged. Racialised relations have wider reference points in social structures that constrain police action. Throughout this book, however, I have tried to emphasise the importance of understanding ways in which relations between people belonging to groups defined by social criteria become and continue to be associated with the idea of 'race'; with how relations are racialised.

Theoretical questions about what Giddens has called structure and action are age-old (Giddens, 1979), but in contemporary work they have been inadequately associated with empirical research. In sociology generally and what is now more frequently called criminology than the sociology of crime and deviance there is a deficit of descriptions and analyses of processes that construct and sustain racialised relations.[1] Research at the middle and micro levels of analysis is needed to understand them more adequately. If 'race' is a social construct – whether understood in terms of a 'new' or 'old' form of racism – it seems to me necessary for sociologists and criminologists to demonstrate how it is constructed and reproduced within the everyday work of the police, or any other occupational or institutional setting for that matter.

This is not to diminish the salience of 'race' as a sociological subject or to advocate the much criticised 'colour-blind' approach. It is not to reduce the subject to an epiphenomenon pure and simple. Neither is it to argue that because 'race' is socially constructed we can somehow easily dismantle and reconstruct its forms. Although the processual nature of interaction has been emphasised throughout this book, the extent to which typifications guiding taken for granted actions solidify within institutions should not be understated (Berger and Luckmann, 1967).

One reason for a stress on social processes within organisations and occupational cultures is to identify possibilities for wider social change, as well as organisational and policy related reform. Unless we are able precisely to demarcate processes and related ideas that sustain racialised relations it becomes very difficult to know where interventions should be directed. Although not an imperative, it is surely important for sociologists to relate their research to policy reform and strategies for change, even though the relationship between research and organisational change is often extraordinarily difficult to fathom. If we do not direct our attention to the smaller scale we risk the reasonable accusation that sociologists have little or nothing to offer most policy makers working in the criminal justice sector.

A need to say something relevant and realistic about policy was one reason for the changes in research about the police and crime during the 1980s. The 'New Criminology' (Taylor, Walton *et al.*, 1973) envisioned a society structured without any need to criminalise – a crime free society – and presumably a society without a formal police. The trouble was that offenders and victims alike had to await wider social change before their pain and disadvantage could be tackled.

After the 1981 riots a 'new realism' gradually developed within the sociology of crime and deviance and administrative, policy related questions found a wider acceptance amongst academics (Young 1986, 1988, 1988). Discrete projects funded by external agencies became a primary symbol of academic credibility, no matter how far they distracted their bearers from theoretical concerns. The pendulum has now swung too far in the other direction and there is an absence of explicit social theory in much criminology.[2] Although the widely accepted policy emphasis of criminology is important, more attention is now required to a sensitive integration of theoretical concerns (Holdaway and Rock, 1996).

Emerging themes

In this chapter I want to focus on some emerging ideas intended to change the extent to which racialised relations, more usually described as race relations, can dominate and sour so much police work. Many of these changes deserve our consideration and have a relevance that extends beyond the racialisation of policing. 'Race' can act as a spotlight to illuminate a more extensive range of social structures and processes that mingles with the specifics immediately facing a policy maker, manager, or whoever.

This idea first became apparent to me during a research project about race issues policy in the probation service (Holdaway and Allaker, 1990). As part of this work chief probation officers identified problems they faced when developing and implementing race issues policy within their area service. It was noticeable that many of the problems they mentioned: giving an appropriate priority to the subject, sustaining staff commitment to the policy, funding its implementation and defining appropriate performance indicators, took on a distinctive cast when viewed in relation to 'race'. It was also apparent, however, that these were fundamental issues for any chief probation officer developing *any* major policy within an area service.

Understandings of 'race' had placed a spotlight on and illuminated generic issues, mainly because it was perceived as a sharply contested issue. The consequences of making a wrong move, of inadvertently failing to implement the policy as intended and, possibly, an equally unintended specialist emphasis on race issues, sharply focused probation managers' minds. Chief officers wanted to avoid the unwarranted slur that they neither cared about the subject nor were 'racists'. 'Race' then tended to over-determine their ideas about policy development. The managerial need, however, was to identify the relationship between generic and specific, racialised issues in need of policy reform. 'Race' needed to be placed within the routines of a chief probation officer's work.

The same problems of failure face chief police officers. Organisational change is not easy and the best plans lead to unintended, detrimental consequences. It is useless to personalise the issue and characterise chief constables as racists, as if this offers both diagnosis and remedy. The issues are more properly and helpfully understood within the context of the organisation of policing and the construction of race relations through the myriad social processes that constitute routine police work.

Monitoring

During our review of the 'race and crime debate' we encountered Paul Gilroy's argument that discussion of the statistics of crime committed by black people is wasteful haggling.[3] Certainly, an indiscriminate use of statistics of offences committed by black and Asian people can become part of a process of the criminalisation of black youth (Solomos, 1993). The construction of rates of offending, their analysis and presentation does not occur in a neutral social context. Some groups may seize an opportunity to make a scapegoat of black people as responsible for 'the crime problem' and, implicitly or explicitly, typify them as naturally given to criminal activity.

This argument, however, is not a objection in principle to the collection of relevant data about the ethnic origin of an offender. It is more a matter of exercising control over how statistics are collected, analysed and presented to safeguard misinterpretation. Racial prejudice and stereotyping, on the other hand, is not open to refutation by the use of statistical information. It is irrational and the use of statistics as an instrument of refutation is irrelevant. At the same time I doubt if we should so easily pass up the argument and opportunity to stereotype and discriminate negatively to whoever wants to use statistics for misleading and damaging ends. Neither is it helpful or accurate to work on the basis that a majority of people slavishly accept the views of the utterly prejudiced.

In this book the limitations of statistically based arguments have been recognised; a great deal can be said about the racialisation of relations after a statistical representation of supposed 'social facts' has been presented. However, properly used, statistics can help the development of appropriate policy responses and more accurate public perceptions of crime *and victimisation* amongst any ethnic group, as well as part of an armoury to decriminalise by a challenge to untruth, the misinterpretation of 'facts', and so on.

The Criminal Justice Act, 1991–Section 95

Although the sociological arguments about the use of official statistics were not debated in the House of Commons and the introduction of the clause was by way of an amendment proposed by a Labour Home Affairs spokesperson, Section 95 of the Criminal Justice Act 1991 lays a duty on the Home Secretary to 'each year publish such information as he considers expedient for the purpose of:

(a) enabling persons engaged in the administration of criminal justice to become aware of the financial implications of the decisions; or

(b) facilitating the performance by such persons of their duty to avoid discriminating against any persons on the ground of race or sex or any other improper ground.

Publication under subsection (1) above shall be effected in such a manner as the Secretary of State considers appropriate for the purpose of bringing the information to the attention of the persons concerned.

Since 1992 the Home Office has annually published a booklet and related materials summarising statistical information about the minority ethnic population in England and Wales; selected official statistics and commentary about the representation of ethnic minorities at a number of stages of the criminal justice system and within the employ of various criminal justice agencies; brief résumés of recent research findings, on-going research initiatives and other policy developments; the introduction of new monitoring systems, and so on. Before long, assuming the establishment of an adequate recording system within the police (and, crucially, other agencies working with the same categories of ethnicity, time frames of data collection and analysis), time series data will be available and trends in the police use of stop and search powers and arrest rates will be available.

Section 95 therefore has the potential to provide evidence of police bias in the use of legal powers. It is one lever to open up the private world of policing to clearer public view. The purpose of Section 95 is of course partly symbolic, demonstrating Home Office willingness to ensure that monitoring of bias in the use of police powers is treated seriously, and partly instrumental in that monitoring makes it possible to use evidence to support or refute – or, more likely, any position in between – claims of racialised discrimination or unfairness. The provision is largely for police use and for other organisations. Constables engaged in tricky encounters with black or any other youth are not expected to suddenly recall to mind statistical evidence that their constabulary has been acting fairly, in statistical terms that is!

There are, however, some dangers for the police in the Section 95 provisions. If their analysis and presentation of data is meaningful all the problems of sample size, multi-variate analysis and consistency of data collection have to be considered by constabularies. This is all the more important because Her Majesty's Inspectorate now requires each chief constable to publish statistics of police stops and searches. We have discussed how aggregate data of arrests or any other outcomes from the use of police powers are grossly inadequate. A recent Home Office circular dealing with these problems has therefore provided a clear guide about, among other issues, the setting of priorities in ethnic monitoring, public consultation as an essential aspect of monitoring, the clear responsibility of particular officers for the monitoring process within constabularies, planning of monitoring cycles, and issues of data collection, analysis and presentation (Home Office, 1994). If chief officers do not follow the guidelines of this circular they will simply distort understanding of their officers' work and, potentially, create a rod for their own back.

All these requirements of monitoring increase the police administrative load, the bureaucratisation of constabularies and puts pressure on resources. I doubt if the research expertise to analyse statistics adequately is present in all but a very few forces. This may be good news for criminologists contracted to undertake the analysis of monitoring data, as the Home Office circular recommends, but the resource demands monitoring places on a constabulary should nevertheless be recognised.

Of potentially greater importance is the management of monitoring within constabularies. 'Race' is not a comfortable issue for any organisation and if the monitoring of police powers is to be successful all ranks must be briefed about the need for ethnic monitoring and ways in which it is relevant to local circumstances. There is a need to gain the confidence and consent of the rank-and-file, including their recognition that public scrutiny of their use of powers and the possibility of identifying racial discrimination is appropriate.

Sergeants and inspectors working on shifts will have to play a crucial role here because when new ideas about policing are introduced they are potentially far more effective agents of change than senior officers. Recent research about the supervision of black and Asian officers by sergeants and inspectors, however, suggests they do not have a clear perspective about policing a multi-racial work-force. They often fail to act when racially prejudiced comments are made by white officers, both in and out of the hearing of black and Asian officers (Holdaway, 1993). We know that chief officers have not published clear race issues policy statements and are therefore dependent on their necessarily sporadic verbal communication with colleagues when they articulate their force's commitment to race equality. In these circumstances an affirmation of the importance of race relations within and without policing is either left to chance or dependent on its being raised by an incident, issue or request from someone dealing with the police at the local level.

Just how these indications of far less than a full commitment to race equality within policing will translate into a realisation of the benefits of ethnic monitoring to the lower ranks requires neither imagination or lengthy comment. The culture of policing is presently not sufficiently adaptable to accommodate fully the idea of ethnic monitoring or adequately support officers who wish to endorse it and put it into operation within their routine work.

This does not mean that ethnic monitoring will be ignored; it is required by HMIC. However, we also know that when monitoring indicators are imposed on the police, and there are now hundreds and hundreds of them, activity is sometimes appropriately accounted to coincide with the definitions of work and its outcomes as defined in the relevant performance indicator. The number of stops of black and Asian people may therefore diminish during the coming years but this does not mean that less black or Asian people are being stopped legitimately or illegitimately. The change may be partly the result of informal police recording practices.

Performance indicators like statistics of stops can therefore only measure the declared outcomes of police action. When particular outcomes are presented statistically to represent existing and changed levels of police action we are still left with the need for an explanation of the reasons for such changes and levels, which only the analysis of social processes can clarify. Detailed analyses of the ways in which relations within and without the police are racialised should therefore accompany the important routine practice of ethnic monitoring (Fitzgerald, 1993).

Section 95 is an important innovation to remind chief officers that they are responsible for their staff's fair use of the law. Organisations and other bodies with a concern for race issues will also be able to more adequately monitor aspects of policing, previously hidden from public view. Like all statistically based analyses, however, ethnic monitoring can only provide an indication of the outcomes of action. The crucial accompaniment to ethnic monitoring within constabularies is cultural change.

The Quality of Service Initiative

Since 1992 the Association of Chief Police Officers (ACPO) has taken the lead in developing what has come to be known as the Quality of Service Initiative, now called Quality of Service Programme (ACPO Quality of Service Committee, 1993). This has its genesis in the results of a public attitude survey jointly undertaken by ACPO, the Superintendents' Association and the Police Federation (Joint Consultative Committee, 1990). It was found that the public did not simply evaluate policing in quantitative terms but qualitative aspects of the delivery of police service also needed to be brought to the fore. A complainant's confidence in an officer dealing with an incident, an officer's courtesy to a 'customer', and so on were found to play a part in public assessments of police service.

In general terms the survey showed that public confidence in the police was less than secure and when British Crime Survey data about the attitudes of white, Afro-Caribbean and Asian people to the police was also taken into consideration it became clear that a pretty fundamental change of policy was required. About 17 per cent of Afro-Caribbean and a similar number of Asian people thought the police were doing a poor or very poor job. Of those having contact with the police in the past year, nearly 30 per cent of Afro-Caribbeans and the same percentage of Asians said the police were doing a poor or very poor job. The conclusion was irresistible – negative views about policing among the public are significantly affected by direct contact with officers.

The quality of police service offered to customers – total quality management in the jargon – was identified by ACPO as a key strategy to enhance public confidence in the police and monitor levels of public satisfaction. Non-discriminatory policing was given recognition in the original ACPO statement and a need to deal with racist and sexist remarks within the organisation was also recognised. Internal consistency should be maintained between a quality of service policy statement published by the chief constable of every constabulary, making a clear commitment to 'fair, courteous and non-discriminatory police service' and internal developments within the constabulary, equal opportunities and race relations policy, for example.

Once the initial strategic policy document was accepted by ACPO, a Quality of Service Committee took the initiative forward. *Getting Things Right* is their response to the need to 'meet the needs and expectations of internal customers (ACPO Quality of Service Committee, 1993).' *Getting Things Right* is mainly about the organisational culture of policing and ways in which it should be changed. Continuity between the original ACPO founding document the *Common Statement of Purpose and Values* and the work of the Quality of Service Committee, however, is far from evident.

It seems incredible that a firm of management consultants was required to reveal to chief officers what a group of their colleagues interviewed during the consultancy defined as the organisational culture of policing.[4] However, neglecting all the academic work available on the police, and with no regard for the particular needs of minority ethnic groups within and without the police, ACPO proceeded with their management consultancy and published a policy document that will sustain the racialised prejudice and discrimination known to be present in the ranks. For example, praising the benefits of officers working as a team the Quality of Service Committee has shown a remarkable lack of reflection about the place of equal opportunities and race issues within their profession. We know that the team emphasis of the rank-and-file excludes many minority ethnic officers from full participation in their work and membership of their 'team' of colleagues. The same could be said of women officers. In no part of the document are racialised relations given any recognition (neither for that matter are gender, sexual orientation and so on). Everything is reduced to a generic notion of customer relations and the particular, known demands of racialised relations are completely neglected.[5]

The idea of quality of service *could* greatly assist the development of a non-discriminatory police service, but before that can occur it is necessary for many chief officers to develop a consciousness of and acceptance that 'race relations' present both generic and specific managerial problems. An absence of evidence of tackling discrimination and prejudice in a pro-active manner leaves the initiative in the police court.

The Quality of Service Initiative swallows total quality management 'hook, line and sinker', failing to question the extent to which it accommodates police staff and other so called customers marginalised by processes of racialisation. If a group of officers from minority ethnic groups had formed part of the consultative process and subjected it to the 'barium test' that race can provide these deficiencies would have been avoided. A customer is not 'Everyman' (sic), as the ACPO policy documents suggest. Within a society of different minority ethnic groups account needs to be taken of those aspects of generic policing that racialise relations between police colleagues and between officers and members of the public. ACPO would have done well to ask a more diverse sample of what they call their internal customers about the culture of policing before they ventured into the business of defining who is and who is not a customer of internal personnel services.

This issue is rather like the question of whether or not there should be a law to create a specific offence to control racial attack and harassment. You might remember an MP's summary of Michael Howard's view – a crime is a crime is a crime. The qualitative differences between assaults and criminal damage motivated by racial discrimination and other offences is not recognised in this perspective and the marginalising experience of racialised relations is given little recognition. Chief officers, more by default than any careful reflection about the impact of their policy development, argue that 'a customer is a customer' and are thereby likely to sustain racialised quality of service policies and practices.

Ethics

Ethics, police ethics, is another strand of the *Common Statement of Purpose and Values* for the police service. The lower ranks must act in strict compliance with rules governing the enforcement of the law and if some guilty people go free as a consequence, so be it. The right thing has been done. This stance contrasts with the rank-and-file emphasis on the conviction of guilty people and a light touch on the means of achieving that end.[6] It is consistent with an attempt to create a non-discriminatory police service.

The quest for a police code of ethics is led from the top of the Home Office. Addressing an international conference on policing, Sir John Woodcock, at the time the highest ranking police officer in England, linked the need to develop a code of police ethics to the occupational culture. 'The first message of my address is, therefore, that the working culture of the police service is shot through with corner-cutting and with expediency (Woodcock, 1991; 1992).'[7] Quoting from a newspaper interview with the then newly appointed Commissioner of the Metropolitan Police, Paul Condon, Woodcock went on to describe the legacy that needed to be overcome by police managers. Condon described the police service he joined in 1967 as 'fairly brutal, poorly trained and poorly educated, despite its rosy image' to which Woodcock added, 'The work-place values of the modern police service have not yet fully cut free of the past and the police service faces a massive task, if it is to hold, as the community now demands, integrity and respect for human rights above all other considerations (ibid, p. 7).'

A grip on the ethical basis of policing is important but it may become slippery when ethical principles are translated into practice. Ethical principles are always contextualised when applied in practice, including the practice of policing. No guarantee can therefore be given that the lower police ranks' acceptance of a statement of policing principles will adequately focus their attention on the means of realising goals and away from the ends of those goals as a good in itself.

Further, English society does not have a strong tradition of human rights, which Woodcock appeals to – certainly not as strong as many of our European partners – and formal appeals to rights are rare in our society. Neither are people necessarily influenced to change their behaviour by an appeal to abstract ethics. The appeal to recognise the ethical basis of policing is extremely important but seems to miss the mark slightly when the processes of racialisation are considered.

A defining characteristic of the police is, as Egon Bittner pointed out long ago, 'the legally legitimate use of force' and injustice is usually the end result of the police misuse of power (Bittner, 1970). The use of force and power in the interests of justice can be constrained by an appeal to transcendent ethics but this is a very long term strategy to change the occupational culture. Breaches of police policy and of law may be understandable within the context of the conflicts and ambiguities of the criminal justice system and of public perceptions of justice. A notion of human rights, however, is a feature of an indivisible ethic.

A breach of a police code of ethics that is defined as an act of injustice can require the use of disciplinary control rather more than the techniques of management. Some acts of police injustice can be restored by conciliation but most cannot wait for the persuasive restoration of rights by negotiation and settlement. Much injustice, not least that committed by police officers in their daily work, requires the use of discipline and a related sanction, and it is senior officers who must enforce that discipline.

Unlike workers in many industrial and commercial organisations, the goods the police use as their primary working resources render them publicly accountable. When used improperly these same resources can straightforwardly infringe what we might call human rights. Ironically, this means that the enforcement of discipline is a central aspect of police management – the very heart of the old militaristic command structure from which modern police managers have wished to free themselves. I speculate whether or not a management consultant reviewing a modern constabulary would produce a report concerned with the importance of discipline within management![8] There seems to be significant conflict between the pursuit of human rights, the use of discipline as a resource and the pursuit of managerial efficiency in police work.

In *Getting Things Right* chief officers uncritically align the police with 'any business or public service'. This is banal. Much more attention has to be given to both the specifies of police work and to racialised relations if the quality of service initiative is to be in any sense effective rather than a rhetorical device to manage the reality of racialised relations. If they were to pay attention to 'race' within the organisational and cultural forms of their organisations, chief officers would be able to clarify the processes that construct and sustain racialised relations within their routine work and be better able to deal with them. Ethics and management, including discipline, could then be more adequately integrated.

Equal opportunities

All constabularies are declared equal opportunities employers and a great deal has been done to enhance the employment opportunities of minority ethnic and female officers. Indeed, the high profile equal opportunities cases brought against chief constables by officers are to some extent symptomatic of the enhanced expectations equal opportunities efforts have promoted among these groups. Another lesson of these cases is nevertheless a lack of clarity or consensus about the purpose of equal opportunities within constabularies.

The content of police equal opportunities statements is pretty even but this does not mean that they are based on a similar foundation of understanding among senior officers. This is hardly surprising given the individualistic, case-based approach of English race and sex discrimination law, and the declared illegality of affirmative action. Earlier in this book I argued that when the close relationship between police work and the use of law is linked to cases of racial discrimination brought by officers, a perception of police equal opportunities policies dwelling on the avoidance of legal actions rather than positive assumptions required to make real progress has been fostered. Positive action is too often misunderstood as affirmative action or positive discrimination.

Misunderstandings about the purpose of police equal opportunities policies have been further compounded by a lack of reflection on their precise objectives. Policies to create more equal opportunities for people from minority ethnic groups can have a number of different goals (Edwards, 1995; Jewson and Mason, 1992).[9] They can be concerned with equality of opportunity at the point of recruitment, promotion and appraisal, as well as the sanctioning of the use of inappropriate language by staff. This means that decisions are double checked for possible bias, tests of competence are reviewed for partiality, rules of non-discriminatory conduct are published, and so on. The objective is future equality of opportunity for all members of the police service by creating work conditions that are free from racialised and other forms of prejudice and discrimination.

A rather different objective for equal opportunities policies is concerned with remedial compensation for past harms, which means an objective to realise equal outcomes from decisions about recruitment, promotion and so on, implying what in America is called affirmative action or positive discrimination. This means that past discrimination has to be taken into account before the conditions within which equality of opportunity can be achieved. The objective is to deal with past harms done to groups defined by 'racialised' criteria. Once the disadvantage of groups is realised, and compensatory action taken, it is more or less assumed that individualised justice will be distributed. For example, past discrimination against black and Asian applicants to the police service requires compensating policies before it is possible to create the conditions for greater equality of opportunity in the future. A compensatory quota of black and Asian officers to be recruited during a particular year is required as well as checking of all policies and procedures for potential bias. These policies and practices, so the argument goes, meet both the demands of group and individual justice.

Another objective of equal opportunities policy is the promotion of diversity within a work-force as a good in itself. The rationale for pursuing this objective is the desirability of creating an organisation that reflects the ethnic diversity of the society it serves. Familiarity with working alongside people from different ethnic backgrounds promotes harmony and trust; a better, more sensitive service can be offered to the public. Here, representativeness and diversity are closely related. Within this perspective, adopted by the Association of Chief Police Officers in their recently published collaborative document with the Commission for Racial Equality (ACPO and CRE, 1993), stress is placed on rectifying, 'the absence of factual information about policing between different ethnic communities, together with a failure to explain any significant differences (ibid, p. 5),' which comes very close to a variant of the multi-cultural perspective.

None of these perspectives on equal opportunities are exclusive and they all raise difficult questions about justice and fairness but, despite their complexity, if chief officers do not clarify the basis of their equal opportunities policies they will not fully grasp why confusion and conflict about the purpose and rationale of policies are found in their constabulary. Senior officers involved in the implementation of policies are unlikely to recognise whether or not claims to equal outcomes or equal starting points are the basis of conflicting expectations within the work-force. They will not be clear about whether or not it is appropriate to bid for and use particular resources for stated ends related to equal opportunities. And they are likely to hold back from pushing at the boundaries of positive action to create greater chances of equal opportunities. Without such clarity, policies well within the bounds of positive action will be perceived by officers as positive discrimination and avoided, which is what I found in interviews with assistant chief constables during my police recruitment research (Holdaway, 1991). The lowest common denominator of equal opportunities with the objective of creating diversity within organisations is then pursued, which is precisely what has happened within the Quality of Service Initiative.

John Edwards clearly reminds us that 'race' is not a moral criterion claimed as the basis for policy and it is not my intention to argue for affirmative action as the basis for police equal opportunities policies (Edwards, 1995). The notions of need and desert related to fairness and justice are more usual criteria for redistributive policies which can and should be employed in the service of equal opportunities for members of minority ethnic groups. Where 'race' has been claimed as a basis of policy, a historical record of oppression stands as its witness and testimony. Neither has the American experience of affirmative action, though recently frustrated by Reaganite policies, been a straight path towards fairness and justice.[10]

The police, however, are some way short of realising the full potential of positive action policy, based on chief officers taking full responsibility for racialised inequalities within and between the ranks; double checking policy related decisions for racialised bias; and an approach founded on what should rather than what should not be done to create more equal opportunities.[11] Their initial task is to identify more clearly the rationale for their equal opportunities policies and to grasp the strategy of positive action in order to refine and develop them.

The discussion so far has dealt with equal opportunities policies and is one step removed, as it were, from the ways in which racialised conflicts arise in constabularies. The legislative approach and the strategy of Total Quality Management adopted by the police also tends to approach racialised relations in an oblique manner. We have seen that the generic customer working within or requiring a service from the police is in the ascendancy, irrespective of his or her ethnic status. Yet when constabularies have introduced access courses to encourage the recruitment of black and Asian applicants specifically racial slurs have been manifested in constabularies (Holdaway, 1991). When officers have taken a chief constable to a tribunal on an allegation of discrimination in employment their experience is moulded by the racialised prejudice and discrimination of colleagues. Exclusion from the team of working colleagues is about 'race'. The real issue within constabularies is 'race' within equal opportunities not equal opportunities *per se*.

It may be managerially convenient to approach the problems of racialised prejudice and discrimination through the language of equal opportunities and 'customer relations' so long as it is realised that the issues involved are racialised discrimination and prejudice. The problem with the police is that one gets the sense that they are not yet squarely facing the issues of racialisation that confront them in their routine work. This is why there is an absence of clear policy for race issues; supervisors have not been given the support to challenge manifestations of 'race'; the occupational cultural themes of 'race' have not been identified and tackled. So long as this situation remains, racialised relations within the work-force will be sustained.

The Black Police Association

Police equal opportunities policies will continue to develop but, since the launch of the Metropolitan Police Black Police Association in October 1994, within a new context. Although a development in one constabulary, the Association is likely to have a much wider impact within the police because it will directly and uniquely articulate the voice(s) of black (and Asian) officers to the senior ranks. In the longer term this impact will resound to challenge the rank-and-file.

We have seen how the association was one result of the 'Bristol Seminars', when all black and Asian officers in the Metropolitan Service discussed and reported on their experience of police employment. They realised they shared similar experiences of prejudice and discrimination and the need for a support network. This began with social gatherings and then a planned black and Asian police association, which was eventually launched as the Black Police Association.

A key feature of the association's profile is the unreserved support of Sir Paul Condon, the Commissioner of the Metropolitan Police Service. Without this the national publicity launch would not have been possible. Condon's tack is not to co-opt the association into a direct negotiating stance, neither is it to welcome the association while quietly refusing it adequate resources. He is demonstrably committed to the association. A chief officer's clearly articulated commitment to work against racialised relations and for equality should not be underestimated. In case studies of police policy and practice to increase the recruitment of black and Asian people I found that a chief constable's commitment had a strong impact on staff working directly in the field and, although often bringing racialised conflict within the work-force to the surface, made a difference to the progress of policy (Holdaway, 1991).

The association's response to Condon's encouragement has been to stress that they are not 'a representative body or to supersede staff associations or other representative bodies (The Black Police Association, 1994).' Their basic stance is to focus attention on two spheres of work: the development of a support network for black officers and influencing policy based on proposals for positive action. Together, these two themes could have significant, beneficial effects on black officers' future experience of and position within police employment.

The support network will continue to foster reflection on a shared experience of racialised relations both between police colleagues and with the public. It is likely that the identity of members of the association will more clearly harmonise around their racialised status and the negative consequences of police employment will be more fully confronted. This does not mean that there will be a growing, polarised conflict defined by sharp differences between the identity and work experience of black and white officers. At times this may and will be the case; specific issues and individual cases of negative discrimination will raise pointed questions about the extent to which realised or unrealised prejudice or discrimination is evident in the police. But it is mistaken to infer from an essentialist view that, as members of the Black Police Association, officers will primarily order their personal and collective identity around being genericised black people. It is more likely that they will regard themselves as black police officers, which is not quite the same.

In *New Ethncities*, Stuart Hall made the following point about the particularity of racialised, or what he calls ethnic, identities,[12]

'This marks a real shift in the point of contestation, since it is no longer only between anti-racism and multi-culturalism but inside the notion of ethnicity itself. What is involved is the splitting of the notion of ethnicity between, on the one hand, and dominant notion which connects it to nation and 'race' and, on the other hand, what I think is the beginning of a positive conception of the ethnicity of the margins, of the periphery. That is to say, a recognition that we all speak from a particular place, out of a particular history, out of a particular experience, a particular culture, without being contained by that position as 'ethnic artists' or film-makers. We are all, in that sense *ethnically* located and our ethnic identities are crucial to our subjective sense of who we are. But this is also a recognition that this is not an ethnicity which is doomed to survive, as Englishness was, only by marginalising, dispossessing, displacing and forgetting other ethnicities. This precisely is the politics of ethnicity predicated on difference and diversity (Hall, 1992, p. 258).[13]

Black police officers work within the context of the rank-and-file occupational culture; they work as black people with their particular historical and cultural legacy; they are police officers. This positioning of black officers cannot be reduced to a racialised essence; neither can it be adequately understood by an extreme version of constructionalism, as if myriad identities are available for appropriation. The black police officer shares a common racialised experience with peers but that experience is manifested within the albeit taken for granted but nevertheless particular of the rank-and-file occupational culture. The intensity of commitment and expression of an occupational identity within this culture is well documented and it has been discussed in earlier sections of this book. The racialisation of the identity of black, and other minority ethnic officers, should therefore be considered within this context.

Interviews with black and Asian serving officers have indicated that they regard themselves as police officers who happen to be black, not black people who are police officers (Wilson, Holdaway *et al.*, 1984; Holdaway, 1991; 1993). The overwhelming majority interviewed opposed policies that approximated in the slightest extent to positive action. Their reasoning was that positive action policies render them second class entrants. Their personal qualifications, skills and qualities had parity with white colleagues.

The officers' day to day work with colleagues was nevertheless highly racialised, through jokes, banter, the way in which many black people were policed, and other means discussed in earlier chapters. In spite of this highly racialised context of employment they did not assert themselves as 'black individuals' or as a pressure group, neither did they hope that such a group would develop. They were police officers who happened to be black and their commitment to policing was not in question.

In part, but only in part, this stance was a response to the power of their white colleagues. They worked alone or with one or two minority ethnic colleagues and did not want to draw attention to themselves, risking the possibility of increased prejudice and discrimination. It was also the case that many of them wanted to get on with the work of policing, which was personally important. They did not regard themselves as passive victims of their white colleagues' jibes but created a response that enabled them to embrace their work as fully as possible.

From this base, the Black Police Association is likely to strengthen the racialised identity of its members and, realising their collective strength, unite them through both a shared experience of social exclusion because of racialised relations with colleagues and, as importantly, a positive commitment to policing. The identity of members is likely to move from being 'police officers who happen to be black' to 'black police officers' – but being a police officer and the partial ordering of identity around that reference point will remain. There is no essence of blackness that will overdetermine their position. As Stuart Hall argues, – . . . a recognition that we all speak from a particular place, out of a particular history, out of a particular experience, a particular culture, without being contained by that position.'

The related objective of working to influence policy reform appropriately articulates the identity of 'black police officer'.[14] If the Black Police Association confines its activities to advocacy for officers bringing a grievance against their employer – and some of their work will no doubt be of this type – 'race' will be separated from the mainstream of police work and identified as a specialism. Their image will be of an issue based group dealing with the problems of individuals. However, with a clear objective to influence policy and the promotion of positive action, the association can ensure that the necessary link between processes of racialisation and routine policing is retained.

This does not subtly co-opt the association into the main stream of policing, blurring the sharpness of their focus on racialised relations. We should remember that the routine experience of the majority of black and Asian officers has been one of considerable, but not total, marginalisation. The formation of a representative association does not dissolve that experience away. Black officers can continue to view the core routines of police work from its periphery, critically appraising the taken for granted processes within and without constabularies that racialise their experience and police work itself. Their positioning offers a vantage point in that they are wholly familiar with the structures and processes of the occupational culture but also peripheral to it and therefore able to identify the points at which racialised prejudice and discrimination are articulated. This is to place racialised relations within the routines of policing, not in some specialist compartment. It is to analyse the racialisation of relations within the particular social space of the occupational culture, which, incidentally, is far more radical than a specialist, issue based stance, and a potentially powerful stimulus for reform.

As the Black Police Association works to establish its position, individual officers will continue to bring cases of discrimination in employment against chief officers. These will give further impetus to the creation of associate membership and regional associations throughout the country. Chief constables will then have to think hard about whether or not they share Paul Condon's commitment and we can expect some interesting stances to be taken by chief constables and officials of the Police Federation, the rank-and-file union, who felt unable to fully support the initial launch of the Metropolitan Association.

The experience of black American officers has been that cases brought against police chiefs and the enforcement of the law, which included quotas and related measures, was a very significant factor in increasing their power base (Leinen, 1984). Although the affirmative action measures supported by law that were once available to black American officers are not contemplated in Britain, resort to law has and will continue to have a considerable significance for chief constables and the Home Office. Anti-discrimination laws are crucial but, as was discussed earlier, within the police they tend to encourage a formal, rule based approach to equal opportunities. The Black Police Association has the opportunity to temper this approach by its contributions to the wider sweep of policy reform required within constabularies.

The American experience also cautions against over-emphasising the association as a crucible for an exclusive, racialised identity. During a recent research visit to Chicago Police I met officials from the Black Police, African American and Asian Police Associations.

My meetings could have been extended to include associations representing Hispanic, Irish, Japanese, Latin American, Jewish, Greek and other minority ethnic groups. The extent to which members of these associations have different experiences of policing is not yet known and some of them are more concerned with charitable work than policy reform. Chicago nevertheless demonstrates how a factionalising of ethnic groups, which do not focus on both the general and particular policy contexts within which they work, can be a negative development. Exclusive ethnic niches contain factions of the work-force, and it is difficult for any of them to identify shared or particular issues for reform.

A further consequence is that chief officers who might be wanting to develop dialogue about reform find it difficult to consult with every group. In the meantime the official police union, which has a type of 'closed shop' agreement with its employer, claims to represent all ethnic groups, when in fact it neglects the voice of black officers.

In spite of these potential problems of disunity, the Black Police Association is likely to face questions about the extent to which it can adequately represent its Asian members. In its earliest stages of development it was proposed as the Black and Asian Police Association but this changed to the Black Police Association, influenced, I think, by other pressure groups working within the criminal justice field. The change may yet prove an error because the evidence is that the work experience of Asian officers is not exactly the same as that of their black colleagues. In a recent project in which black, Asian and white resigners from the police service were interviewed, I found that some, but not all, Asian resigners had experienced conflict between their culture and the culture of the police organisation which did not concern black officers.[15]

The other dimension to take into consideration is gender. Black and Asian women working within the police service have a rather different experience of employment than their male peers. That experience is yet to be described and analysed. One of the problems with social science analysis of exclusion is that it tends to parrot the importance of recognising relationships between social divisions of 'race', gender, age and disability but pays far too little attention to how these relationships can be adequately described and analysed. This returns us to the problems of phenomenalism and essentialism, which cannot be adequately solved by the expression of statistical relationships based on regression analysis. Neither can they be solved by tacking on or reminding readers that a relationship exists. Detailed, sensitive research methods that depend on the involvement of the researcher in the immediate context researched is the initial requirement. Then data should be analysed within an essentialist and phenomenal framework (Rock, 1973; 1974).

If it becomes stronger, the Black Police Association will change the environment within which officers interact with people from minority ethnic groups. At the moment there is no evidence that the values and tactics of policing employed by black and Asian officers are radically different from those of white officers (Sherman, 1983). The tenor of the occupational culture will not be entirely changed by the raised consciousness of one group of minority ethnic officers but some features that sustain racialised relations could be re-formed. The objection of black and Asian officers to the use of racialised language and different treatment within the ranks, for example, will in time extend to relations without the service. Black officers will object when their colleagues racialise relations with black youths.

The limitations of such change have to be recognised but it is nevertheless appropriate to take into consideration the extent to which, as Carl Weick put it, we 'enact the environment', which is to say that the wider structure of racialised relations is not autonomous, unchanged by the smaller interactional patterns of routine relations between minority ethnic officers and youths from different minority and majority ethnic groups (Weick, 1969; 1976; 1979; Manning, 1980).

The Association of Black Police Officers is and in the future will increasingly become an agent of empowerment for serving and recruiting from minority ethnic groups. This is not to place the burden of change exclusively on their shoulders. A key aspect of positive action is for senior officers with managerial obligations to accept this responsibility. It is, however, important to take full account of black officers' shared and yet distinctive experience of police employment. In this sense the racialisation of black and Asian officers' identity and interpretation of police employment – and maybe police work – is a positive process. And as a positive, empowering process it is likely to avoid the constant negative stance of 'anti-racism', which rarely if ever informs people working in organisations what amounts to good practice, except in terms of high flown principles (Burney, 1988; Gilroy, 1990). The constant receipt of negative messages never builds peoples' confidence or assists reform. Though important in themselves, the repetition of principles eventually prompts inaction and boredom. It is necessary to articulate how principles can be translated into policy and practice. Because its members have been immersed in the culture of policing and are sensitive to its nuances it becomes possible for the Black Police Association to propose detailed, positive reforms which can enhance change and, if they are not accepted by chief officers, require an account of why they are not feasible.

The Black Police Association also points us to the possibility that, although processes of racialisation can be exclusionary, they need not be. It is folly to offer predictive capacities to sociology, which is more concerned with identification of the unintended consequences of action than 'I told you so'.[16] The indication from the Black Police Association, however, is that the racialisation of identity can be a positive point of organisation and the development of social processes to promote change within organisations and beyond their structural boundaries (Gilroy, 1987; Small, 1994). Racialised identities in the context of policing, and other organisations, *could* be a key aspect of processes of inclusion. This, however, requires a relinquishing of some power by the chief officer and, by implication, a strengthening of the power of a racialised minority group, who organise *their concerns* into a policy stance.

Understanding the racialisation of relations

A critique of much criminological research about 'race' has run a thread throughout this book. One strand of the criticism has centred on the need for criminology to be underpinned by a sociological perspective, which I have narrowed to a preference for the 'social construction' framework of analysis. This also covers a wide terrain of sociological perspectives on research but my preference has been for a move beyond macro sociology to the middle and micro levels of analysis that allow us to identify social processes creating and sustaining the racialisation of relations. Concepts like 'ideology', as understood, for example, within a Marxist schema, or the postulation of an implicit need for a societal 'Other' are too imprecise and empirically slippery adequately to describe processes that sustain racialised relations. Far more detailed, sensitive analysis is required.

I have also tried to argue that sociology should avoid the all too frequent either/or type of argument. Understandings of 'race' tend to be either reduced to an essentialist or phenomenalist perspective, when both essentialism and phenomenalism should be taken into account.[17] Attention needs to be directed to core and peripheral meanings of 'race', to the documentation of sameness and diversity. From this perspective sociological research is concerned with both the shared *and* distinct experiences of racialisation of minority ethnic people: with shared and distinct processes of social exclusion applicable to racialised, engendered and other relationships; with continuities between racialised identities among people from minority and majority backgrounds;[18] and with negative and positive consequences of racialised relations.

Throughout, the racialised subject has been preserved from either victim status or passivity, and we have avoided embracing what might be called the 'deconstructionalism' that has all too often explained away the Subject (so why continue with a capital S?). If these emphases become the orientation of a sociology of racialised relations it is possible to move away from the passive or victim status so often attributed to members of socially defined groups. A notion of human creativity is retained. In the wake of opposition and imbalances of power between racialised groups, black, Asian and other minority ethnic people have crafted diverse responses within and between societies. (Hannerz, 1969; 1980 are examples of the empirical use of similar ideas.) Stephen Small makes the point in his recent *Racialised Boundaries*:

> Despite relentless constraints, Black people still excel in certain areas, while in others our strength and striving must be reason for celebration (though not exaggeration) and grounds for inspiration. It is the foundation upon which we must build (Small, 1994, p. 70).

Racialised identities and related social processes and structures are not build around constant opposition to 'white society', though at times they may be. Neither are they moulded by a form of co-option. Diverse identities are constructed with an integrity demanding more than an attribution of epiphenomenal status by proponents of the sociologies of systems. This, incidentally, does not mean that sociology and criminology are consequentially reduced to description (although that would be no bad thing for a time), or an analysis that never extends beyond the immediate appearance of phenomena. Wider structures of power have to be taken into account and, although extremely difficult to analyse satisfactorily, historical relations that frame the present are integral. More appreciation of small gains derived from the study of the racialisation of relations within institutions and organisations would save us from the 'grand sociological gesture' (Mason, 1992). A deeper appreciation of human possibilities than is presently evident in much sociology and criminology is required (Matza, 1969; Rock, 1973; 1974).

One of the defining features of criminology has been its applied reform orientation. This has too often led research to the social problems of the hour, latterly because this is where governments and other funding bodies want to direct their bank balance. The trouble with this stance is the growth of the 'jobbing criminologist' who lives for the next project and grant. Where policy recommendations are written into research reports they usually concern the discrete problem under consideration; and where a wider field of knowledge is taken into account the next project and grant rather than the relevance of past conceptualisations of the same or similar phenomena tend to take priority.

There is nothing intrinsically wrong with this approach (maybe!), but it deflects us from one of the key tasks of the academic, which is to range across findings from apparently discrete research projects to look for continuities and differences; to theorise; and contribute to policy development. Where theory is evident it is often prey to that curse of sociology – fashion. The study of racialised identities, including new racialised identities and organisational processes, for example, need not be over-constrained by post-modernism, which has once again discovered fragmented identities, the particularity and the construction of phenomena. Suffice it to say that from my perspective a rich stream of thought flows from the writings of George Herbert Mead, the Chicago interactionist, that is more than ample for analysis of these subjects but yet to be adequately exploited (Blumer, 1963; Goffman, 1969; 1970; 1971; Mead, 1934).

None of this is to suggest that policy concerns are or should be divorced from theoretical questions. Elsewhere I have argued that the early development of the study of the police was influenced more by theoretical than policy related puzzles (Holdaway, 1987). Theoretical questions then led to considerations of policy. The challenge is to find an appropriate balance between both. This is another point of added value, to misuse managerial jargon, in the use of a social constructionalist framework. It offers a great deal to policy reform, precisely because it is explicitly sensitive to the description and analysis of organisational and other processes that connote and denote the meaning of 'race'.

One intention of the discussion of the ways in which police actions racialise the employment relations of black and Asian officers was to identify precisely those aspects of the occupational culture that need to be reformed. This avoided a specialist focus on 'race', embedding the racialisation of relations within the normative characteristics of the occupational culture. Team work, stereotypical thinking, and other features found within the occupational culture affect members of all perceived minorities but also racialise and exclude minority ethnic officers. We also saw how the Association of Chief Police Officers' Quality of Service Initiative fails to take account of the capacity of the occupational culture to racialise the employment experience of some officers, partly because it is dependent on the quick fix but much beloved work of management consultants, and also crucially, because it is an uncritical theoretical approach to analysing the police as an organisation.

In the chapters about the extent of criminal victimisation amongst ethnic minorities we also commented on the limitations of statistical approaches to understanding racial discrimination. Outcome evaluations beg an analysis of the social processes that in the first place and, when taken for granted, create and sustain racialised relations between offender and victim and victim and police officer. Without doubt many of the processes that racialise offences committed on minority ethnic victims lie outside the immediate and lasting influence of the police. Housing policies, schooling, neighbourhood planning, and related, but not determinate, wider distributions of economic resources press upon and constrain police work.

At times the police work with the grain of social inequality, including racialised inequality. However, this should not deflect attention to wider questions more usually the province of 'macrosociology' of one kind or another. As the police respond to racialised subjects in the course of their work, whether it be in the sphere of policy development or the practice of police work on the streets, they help to sustain or diminish the negative consequences of racialisation. This may include consideration of senior and rank-and-file officers' unwillingness to act as much as the deliberate or unintended

consequences of their action. Whatever the explanation, our understanding of the ways in which these so called wider structures of
racialised relations must include documentation and analysis of the
common-sense meanings and related action of racialised subjects.

This brings us full circle to the comments of the police officer
quoted in the opening of this book. 'Race' is a term with no validity
attached to it by natural scientists. It has nevertheless been found
that 'race' is a category and criterion by which police services and
other resources are distributed. An environment of 'racialised relations' is enacted by taken for granted routines of police work. The
mundane then has a significance that extends beyond its taken for
granted character.

How are relations between police and people racialised? This book
has hopefully offered some answers and provoked further questions.
Let's end with another opportunity to consider the police officer's
explanation of racialised relations.

'Blacks today are repaying whites for their bad treatment in colonial
days. They aren't just against police but against all white people. The
police are an obvious target because they represent white supremacy.
Really, until blacks have taken over and evened up the score, the
problem won't be solved. I don't blame them really, when they get stuck
in places like Brixton. I know that PCs call them spooks, niggers and
sooties, but deep down the majority of PCs aren't really against them,
although there are some who really hate them and will go out of their
way to get them. I call them niggers myself now, but I don't really mean
it. I think a relief takes on a personality of its own. Although you still
have your own personality you lose a lot of it to the relief group
personality (Smith, D. *et al.*, 1986; p. 393).'

Notes and References

1. Thinking about 'race'

1. In this book the terms, black, Asian and white are, as is common, used to classify people.
2. Sociology is of course not a unified discipline. It will become clear that I think some forms of sociology are indeed little more than a form of presumption dressed in fancy language.
3. The principles of reasoning and methods of data collection and analysis to which I refer are themselves highly contestable. Full discussion of them is not within the scope of this book.
4. All methods of social research have theoretical assumptions embedded within them. I am not about to claim an atheoretical purity for any form of sociological method. As far as theoretical reflection is concerned, its ultimate strength lies in its applicability to 'real world' contexts and I am therefore proposing an empirical sociology.
5. This does not mean, for example, that we can be content with leaving happy people in poverty. I am not arguing any such point. It is nevertheless crucial to understand that the integrity of the worlds we document will not be straightforwardly reformed by changing material circumstances.
6. A great deal of the discussion of race relations within social work has adopted this stance. For example, see C.D. Project Steering Group, 1991; Dominelli, 1992.
7. But not, for example, in Chicago or New York, where different classifications of 'race' are employed.
8. See Bettleheim, 1943 for examples of resistance in the concentration camp. Also see Bauman, 1989.
9. For discussion of this see Banton, 1967.
10. I am not suggesting there is a simple, direct relationship between this history and the present structural position and consciousness of black and Asian people in England. This issue will be discussed in greater detail later.

11. See Gilroy (1987) for a discussion of the ways in which black people have been defined as 'trouble'.

2. Victim's of crime in Britain

1. For a more recent analysis of the labour market position of black and Asian people, who have always had different employment profiles, as have men and women within and between those groups, see Brown, 1992; Jones, 1993; Owen, 1994.
2. It is extremely important not to portray black and Asian people as passive victims within the labour market. Important changes have been secured to enhance their mobility. We are nevertheless recognising the base from which such mobility began and the continuing effects of immigrant status.
3. For a fuller discussion of this point see Fitzgerald and Ellis, 1989.
4. Surveys have also been conducted in the USA and in Europe. See Whitaker, 1990; Albrecht, 1991.
5. Racial classifications were used in the most recent 1991 survey.
6. But note that the number of black women interviewed was very small.
7. This is also a point to be made about all victims. Here I am focusing on the particular needs of minority ethnic groups.

3. Recial attack in Britain

1. At the time of writing the Home Affairs Committee is conducting another inquiry into racial attacks and harassment. They have not yet published their report or detailed evidence presented by various organisations, which means that it is not possible to take account of a potentially important source of information.
2. The Home Affairs Committee has regularly investigated racial attack at about three-yearly intervals. The committee can only publish reports and in them offer advice to government, the police and so on. Chief constables are not obliged to implement their recommendations and it is only by returning to the subject that the need for reform can be pressed.

4. The cultural mediation of 'race'

1. I should also point out that I am not entirely comfortable with my conclusion. Ideas about 'belonging' are perhaps more suited to ethnic status and we have an example of ethnocentrism rather than racial prejudice.

2. Some studies have nevertheless included elements of direct observation of policing within substantial work. See, for example, Keith, 1993.
3. For the American context of debate see Wolfgang and Cohen, 1970.
4. This is to describe realism in the most basic terms.
5. Paul Gilroy was one of the writers Lea and Young criticised in *What is to be Done about Law and Order*. His ideas have now been revised and the diversity of culture is at the forefront of his analysis (Gilroy, 1992).

5. British police responses to riots

1. The 'Sus Law' was the popular name of a police power to arrest people loitering in a public place to commit an offence. Arrests were made on uncorroborated police evidence and there was considerable public concern about the extensive use of the law against black people. See Brogden. (1981).
2. Scarman took some bearings from the American Kerner Commission on civil disorders (Kerner, 1968). The US literature on 'race riots' is pretty extensive and cannot be discussed here.
3. I am being somewhat arbitrary here and recognise that there are many others. Scarman's emphasis on a balance between police discretion and as consensual relations as possible with the public, for example, has had a considerable impact.
4. This article describes the organisation of training and I draw on it for most of this discussion. Also see Southgate, 1988.
5. I have in mind cases like those of PC Singh against the Chief Constable of Nottinghamshire, and WPC Sarah Locker against the Commissioner of the Metropolitan Police.
6. The Home Office can only advise but of course it can encourage compliance by a range of strategies.
7. This will change in the near future when a Police Board for London is established.
8. These changes did not occur in one fell swoop but over a period of years.

6. An enemy within – racialized relation, within the British police.

1. In this chapter I draw on my book *Recruiting a Multi-Racial Police*, HMSO, London, 1991 and *Race Relations and Police Recruitment*, published in the British Journal of Criminology, vol. 31, no. 4, 1991.
2 Leicestershire Constabulary is the exception here. The Police Federation has published a 'Statement of Intent' in which a commitment is made to the eradication of any racist or sexist behaviour within the service. The Commissioner of the Metropolitan Police, Sir Paul Con-

don, has also expressed strong views about the eradication of racism within his force. It is interesting to note that the Probation Service has taken a very different stance on this issue. The Association of Chief Officers of Probation has published a recommended anti-racism policy statement and done much work to develop exemplar codes of practice (Holdaway and Allaker, 1990).

3. *n.* is 43.
4. For further examples see (Wilson, Holdaway *et al.*, 1984).
5. The interviews were carried out in 1989.
6. All the quotes in this section are taken from this as yet unpublished study. The study includes a sample of white resigners.
7. Other occupations also have unwritten rules about the use of alcohol and a willingness to consume alcohol is of course part of a broader value placed on consumption by men. There is nothing about this point that is intrinsic to the police.

7. Emerging theme

1. The sociology of race relations has some studies of relevance here. Robert Miles has analysed such processes at the macro level and his almost exclusive concern is with political and economic processes. My emphasis is at a much smaller scale of analysis, of which Richard Jenkins's work is but one example (Jenkins, 1986).
2. See the encyclopaedic Oxford Handbook of Criminology, for example (Maguire, Morgan *et al.*, 1994).
3. There is more to Gilroy's argument than I present here. But unless we accept his theoretical stance we cannot agree with his view on the use of crime and other statistics.
4. This is a matter for a separate discussion but anyone familiar with the published literature about the occupational culture will be interested in the analysis presented by the Quality of Service Committee. There is also an interesting comment by the management consultants who undertook the exercise about the organisational culture. Referring to the officers and presumably ACPO representatives on the working party she says, 'No one is secure in their knowledge of the culture of the police service, and the extent of change it has undergone since 1985. Those who are charged with managing this change need to know where they are starting from.'
5. The ACPO/Commission for Racial Equality publication is similar and we have discussed it earlier.
6. Features of the occupational culture, incidentally, that did not come to light in the ACPO consultancy about the occupational culture!
7. Again features omitted from the ACPO consultation report.
8. There is no space to develop the point here but Michael Chatter-ton's important work on the use of information technology by the

police leads him to argue that such technology and the use of the HMIC's matrix of performance indicators and other management devices can expose the low-visibility of routine policing to greater public view.

9. My discussion here is greatly reliant on John Edwards's excellent *Race book When Counts* (1995)

10. For example, a middle class of blacks rather than all blacks seem to have benefited, perhaps disproportionately (Small, 1994).

11. Again, it is important to stress that many constabularies have developed significant equal opportunities policies, far more so than universities, for example. We are not discussing a stagnant situation but how constabularies can become even more aware of the policy questions they face.

12. This was a talk to film makers.

13. Also see Gilroy, 1990.

14. This is of course to simplify 'identity'. Other reference points, with family, friends, leisure, consumption, and many more will also be important.

15. It is argued by some of these groups that a differentiation between black and Asian people weakens the bargaining power of representative associations. The English, a term summarising a diverse population, is presented as a single group so why should black and Asian people, who share the single experience of racialised prejudice and discrimination, be differentiated?

16. Which is not to say that sociology cannot be of assistance to the development of good policy and practice in any sphere of work.

17. Biological essentialism plays no part in this view.

18. This requires whiteness and 'English identity' to be the subject of inquiry.

Bibliography

ACPO (1990) *Setting The Standards For Policing: Meeting Community Expectation* (London, Association of Chief Police Officers)

ACPO and CRE (1993) *Policing and Racial Equality* (London, ACPO and the Commission for Racial Equality).

ACPO Quality of Service Committee (1993) *Getting Things Right* (London, Association of Chief Police Officers).

Adorno, T. (1950) *The Authoritarian Personality* (New York, Harper).

Albrecht, H.J. (1991) 'Ethnic minorities: crime and criminal justice in Europe' *Crime in Europe* (London, New York, Routledge).

Alex, N. (1969) *Black in Blue* (New York, Century Crofts).

Allan, S. and M. Macey (eds.) (1988) *Race and Social Policy* (London, ESRC).

Althusser, L. (1971) *Lenin and Philosophy* (London, New Left Books).

Anderson, B. (1991) *Imagined Communities. Reflections on the Origins and Spread of Nationalism* (London, Verso).

Ball, D. (1973) *Microecology: Social Situations and Intimate Space* (Chicago, Bobs-Merill)

Banton, M. (1967) *Race Relations* (London, Tavistock).

Banton, M. (1977) *The Idea of Race* (London, Tavistock).

Banton, M. (1979) 'Analytical and folk concepts of race and ethnicity' *Ethnic and Racial Studies*, 2, n. 2: pp. 127–8.

Banton, M. (1983) 'Categorical and Statistical Discrimination' *Ethnic and Racial Studies*, 6, n. 4: pp. 61–80.

Banton, M. (1987) *Promoting Racial Harmony* (Cambridge, Cambridge University Press).

Banton, M. (1994) *Discrimination* (Buckingham, Open University Press).

Banton, M. and J. Hawood (1975) *The Race Concept* (Newton Abbott, David and Charles).

Barker, M. (1981) *The New Racism* (London, Junction Books)

Barth, F. (ed.) (1969) *Ethnic Groups and Boundaries: The Social Organisation of Cultural Difference* (Boston, Little, Brown and Company).

Bauman, Z. (1989) *Modernity and the Holocaust* (Cambridge, Polity).

Benyon J. and J. Solomos (eds) (1987) *The Roots of Urban Unrest* (Oxford, Pergamon).

Benyon, J. (1986) *A Tale of Failure: Race and Policing* (University of Warwick, Centre for Research In Ethnic Relations).

Berger, P. and T. Luckmann (1967) *The Social Construction of Reality* (Harmondsworth, Penguin).

Bettleheim, B. (1943) 'Individual and mass behaviour in extreme situations' *Journal of Abnormal and Social Psychology* 38: pp. 417–52.

Bittner, E. (1967) 'The Police on Skid Row' *American Sociological Review*, 32, no. 5: pp. 699–715.

Bittner, E. (1970) *The Functions of the Police in Modern Society* Washington, National Institute of Mental Health.

Blom-Cooper, L. and R. Drabble (1982) 'Police perceptions of crime: Brixton and the operational response' *British Journal of Criminology*, 22: pp. 184–7.

Blumer, H. (1968) *Symbolic Interaction* (Englewood Cliffs, N.J., Prentice-Hall).

Bowling, B. (1993) 'Racial Harassment and the Process of Victimisation' *British Journal of Criminology*, 33, no. 2: pp. 216–30.

Broadwater Farm Inquiry (1986) *The Broadwater Farm Inquiry* (London, London Borough of Haringey).

Brogden, A. (1931) ' "Sus" is dead but what about "sas"?', *New Community*, 9(1).

Brown, C. (1984) *Black and White in Britain: The Third PSI Survey* (London, Policy Studies Institute).

Brown, C. (1992). ' "Same Difference": the persistence of racial disadvantage in the British employment market' *Racism and Anti racism: Inequalities, Opportunities and Policies* (London, Sage).

Brown, L. and A. Willis (1985) 'Authoritarianism in British Police Recruits: Importation, Socialisation or Myth' *Journal of Occupational Psychology*, 58, no. 1: pp. 97–108.

Burney, E. (1988) *Steps to Racial Equality: Positive Action in a Negative Climate* (London, Runnymede Trust).

Cain, M. (1973) *Society and the Policeman's Role* (London, Routledge and Kegan Paul).

Carmichael, S. and C. V. Hamilton (1968) *Black Power; the Politics of Liberation in America* (London, Jonathan Cape).

Cashmore, E. and B. Troyna (1983) *Introduction to Race Relations* (London, Routledge and Kegan Paul).

Cashmore, E. and B. Troyna (eds.) (1982) *Black Youth in Crisis* (London, George, Allen and Unwin).

Central Council for Training and Education in Social Work (1991) *One Small Step Towards Racial Justice: The Teaching of Antiracism in Diploma in Social Work Programmes* (London, CCETSW).

Chatterton, M. R. (1979) 'The supervision of patrol work under the fixed points system', in S. Holdaway (ed.), *The British Police* (London, Edward Arnold).

Chatterton, M. R. (1992) *Controlling Police Work. Strategies and tactics of the lower ranks – their past and future relevance*. Paper presented at conference 'Social Order in Post Classical Sociology', University of Bristol,

Chatterton, M. R. and M. Rogers (1989) 'Focused Policing' *Coming to Terms with Policing* (London, Routledge).

Cohen, P. (1993) *Home Rules* (London, New Ethnicities Unit, University of East London).

Cohen, P. (1993) 'The Perversions of Inheritance' in P.Cohen and H. Bains (eds.), *Multi-Cultural Britain* (Basingstoke, Macmillan pp. 9–118).

Colman, A. and A. Gorman (1982) 'Conservatism, Dogmatism and Authoritarianism in British Police Officers' *Sociology*, 16: pp. 1–11.

Conley, J. A. (1982) *Assessment of Affirmative Action in Criminal Justice Agencies* (Washington, National Institute of Justice).

Connelly, N. (1989) *Race and Change in Social Services Departments* (London, Policy Studies Institute).

Connelly, N. (1990) 'Social Services Departments: The Process and Progress of Change' in W. Ball and J. Solomos (eds.), *Race and Local Politics* (Basingstoke, Macmillan).

CPTU Community, F. a. Q. R. T. (1993) *Final Report – Minimum Effective Training Levels* (Harrogate, Home Office Central Planning Unit).

CRE (1981) *Racial Harassment on Local Authority Housing Estates* (London, Commission for Racial Equality).

CRE (1988) *Learning in Terror: A Survey of Racial Harassment in Schools and Colleges in England, Scotland and Wales, 1985–87* (London, Commission for Racial Equality).

Dear, G. (1972) 'Coloured Immigrant Communities and the Police' *The Police Journal* (April–June): pp. 128–150.

Dominelli, L. (1988) *Anti-Racist Social Work* (London, BASW/Macmillan).

Edwards, J. (1987) *Positive Discrimination, Social Justice and Social Policy* (London, Tavistock).

Edwards, J. (1994) 'Group Rights v. Individual Rights: The Case of Race Conscious Policies' *Journal of Social Policy*, 23, no. 1: pp. 55–70.

Edward, T. (1995) *Who Rue Courts: The Morality of Racial Prejudice in Britain and America.* (Laura, Rouetledge).

Eriksen, T. H. (1993) *Ethnicity and Nationalism: Anthropological Perspetives* (London, Pluto Press).

Field, S. (1982) *Public Disorder* (London, HMSO).

Field, S. (1984) *The Attitudes of Ethnic Minorities* (London, HMSO).

Fielding, N. (1988) 'Competence and culture in the police' *Sociology*, 22, no. 1: pp. 45–65.

Fielding, N. (1988) *Joining Forces: Police Training, Socialisation and Occupational Competence* (London, Routledge).

Fitzgerald, M. (1990) 'Legal approaches to racial harassment in council housing: the case for reassessment' *New Community*, 16, no. 1: pp. 93–106.

Fitzgerald, M. (1993) 'Racism': Establishing the Phenomenon in D. Cook and B. Hudson (eds.), *Racism and Criminology* (London, Sage).

Fitzgerald, M. and T. Ellis (1989) 'Racial Harassment: The Evidence' *Current Issues in Criminological Research: British Criminology Conference vol. 2* (Bristol, Bristol Centre for Criminal Justice).

Gambetta, D. (ed.) (1988) *Trust: The Making and Breaking Co- operative Relations* (Oxford, Blackwell).

Gaskell, G. and P. Smith (1981) *Are young blacks really alienated* (New Society)

Gaskell, G. and P. Smith (1985) 'Young Black's Hostility to the Police: An Investigation into its causes' *New Community*, 12, no. 1: pp. 66–74.

Giddens, A. (1979) *Central Problems in Social Theory* (London, Macmillan).

Gilroy, P. (1983) 'Police and Thieves' in The Centre for Contemporary Cultural Studies, *The Empire Strikes Back: Race and Racism in Britain* (London, Hutchinson).

Gilroy, P. (1987) *There Ain't no Black in the Union Jack* (London, Hutchinson).

Gilroy, P. (1990) 'The End of Anti-Racism' in W. Ball and J. Solomos (eds.), *Race and Local Politics* (Basingstoke, Macmillan).

Gilroy, P. (1992) 'The End of Antiracism' in J. Donald and A. Rattansi (eds.), *'Race' Culture and Difference* (London, Sage).

Gilroy, P. (ed.) (1982) *The myth of black criminality* Socialist Register, 1982 (London, Merlin).

Goffman, E. (1969) *The Presentation of Self in Everyday Life* (Harmondsworth, Penguin).

Goffman, E. (1970) *Stigma: Notes on the Management of Spoiled Identity* (Harmondsworth, Penguin).

Goffman, E. (1971) *Relations in Public: Micro studies of the Public Order* (Harmondsworth, Penguin).

Gordon, P. (1985) *Policing Immigration: Britain's Internal Controls* (London, Pluto Press).

Gordon, P. (1986) *Racial Violence and Harassment* (London, Runnymede Trust).

Hall, S. (1992) 'New Ethnicities' in J. Donald and A. Rattansi (eds.), *'Race', Culture and Difference* (London, Sage) pp. 252–259.

Hall, S. *et al.* (1978) *Policing the Crisis* (London, Macmillan).

Hannerz, U. (1969) *Soulside: Inquiries into Ghetto Culture and Community* (New York and London, Columbia University Press).

Hannerz, U. (1980) *Exploring the City: Inquiries Towards an Urban Anthropology* (New York, University of Columbia Press).

Harris, L. (1982) *Attitudes to Careers of Young Asian Men in Britain* (London, Louis Harris Group).

Her Majesty's Chief Inspector of Constabulary (1994) *Annual Report 1993* (London, HMSO).

Her Majesty's Inspectorate of Constabulary (1992) *Equal Opportunities in the Police Service* (Home Office).

Hobbs, D. (1988) *Doing the Business: Entrepreneurship, the Working Class and Detectives in the East End of London* (Oxford, Clarendon Press).

Hochstedler, E. (1984) 'Impediments to Hiring Minorities in Public Police Agencies' *Journal of Police Science and Administration* **12**, no. 2: pp. 227–40.

Holdaway, S. (1977) 'Changes in Urban Policing' *British Journal of Sociology*, 28, no. 2: pp. 119–37.

Holdaway, S. (1978) 'The reality of police race relations: towards an effective community relations policy' *New Community*, 6, no. 3: pp. 258–67.

Holdaway, S. (1983) *Inside the British Police: A Force at Work* (Oxford, Blackwell).

Holdaway, S. (1987) 'Discovering Structure: studies of the police occupational culture' in M. Weatheritt (ed.), *The Future of Police Research* (Aldershot, Gower).

Holdaway, S. (1988) *Crime and Deviance* (Basingstoke, Macmillan).

Holdaway, S. (1991) *Recruiting a Multi-Racial Police Force* (London, HMSO).

Holdaway, S. (1993) *The Resignation of Black and Asian Officers from the Police Service: A Report to the Home Office* (London, Home Office).

Holdaway, S. and J. Allaker (1990) *Race Issues in the Probation Service: A Review of Policy* (Wakefield, Association of Chief Officers of Probation).

Holdaway, S. and P. Rock (eds.) (1996) *The Social Theory of Criminology* (London, UCL Press).

Holdaway, S. (ed.) (1979) *The British Police* (London, Edward Arnold).

Home Affairs Committee (1982) *Racial Attacks. Second Report from the Home Affairs Committee. Session 1981–2, HC 106* (London, HMSO).

Home Affairs Committee (1986) *Racial Attacks and Harassment. Third Report from the Home Affairs Committee. Session 1985–6, HC 409* (London, HMSO).

Home Affairs Committee (1989–90) *Racial Attacks and Harassment* (London, HMSO).

Home Office (1981) *Racial Attacks: Report of a Home Office Study* (London, Home Office).

Home Office (1982) *Report of a Study Group: Recruitment into the Police Service of Members of the Ethnic Minorities* (Home Office).

Home Office (1986) National Conference of Recruiting Officers, Letter from Mr Douglas Hogg, Parliamentary Secretary of State at the Home Office, to all Chief Constables (Home Office).

Home Office (1986) The National Conference of Police Recruiting Officers 14th–15th October, Record of Proceedings (Home Office).

Home Office (1989) *Equal Opportunities in the Police Service* Circular 87/1989.

Home Office (1989) *The Response to Racial Attacks and Harassment: Guidance for the Statutory Agencies: Report of the Inter-Departmental Racial Attacks Group* (London, Home Office).

Home Office (1990) *Equal Opportunities in the Police Service: Progress Report*.

Home Office (1990) Ethnic Minority Recruitment into the Police Service Circular 33/1990.

Home Office (1991) *Equal Opportunities in the Police Service: Progress Report.* (Home Office)

Home Office (1992) *Race and the Criminal Justice System* (London, Home Office).

Home Office (1993) Evidence to the Inquiry into Racial Attacks and Harassment (London, House of Commons).

Home Office (1994) *Ethnic Monitoring Guidance* Circular 34/1994.

Hough, M. (1980) 'Managing with less Technology' *British Journal of Criminology*, 20, no. 4: pp. 344–57.

Hough, M. and P. Mayhew (1983) *The British Crime Survey* (London, HMSO).

Hough, M. and P. Mayhew (1985) *Taking Account of Crime: Key Findings from the 1984 British Crime Survey* (London, HMSO).

House of Commons (1994) *Racial Attacks and Harassment: Home Affairs Committee, 3rd Report* (London, HMSO).

House of Commons Select Committee on Race Relations and Immigration (1972) *Police/Immigrant Relations* (London, HMSO).

Howe, D. (1981) *From Bobby to Babylon* (London, Race Today Collective).

Hunte, J. (1966) *Nigger hunting in England* (London, Institute of Commonwealth Studies).

Institute of Race Relations (1978) *Police Against Black People: Evidence Submitted to the Royal Commission on Criminal Procedure* (London, Institute of Race Relations).

Jackson, P. (1989) 'Street Life: the politics of Carnival' *Environment and Planning* D, no. 6: pp. 248–61.

James, D. (1978) 'Police Black Relations: The Professional Solution' in S. Holdaway (ed.), *The British Police* (London, Edward Arnold).

Jefferson, J. (1990) *The case against paramilitary policing* (Milton Keynes, Open University Press).

Jefferson, T. (1987) 'Beyond Paramilitarism' *British Journal of Criminology*, no. 27: pp. 47–53.

Jefferson, T. (1993) 'Pondering Paramilitarism: A Question of Standpoints?' *British Journal of Criminology*, 33, no. 3: pp. 374–81.

Jefferson, T. (1993) 'The Racism of Criminalization: Policing and the Reproduction of the Criminal Other' in L. Gelsthorpe (ed.), *Minority Ethnic Groups in the Criminal Justice System* (Cambridge, Cambridge University, Institute of Criminology), pp. 26–46.

Jefferson, T. and M. A. Walker (1992) 'Ethnic Minorities in the Criminal Justice System' *The Criminal Law Review*, pp. 83–95.

Jefferson, T. and M. Walker (1993) 'Attitudes to the Police of Ethnic Minorities in a Provincial City' *British Journal of Criminology*, **33**, no. 2: pp. 251–66.

Jenkins, R. (1986) *Racism and Recruitment* (Cambridge, University of Cambridge).

Jenkins, R. and J. Solomos (eds.) (1987) *Racism and equal opportunities policy in the 1980s* (Cambridge, Cambridge University Press).

Jewson, N. and D. Mason (1992). 'The theory and practice of equal opportunities policies: liberal and radical approaches' in P. Braham *et al.* (eds.), *Racism and Antiracism: Inequalities, Opportunities and Policies* (London, Sage).

Joint Consultative Committee (1990) *Operational Policing Review* Surbiton,

Jones, T. (1993) *Britain's Ethnic Minorities* (London, PST).

Jones, T. M., Maclean, *et al.* (1986) *The Islington Crime Survey* (Aldershot, Gower).

Keith, M. (1987) 'Something happened: explanations of the 1981 riots' in P. Jackson (ed.), *Race and Racism* (London, Allen and Unwin).

Keith, M. (1988) 'Squaring Circles' *New Community*, 15, no. 1: pp. 63–77.

Keith, M. (1988) 'Riots as a "social problem" in British cities' in M. Cross and M. Keith (eds.), *Social Problems in the city* (Oxford, OUP).

Keith, M. (1991) 'Policing a perplexed society?: no-go areas and the mystification of police-Black conflict' in E. Cashmore and E. McClaughlin (eds.), *Out of order? Policing Black People* (London, Routledge).

Keith, M. (1993) 'From punishment to discipline? Racism racialisation and social control' *Racism, the city and the state* (London, Routledge).

Keith, M. (1993) *Race, Riots and Policing: Lore and Disorder in A Multi-Racist Society* (London, UCL Press).

Kerner, O. (1968) *Report of the National Advisory Commission on Civil Disorders* (Washington, US Government Printing Office).

Kimber, J. and L. Cooper (1990) *Victim Support Racial Harassment Project: final report* (London, Victim Support).

Klug, F. (1982) *Racist Attacks* (London, Runnymede Trust).

Lambert, J. (1970) *Crime, Police and Race Relations* (London, Oxford University Press).

Lawrence, D. (1987) 'Racial Violence in Britain: Trends and a Perspective' *New Community*, 14, no. 1/2: pp. 151–60.

Lea, J. and J. Young (1982) 'Race and Crime' *Marxism Today*, August pp. 29–30.

Lea, J. and J. Young (1982) 'The Riots in Britain 1981: Urban Violence and Marginalisation' in D. Cowell *et al.* (eds.), *Policing the Riots* (London, Junction Books), pp. 5–20.

Lea, J. and J. Young (1984) *What is to be done about Law and Order?*

Legal Action Group (1990) *Making the law work against racial harassment* (London, LAC).

Leinen, S. (1984) *Black Police: White Society* (New York, New York University Press).

London Borough of Lambeth (1981) *Final Report of the Working Party into Community/Police Relations in Lambeth* (London, London Borough of Lambeth).

London Borough of Newham (1987) *Crime in Newham: Report of a Survey of Crime and Racial Harassment in Newham* (London, London Borough of Newham).

London Borough of Newham (1987) *Crime in Newham: The Survey* (London, London Borough of Newham).

Maguire, M. R. Morgan, *et al* (ed.) (1994) *The Oxford Handbook of Criminology* (Oxford, Clarendon Press).

Manning, P. (1977) *Police Work* (Cambridge, Mass, MIT Press).

Manning, P. K. (1980) *The narc's game: organisational and informational limits to drug enforcement* (Cambridge, Mass, MIT Press).

Mason, D. (1982) 'After Scarman: A note on the concept of institutional racism' *New Community*, 10, n. 1

Mason, D. (1992) *Some Problems with the Concepts of Race and Racism* (Leicester, University of Leicester, Department of Sociology).

Mason, D. (1994) 'On the dangers of disconnecting Race and Racism' *Sociology*, 28, no. 4: pp. 845–58.

Matza, D. (1969) *Becoming Deviant* (Englewood Cliffs, Prentice-Hall).

Maung, A. N. and C. Mirlees-Black (1994) *Racially motivated crime: a British Crime Survey analysis* (London, Home Office).

Mayhew, P., D. Elliott, *et al.* (1989) *British Crime Survey 1989* (London, HMSO).

Mayhew, P., N. A. Maung, *et al.* (1993) *The 1992 British Crime Survey* (London, HMSO).

McFarland, E. and D. Walsh (1987) *Refugees in Strathclyde* (Glasgow, Scottish Ethnic Minorities Research Unit).

Mead, G. H. (1934) *Mind, Self and Society* (Chicago, University of Chicago Press).

Merton, R. K. (1938) 'Social structure and anomie' *American Sociological Review*, 3: pp. 672–82.

Metropolitan Police: Analysis Team (1990) *The Metropolitan Police Seminars Looking into Recruiting and Retention of Officers, Particularly Black and Asian Officers: Analysis of Data from Seminar July 1990* (London, Metropolitan Police).

Metropolitan Police (1990) *Analysis of data from seminars looking into recruiting and retention of officers, particularly black and Asian officers* (London, Metropolitan Police).

MIL (1979) *Attitudes to the Police: Report on a Survey Amongst West Indians* (London, MIL Research Ltd).

Miles, R. (1982) *Racism and Migrant Labour* (London, Routledge and Kegan Paul).

Miles, R. (1989) *Racism* (London, Routledge).

Mills, C. W. (1959) *The Sociological Imagination* (New York, Oxford University Press).

Modood, T. (1992) *Not Easy Being British: Colour, Culture and Citizenship* (London, Runnymede Trust and Trentham Books).

Morgan, R. (1987) 'Police accountability; current developments and future prospects' in M. Weatheritt (ed.), *The Future of Police Research* (Aldershot, Gower), pp. 169–84.

Morgan, R. (1989) ' "Policing by consent": legitimating the doctrine' in D. Smith and R. Morgan (eds.), *Coming to Terms with Policing* (London, Routledge) pp. 217–34.

Morris, T. P. (1976) Commentary by Professor Morris on the Memorandum by the Metropolitan Police *Vol. 3. Select Committee on Race and Immigration, 1976–77 Session.*

Newing, J. and R. R. Crump (1974) *Footpad Crime and its Community Effect in Lambeth* (A7 Division, Unpublished Report, New Scotland Yard).

Oakley, R. (1989) 'Community and race relations training for the police: a review of developments' *New Community*, 16, no. 1: pp. 61–80.

Oakley, R. (1993) 'Race Relations Training In The Police' in L. Gelsthorpe (ed.), *Minority Ethnic Groups in the Criminal Justice System* (Cambridge) pp. 49–67.

Oakley, R. (1993) *Racial Violence and Harassment in Europe* (Council of Europe).

Omi, M. and M. Winant (1986) *Racial formation in the United States* (London, Routledge).

Owen, D. (1994) *Ethnic Minority Women and the Labour Market: analysis of the 1991 Census* (Manchester, Equal Opportunities Commission).

Park, R. and E. Burgess (ed.) (1925) *The City* (Chicago, University of Chicago Press).

Pearson, G. (1976) 'Paki-Bashing' in a North-East Lancashire cotton town: A case study and its history' in G. Mongham and G. Pearson (eds.), *Working Class Youth Culture* (London, Routledge and Kegan Paul).

Pearson, G., A. Sampson, *et al.* (1989) 'Policing Racism' in D. Smith and R. Morgan (eds.), *Coming to Terms with Policing: Perspectives on Policy* (London, Routledge).

Police Training Council (1983) *Community and Race Relations Training for the Police* (London, Home Office).

Pope, D. (1976) *Community Relations: The Police Response* (London, Runnymede Trust).

Pryce, K. (1979) *Endless Pressure* (Harmondsworth, Penguin).

Reiner, R. (1985) *The Politics of the Police* (Brighton, Wheatsheaf Books).

Reiner, R. (1991) *Chief Constables* (Oxford, Oxford University Press).

Research Services (1990) *Customer Satisfaction Survey* (London, Research Services Limited).

Rex, J. (1973) *Race, Colonialism and the City* (London, Routledge and Kegan Paul).

Rex, J. (1982) 'West Indian and Asian youth' in E. Cashmore and B. Troyna (eds.), *Black Youth in Crisis* (London, George, Allen and Unwin).

Rex, J. and D. Mason (eds.) (1986) *Theories of Race and Ethnic Relations* (Cambridge, Cambridge University Press).

Rex, J. and R. Moore (1967) *Race, Community and Conflict* (London, Oxford University Press).

Rock, P. (1973) 'Phenomenalism and Essentialism in the Sociology of Deviance' *Sociology*, 7, no. 7: pp. 17–29.

Rock, P. (1974) 'Conceptions of Moral Order' *British Journal of Criminology*, 14, no. 2: pp. 139–49.

Rock, P. (1979) *The Making of Symbolic Interactionism* (London, Routledge and Kegan Paul).

Sampson, A. and C. Phillips (1992) *Multiple Victimisation: Racial Attacks on an East London Estate* (London, Home Office).

Saulsbury, W. E. and B. Bowling (1991) *The Multi-Agency Approach in Practice: The North Plaistow Racial Harassment Project* (London, Home Office).

Scarman OBE, Rt. Hon. the Lord (1981) *The Brixton Disorders, 10–12 April 1981* (London, HMSO).

Schutz, A. (1967) *Collected Papers 1: The Problem of Social Reality* (The Hague, Martinus Nijhoff).

Seagrave, J. (1989) *Racially Motivated Incidents Reported to the Police* (London, Home Office).

Select Committee (1971–1972) *Select Committee on Race Relations and Immigration. Police/Immigrant Relations* (London, HMSO).

Select Committee (1976–1977) *Select Committee on Race Relations and Immigration. The West Indian Community* (London, HMSO).

Shaw, C. and H. McKay (1942) *Juvenile Delinquency and Urban Areas* (Chicago, University of Chicago Press).

Sherman, L. W. (1983). 'After the Riots: Police and Minorities in the United States' in N. Glazer and K. Young (eds.), *Ethnic Pluralism and Public Policy* (London, Heinemann).

Skogan, W. G. (1990) *The Police and Public in England and Wales* (London, HMSO).

Skolnick, J. (1966) *Justice Without Trial: Law Enforcement in a Democratic Society* (New York and London, Wiley).

Small, S. (1983) *Police and People in London, Vol. II: A Group of Young Black People* (London, Policy Studies Institute).

Small, S. (1994) *Racialised Barriers* (London, Routledge).

Smith, D. *et al.* (1986) *Police and People in London* (Aldershot, Gower).

Smith, D. J. (1994) 'Race, Crime and Criminal Justice' in M. Maquire *et al.* (eds.), *The Oxford Handbook of Criminology* (Oxford, Clarendon Press).

Smith, S. J. (1989) *The Politics of 'Race' and Residence: Citizenship, Segregation and White Supremacy in Britain* (Cambridge, Polity).

Solomos, J. (1993) 'Constructions of Black Criminality: Racialisation and Criminalisation in Perspective' in D. Cook and B. Hudson (eds.), *Racism and Criminology* (London, Sage).

Southgate, P. (1984) *Racism Awareness Training for the Police* (London, Home Office).

Southgate, P. and D. Crisp (1992) *Public Satisfaction with Police Services* (London, Home Office).

Southgate, P. (ed.) (1988) *New Direction in Police Training* (London, HMSO).

Stevens, P. and C. Willis (1979) *Race, Crime and Arrests* (London, Home Office).

Stinchcome, A. (1963) 'Institutions of Privacy in the Determination of Police Administrative Practice' *American Journal of Sociology* 69(2): pp 150–60

Taylor, I., P. Walton, *et al.* (1973) *The New Criminology* (London, Routledge and Kegan Paul).

The Black Police Association (1994) *The Black Police Association* (London, Metropolitan Police).

The Guardian (1973) 'The Hard Road To Harmony' 23 October, 1973, p. 16.

The Independent (1993) 25 September, p. 8.

The Runnymede Trust (1976) *Runnymede Bulletin*, London, No. 4.

The Runnymede Trust (1993) *Equality Assurance in Schools: quality, identity, society* (London, Runnymede Trust).

The Runnymede Trust (1993) *Racially-Motivated Attacks and Harassment: Submission to the Home Affairs Committee* (London, Runnymede Trust).

Tuck, M. and P. Southgate (1981) *Ethnic Minorities, Crime and Policing* (London, HMSO).

Waddington, P. A. J. (1984) 'Black Crime the "Racist" Police and Fashionable Compassion' *The Kindness That Kills* (London, SPCK).

Waddington, P. A. J. (1986) 'Mugging as a Moral Panic' *British Journal of Sociology*, XXXVII, no. 2 pp. 37–46.

Waddington, P. A. J. (1991) *The Strong Arm of the Law* (Oxford, Oxford University Press).

Waddington, P. A. J. (1993) 'The Case Against Paramilitary Policing Considered' *British Journal of Criminology*, 33, no. 3: pp. 353–73.

Waddington, P. A. J. (1994) 'Coercion and accommodation: Policing public order after the Public Order Act' *British Journal of Sociology*, forthcoming.

Waddington, P. J. A. (1987) 'Towards Paramilitarism? Dilemmas in Policing Civil Disorder' *British Journal of Criminology*, 27, no 3: pp. 37–46.

Walker, M. (1987) 'Interpreting Race and Crime Statistics' *Journal of the Royal Statistical Society*, A150 (Part 1): pp. 39–56.

Walker, M. A. (1992) 'Arrest Rates and Ethnic Minorities: a Study in a Provincial City' *Journal of the Royal Statistical Society*, 155, no 2: pp. 259–72.

Walklate, S. (1992) *Victimology: The Victim And The Criminal Justice Process* (London, Unwin Allan).

Walsh, D. (1987) *Racial Harassment in Glasgow* (Glasgow, Scottish Ethnic Minorities Research Unit)

Watson, G. (1970) *Passing for White* (London, Tavistock).

Weick, K. (1969) *The Social Psychology of Organising* (Reading, Mass, Addison-Wesley).

Weick, K. (1976) 'Educational Organisations as Loosely Coupled Systems' *Administrative Science Quarterly*, 21, no. 1: pp. 1–12.

Weick, K. (1979) 'Cognitive processes in organisations' *Research in Organiza-tional Behaviour* (Connecticut, JAI Press) pp. 41–74.

Whitaker, C. (1990) *Black Victims* (Washington, US Bureau of Statistics).

Willis, C. (1983) *The Use, Effectiveness and Impact of Police Stop and Search Powers* (London, Home Office).

Wilson, D., S. Holdaway, *et al.* (1984) 'Black Police in the United Kingdom' *Policing*, 1, no. 1: pp. 20–30.

Wolfgang, M. E. and B. Cohen (1970) *Crime and Race: Conceptions and Misconceptions* (New York, Institute of Human Relations Press).

Woodcock, J. (1991) 'Overturning Police Culture' *Policing*, 7, no. 3: pp. 1–12

Woodcock, J. (1992) *Trust in the Police – The Search for Truth* (International Police Exhibition and Conference, The Barbican, London).

Young, J. (1971) *The Drugtakers* (London, Paladin).

Young, J. (1986) 'The future of criminology' in R. Mathews and J. Young (eds.), *Confronting Crime* (London, Sage).

Young, J. (1988) 'Radical criminology in Britain' *British Journal of Criminology*, 28: pp. 159–83.

Young, J. (1988) 'Risk of crime and fear of crime: A realist critique of survey-based assumptions' in M. Maquire and J. Ponting (eds.), *Victims of Crime: A New deal* (Milton Keynes, Open University Press).

Young, K. (1983) 'Ethnic Pluralism and the Policy Agenda in Britain' in N. Glazer and K. Young (eds.), *Ethnic Pluralism and Public Policy* (London, Heinemann).

Young, K. and N. Connelly (1981) *Policy and Practice in the Multi-Racial City* (London, PSI).

Zedner, L. (1994) 'Victims' in M. Maquire *et al.* (eds.), *The Oxford Handbook of Criminology* (Oxford, Clarendon Press).

Index

221